The Invention
of the Park

Recreational Landscapes
from the
Garden of Eden to
Disney's Magic Kingdom

KAREN R. JONES
and
JOHN WILLS

polity

First published in 2005 by Polity Press

Polity Press
65 Bridge Street
Cambridge CB2 1UR, UK.

Polity Press
350 Main Street
Malden, MA 02148, USA

ISBN: 0-7456-3138-X
ISBN: 0-7456-3139-8 (pb)

A catalogue record for this book is available from the British Library and has been applied for from the Library of Congress.

Typeset in 10½ on 12 pt Bembo
by Servis Filmsetting Ltd, Longsight, Manchester
Printed and bound in Great Britain by MPG Books Ltd, Bodmin, Cornwall

For further information on Polity, visit our website: www.polity.co.uk

Contents

Introduction: Defining the Park

On some level we all know the park. It's a realm of relaxation, a Sunday stroll, a refuge from the working week. It's a kaleidoscope of colourful rides, themed worlds, and cartoon characters. It's a green place, an earthy realm, somewhere that hobbits and fairies might prosper. It's a meeting point, a talking point, a place for protest, a place where culture and nature collide.

How do we know the park? Often from our practical interactions with it. Local parks linger in our memories – their sights, sounds and smells. We also know the park through multiple fictions. From the very beginning, the park has been part of our creative voice. Its presence around the world is testament to a greater human quest for optimism and adventure. Put simply, the park is our invention.

In 1591, William Shakespeare recounted the epic loss of France by England in the historical play *Henry VI*. In it, Shakespeare employed the park as a prime symbol of classical English landscape. Rules of land enclosure applied to both deer and man. Lord Talbot, stalwart warrior for the English cause, declared at the siege of Bordeaux:

> I hear the enemy:
> Out, some light horsemen, and peruse their wings. –
> O, negligent and heedless discipline!
> How are we park'd and bounded in a pale, –
> A little herd of England's timorous deer,
> Maz'ed with a yelping kennel of French curs!
>
> *1 Henry VI*, IV. ii.

Later on in the work, a park near Middleham Castle, Yorkshire served as the venue for the imprisonment of King Edward IV. His loyal followers, led by Gloucester, hid in the 'chiefest thicket' with the plan of liberating the monarch during one of his park-based hunting trips (*3 Henry VI*, IV. v). The park environment furnished the King's freedom.

As a landscape valued chiefly for its aesthetics, the park was destined to make the transition from the written word to the silver screen. In 1908, J. Stuart Blackton filmed a silent movie version of Shakespeare's *Romeo and Juliet* in Central Park, New York. Bethesda Fountain serviced as Verona. Shakespearian prose was duly condensed for the silent format. Central Park went on to feature in more than 150 films during the twentieth century, including titles as diverse as *Breakfast at Tiffany's* (1961) and *Ghostbusters* (1984). The much lauded city park became part of the iconography of Woody Allen's movies. Originally designed by landscape architect Frederick Law Olmsted as a vignette of social uplift, Allen transformed Central Park into the refuge of a neurotic comic. In the 1990s, the cafe 'Central Perk' served as a regular hang-out in the popular television series *Friends*, the amiable coffee-house taking the idea of the park as a friendly gathering place indoors.

In the history of film, parks have served as celluloid canvases, providing stunning backdrops to classic dialogue and riveting action sequences. Myriad Hollywood westerns used Monument Valley, Utah, since 1958 a Navajo Tribal Park, as an iconic stage for gun-fights, wagon trail-blazing and Indian ambushes. The classic 'cowboys in space' movie *Star Wars* (1977) employed Death Valley National Park as filmic substitute for the fantasy world of Tattoine, the arid, hostile land where Luke Skywalker grew up. Recently, Peter Jackson filmed key sections of Tolkien's *Lord of the Rings* (2001–3) at Tongariro National Park in New Zealand. Mythic Middle Earth was pictured as park-like in image. The unbridled success of the film trilogy in turn sparked a tourist exodus to New Zealand in the hope of soaking up the spectacular landscapes of Middle Earth. Intriguingly, enigmatic writer J. R. R. Tolkien may have taken inspiration from another neck of the woods. Taking part in an archaeological dig at Lydney Park, Gloucestershire, England, in 1929, Tolkien came across a Roman temple. Named Dwarf's Hill, the temple featured a legend telling of hobgoblins and dwarves that once resided there. Tolkien was working on *The Hobbit* at the time.

Hence the life of the park is revealed through fiction, film and fantasy. Parkscapes have made great film sets and theatre stages; they have inspired us and allowed our inspirations to take physical form. But what do really know about the park itself. What is its story?

DEFINING THE PARK

park [pärk] n.
1. a large public green area in a town, used for recreation: *a walk around the park*
– a large area of land kept in its natural state for public recreational use
– (also wildlife park) a large enclosed area of land used to accommodate wild animals in captivity
– a stadium or enclosed area used for sports
– a large enclosed piece of ground, typically within woodland and pasture, attached to a large country house: *the house is set in its own park*
2. an area devoted to a specified purpose: *an industrial park*

New Oxford American Dictionary (2001)

Cultural critic Raymond Williams once deemed 'nature' to be 'perhaps the most complex word in the [English] language'. 'Park' comes a close second. Deriving from 'parc' in Middle English and *parricus* in medieval Latin, the park was first employed to describe enclosed preserves for 'beasts of the chase'. Since that time, the remit of the park has broadened far beyond its hunting purposes. To indulge in naturalistic metaphors, the park has both 'evolved' and, like the archetypal rose, found itself variegated by generations of custodians. The park connotes nation building, spirituality and fantasy. It is an innately aesthetic place, a realm where image and perception rule. It also has its share of interpretive paradoxes. While for some the park conjures images of gentrified elites strolling in private royal estates, for others the park is a bastion of democracy, a city space set aside for working-class people. Thinking of the park as a locus of contemplation and peace makes sense with a wilderness park, but hardly applies to a theme park, where entertainment and dramatic action take precedence. Put simply, the park means many things to many people.[1]

The meaning of the park has altered significantly over time. While the rest of the book details such changes, for now, the process is best observed in microcosm, in the unlikely guise of parks found on the written page, in dictionaries. Whereas older editions of the *Oxford English Dictionary* began by highlighting the European hunting reserve as the obvious park type, more recent compendiums have added new categories of parkscape, in turn reducing the significance of the 'original' starting point. The definition of the 'park' offered above by the *New Oxford American Dictionary* underscores the shifting meaning of the idea itself. No longer is such a landscape based on the nobility pursuing beasts of the chase. Instead, the *New Oxford American* prioritizes the democratic city park (most often touted as the invention of Connecticut-born Frederick Law Olmsted) as a principal route towards understanding what the phrase means in the twenty-first century. 'A walk around the park' is offered as a pithy suggestion of what we should do if, by chance, we find ourselves in such a setting as Olmsted's Central Park, having made the wrong turn when heading for a shopping district.

A number of core ideas about the park are also set down in written form. The first purpose of the park is as a forum for exercise ('to walk'), to explore the geographical limits of the park, its boundaries of open space. For some, this can be an uncomfortable suggestion – as Woody Allen said in *Stardust Memories* (1980) on watching joggers in Central Park: 'Look at all these people, trying to stave off the inevitable decay of their bodies.' The park is none the less a place of human movement. We also learn that, in its modern guise at least, the park appears open to all. With the 'public' mentioned twice in the *New Oxford American* definition, notions of freedom and democracy come to the fore. Reading down the list of subcategories, the park also emerges as a space associated with nature. It is 'a green area' in the town, an expansive territory preserved in a 'natural state', a zoological collection and a country estate. Such locales become 'parks' partly due to the quality of their organic features, but also through the process of enclosure. Typically enclosed by fences or berms, they are cordoned off from surrounding cityscapes or agricultural fields. In the case of the wildlife park, the logic of enclosure is taken to the next level with the keeping of animals in cages. Enclosure renders the park a distinct space. Finally, recreation is a hallmark of park design – 'it is *for* public recreational use', whether for strolling, exploration or simply watching others play in sports stadiums.

Dictionary terminology can thereby assist our understanding of the park idea. We obtain a clear impression of a typical park landscape based on, for all intents and purposes, a brief textual entry. The definition also raises some interesting lines of enquiry. While nature appears crucial to understanding the park, what exactly we mean by the term is not entirely obvious in the reading. The park can be used to preserve land in 'its natural state', yet it also facilitates the capture and control of flora and fauna, hardly indicative of 'natural' conditions. Moreover, how are parks different from other crafted pleasure landscapes such as gardens? Size, social function, the presence of animals, and organized activities provide a few distinctions. From the outset, there appear to be very different 'natures' on offer in the various parkscapes, underlining the concern of Raymond Williams over the cultural ambiguity attached to language. The 'industrial park' mentioned in the text meanwhile challenges our comprehension of the park label. Such spaces venture an apparent clash with park conventions by their scarce natural and recreational features. Can we, as the dictionary claims, simply tag the epithet 'park' on to any 'area devoted to a specific purpose'? Is the park moniker demeaned if we name business regions, scientific research hubs, and even makeshift collections of trailers park landscapes?

As will be evident throughout this work, the park idea is a fluid and adaptable concept. While the stereotypical image of the park as a place of family recreation in green pastures may hold true for many locations detailed in this book, this is not the whole story. There is clearly more than one type of park, and more than one purpose to parks. This study examines at least ten different types of park, spread across seven chapters. Successive chapters detail ancient parks, the English landscape park, the city park and the baseball park, the national (or nature) park, the amusement park, the zoological (or animal) park, with trailer parks, industrial parks and culture parks the subject of the final chapter. We travel from the Garden of Eden to the Hanging Gardens of Babylon, take a stroll in Versailles and Central Park, explore Yellowstone and Kruger national parks, and end up in Disneyland. Such diverse, trans-continental landscapes represent popular landmarks of parkdom. When people first consider the idea, they are liable to think of these places. As the most famous parks in the world, it is only natural to expect scholars to have lavished their attentions on such 'crown jewels'. In the main, academics have focused their studies on renowned parks such as Yosemite in the USA (Alfred Runte providing the seminal tome) and Kruger in South Africa (see the scholarship of Jane Carruthers). Disney has grabbed the attention of cultural studies stalwarts, eager to deconstruct the Disney experience in all its cartoonish wonder. Janet Wasko's *Understanding Disney* (2001) provides a valuable starting point in this regard. Parks have also piqued the interest of those studying landscape architecture and horticulture – for example, Elizabeth Barlow in *Landscape Design* (2001) and John Dixon Hunt in *Gardens and the Picturesque* (1992). Central Park has been scrutinized for its democratic impulses (in Rosenzweig and Blackmar's impressive *The Park and the People* (1992)), the Grand Canyon for its invocation of cultural nationalism (in Stephen Pyne's bite-sized but insightful *How the Canyon Became Grand* (1998)). However, while we understand a fair amount about Disney and Yosemite, we know far less about other landscapes in the global park system. Very little has been published on some truly exceptional landscapes (such as Canada's first national park, Banff, or Hagenbeck Zoo in Germany), while unusual parks, such as Hiroshima Peace Memorial Park or Nevada National Environmental Research Park, have escaped attention entirely. Few scholars have written on the park idea as a whole, or compared the wide array of designs and features on display. The park has not been treated as a single entity, but rather many different ones, and it is time to bring them together.

The park is a truly global product, and *The Invention of the Park* points to this fact. Where possible, global examples have been employed to demonstrate the variegated nature of parks worldwide. By discussing such diverse landscapes as ancient Persian paradises and Chinese industrial sites, the park idea is touted for what it really is – a truly international phenomenon. However, constraints of time and space have imposed themselves on this study. As Americanists, we have naturally favoured examples from the English-speaking world, and (at times unfairly) neglected the rich park heritage of countries such as Germany and Italy. The limits of this book also reflect the finite boundaries of existing academic literature. Most texts assert the Western origins and Anglo-American countenance of the 'park' label. The majority of park studies remain concentrated on 'honeypot' locales such as Yellowstone and Disneyworld. Gaps in coverage aside, we remain committed to the idea that the park has never existed as a solely Western property.[2]

In order to consider so many park types and take in as many countries as possible, our treatment is necessarily broad in scope. The only park genre consciously absent from this enquiry is the kind you find on vehicles with automatic transmissions. Other park types are invariably raised throughout. The zoological park is granted a whole chapter. Some might consider the zoo little more than a collection of animals; however, the historic development of the zoological park demonstrates keen links with the greater park movement. Zoos are, after all, places where humans corral beasts of the chase, ponder relations between species, and have fun. Elsewhere, theme parks, industrial parks and even virtual parks all gain mention. Such breadth of coverage has inevitably led to significant omissions. Suburban settlements or individual streets boasting the park epithet are ignored, while some of your own favourite recreational hotspots may not appear on these pages. The essential aim of the book is not to document all the world's parks (a well-nigh impossible task), but to elaborate on the evolution of the park idea (and ideal) over time. The park is throughout classified as a cultural artefact, a product of evolving societies and lingering ties to the natural world. The truly social function of the park is evidenced by its continual appearance in the popular vernacular – from elite calls for 'park time' (meaning a leisurely break) in seventeenth-century London to recent celebrations of working class 'park life' (replete with pigeon feeding and handholding) by the likes of Britpop rockers Blur.

APPROACHING THE PARK

PARK, a space of ground used for public or private recreation, differing from a garden in its spaciousness and the broad, simple, and natural character of its scenery, and from a 'wood' in the more scattered arrangement of its trees and greater expanse of its glades.

Frederick Law Olmsted, 'Park', in *The American Cyclopedia* (1875)

As the man who helped to define both the city and the national park concepts in the nineteenth century, and took responsibility for the design of such illustrious landscapes as Central Park and Prospect Park, Frederick Law Olmsted understood better than most the park idea. Olmsted's life revolved around visiting, planning and overseeing the construction of parks across North America. With his business partner, Calvert Vaux, Olmsted revolutionized landscape design in the United States. Olmsted treated the park as nature's canvas to be fine-tuned by human engineering. His encyclopaedic definition of 1875 began with the English landscape park, where nature had been moulded over centuries to suit gentrified, dignified whims. Olmsted admired the aesthetic composition of old English parks, noting, in their great organic beauty, an ability 'to stimulate simple, natural, and wholesome tastes and fancies'. By meticulous manipulation of the aesthetic scene, generations of English gardeners maintained immaculate, immersive parkscapes. The age of trees, the careful choice of foliage, the relationship of man and nature all factored into Olmsted's earliest notions of the park idea. For Olmsted, the park was something different from civilization and urbanity. In its 'open, free, tranquil character', it provided the city with 'an antithesis to its bustling, paved, rectangular, walled-in streets'. Olmsted recognized the distinctiveness of the parkscape when compared to gardens and woods. The grand scale of parks dwarfed smaller private gardens, while the planned logic of the park set it aside from the chaotic, free-flowing forest.[3]

As well as nature's creation, Olmsted envisaged the park as a social structure, and, more significantly, as a place where society could be, if not perfected, at least improved. Olmsted's plans for a great South Park in Chicago in the 1870s (later realized in two separate enclaves, Washington and Jackson) included both the remaking of nature and the remaking of man. Olmsted found the natural landscape of Chicago a challenge, given its flatness and 'poor soil' (he later called the region 'most unfavourable to parks'). In Olmsted's view, a 'fine park' needed turf, foliage and water. With South Park, only water came easily. Cultural wants also needed to be met. Olmsted envisioned Chicago's

South Park as 'the principle recreation ground of the city', suited to baseball as much as parades, Sunday school outings as well as family picnics. The park, to Olmsted, promised social betterment and rejuvenation. The park idea rested on society, on human needs, just as much as it tapped nature's roots.[4]

As Olmsted pertinently surmised, the park idea relates to both nature and society. It is, in equal parts, about our constructions (and conceptions) of the natural world and our hopes and fears for the social world about us. Approaching the park as an organic artefact, we learn a great deal about human relations with the natural world. The park in many ways reflects what we envisage as 'ideal nature'. Landscape architects make parks into organic utopias, places brimming with lush flora, charismatic fauna, water pools, play areas – all facets of nature that we consistently enjoy. Some (national) parks are deemed 'wildernesses': their wild character, seen to encapsulate a non-human pre-lapsarian realm, appealing to human sensibilities for escape and a temporary reconnection with savagery and survivalism. The park also serves as a spiritual refuge – a realm of contemplation, with nature cast as an ideal setting for individual soul searching. Nature, in such instances, is granted positive traits, imbued with the ability to enrich people's lives. The freedom of creatures in protected wilderness somehow frees us from our social responsibilities, our everyday burdens.

At the same time, parks are controlled landscapes. Whether under the stewardship of landscape architect, gardener or ranger, the park is shaped and patrolled by social forces. From caged animals in countless zoological parks to imposed boundaries surrounding national park refuges, the natural world remains under our purview, our jurisdiction. Parks, as we shall see, bespeak a human need to control, as well as enjoy, the organic experience.

In the 1920s, Robert E. Park and Anthony Burgess, two prominent members of the Chicago School of Sociology, ruminated on the city as a living organism. In their opinion, the industrial city of Chicago operated akin to a natural environment, and thus could be studied as such. People, like animals, abided by Darwinian laws of evolution. They competed for resources, moved between territories, and some groups faltered where others succeeded. This notion of urban ecology heavily influenced the thought of the Chicago School at the time. In 1925, Burgess and Park published *The City*. The work included a diagram consisting of several concentric circles, each equating to distinct zones of Chicago. It became one of the most famous illustrations in sociology, providing a basic framework for mapping, researching and understanding urban environments. While the diagram was usefully employed to chart class divides, ethnic enclaves and housing districts in Chicago, the park never appeared on the sociological map. Yet parkscapes have undoubtedly influenced urban life. Olmsted's plans for South Park evolved into a substantial park district on the South Side constructed in the late 1870s. Bandstands, croquet and nature walks beckoned. Though posited as a democratic melting pot, Chicago's park network in reality drew first and foremost the privileged few. By the 1920s, when Park and Burgess were publishing their own city plan, Chicago's parks were caught up in racial and class conflicts, with gang violence commonplace in Washington Park.[5]

This study considers 'park ecology', not just in the sense of animal movements and landscape design, but, in homage to the Chicago School, in terms of public movements, ideals and actions. Crucially, we approach the park as a social as well as an environmental artefact. As a social construction, the park idea is consistently influenced by cultural norms and values. Early parks in Assyria and later on in Europe reflected the power of the nobility, with parkscapes serving as ornate symbols of royal prestige. Rejuvenated by fresh democratic impulses, parks in the nineteenth century were opened to all and sundry. Over the centuries, parks reflected popular notions of nationhood, citizenship and politics. In the 1950s, Disneyland emerged as one of the first consumer-friendly parks. Its stores, stalls and themed products intersected with a post-war rush to buy happiness. A new emblem of middle-class affluence and mass purchase, the theme park joined an array of alluring commodities, from the home TV set to kitchen appliances. Mass advertising helped make it happen.

In essence, the park as studied here is a product of society. Its design shifts subtly in accordance with fluctuating human desires and wants. The concept has proved highly malleable. Take Wivenhoe Park, for instance, the locale where most of this book was written. Today, it stands as a university campus – yet a hundred years ago it was a country park. Where once only the privileged elite strolled, now an array of international students gather (not to mention rabbits and Canada geese).

People find different pleasures within the park fraternity. Some discover happiness through family picnics in open greenery, the park idea allied with notions of play, safety, fun and reassurance. Others use the park to escape reality, to ponder what could be, and immerse themselves in a fantasy landscape. Theme parks bring out the child in visitors, and strive to be sterile, clean environments suited to kids. Industrial parks, by contrast, provide (naturalized but still nine till five) workplaces, while wilderness parks offer experiences of nature 'red in tooth and claw'. For some, the appeal of parks lies in their social purposes, for others it is grounded in their raw nature. Some park values are timeless and enduring, others the products of specific decades and fashions. The park idea intrigues through such a varied intersection with cultural forces. In turn, the landscape represents a useful crucible for the examination of mainstream social values.

If the park can be reduced to a single cultural indicator, it is that of optimism. Contained within the evolution of the park idea is an enduring quest for utopian living. From the Garden of Eden to Disney's Magic Kingdom and beyond, the park has serviced an almighty exploration of hope. While the park has sanctioned racism, class exclusion and the removal of indigenous peoples, the park diaspora also holds within it landscapes famed for their romance, beauty and perfection. The park idea is also an ideal to be explored throughout this book.

1 From Ancient Groves to Versailles

While the park signifies an intrinsic part of recreational life in the twenty-first century, the park idea is not strictly a creation of modern society. Instead, its history stretches back thousands of years. The park has long been the subject of popular mythology. Colourful descriptions of ancient groves appear in folklore and fables from all over the world.

ASSYRIAN PARKS AND PERSIAN PARADISES

The earliest known literary description of a park-like landscape comes from the *Epic of Gilgamesh*, a legendary tale from the Sumerians of the ancient Near East. Written *c*.2000 BC and preserved in tablet form at Assyrian King Ashurbanipal's palace at Nineveh (near today's Mosul, in Iraq), the *Epic* relates the story of two friends: Gilgamesh, part human, part deity, and Enkidu, a wild man of the woods. Embarking on a quest to discover the secret of immortal life, the two heroes venture into a sacred cedar forest guarded by an ogre named Humbaba. With its own gateway and fence of wooden stakes, the enclave would today be recognized as a hunting park. The grove contains towering dendrons, dense thickets, fragrant plants and well-tended trails. Once inside, Gilgamesh and Enkidu begin to cut down the trees, thereby provoking the wrath of the gatekeeper. An epic battle ensues. Gilgamesh decapitates Humbaba, then fells the tallest cedars in the forest to craft a gate for the city of Uruk.

From 1250 BC, grand hunting preserves graced the landscape of northern Mesopotamia (an area once identified with the Garden of Eden, according to biblical geography). Assyrian kings forged preserves in the Tigris–Euphrates Valley for their sporting entertainment. Emphasis was placed not on growing trees, as in Humbaba's park, but on nurturing beasts of the chase. Within enclosed areas roamed native herbivores as well as rare exotic animals including lions, ostriches, lynx and gazelle. Keepers placed ditches and fences around parks to prevent game from escaping and unwelcome predators from wandering in. The Assyrian park served as a private arena for the propagation of valuable trophy animals. It also elicited an important connection between gentlemanly status, ritualized hunting and parkscapes.

Expressly created for the pleasure of the monarch, the hunting reserves of ancient Assyria represented idealized landscapes. Organic designs paid homage to nature's beauty as well as the thrill of the chase. Consciously separated from the surrounding environment, the park was marked by its lush vegetation, abundant water supply and impressive faunal complement. Planted palms and cypresses offered shade, while canals irrigated an otherwise arid environment.

That the Assyrians paid heed to the aesthetic value of nature was most evident in the Hanging Gardens of Babylon. Established by King Nebuchadnezzar from 604 BC, the Hanging Gardens were reputedly designed to lift the spirits of Queen Amyitis who missed the rugged scenery of her Media home. The king instructed gardeners to craft an artificial tree-covered mountain with lofty groves in the bustling city of Babel to provide relief from the surrounding plains. The Gardens won plaudits from travellers, who admired the vaunted terraces adorned with cypress, pomegranate, palm, juniper and myrtle. An elaborate system of chain pumps ensured that the ensemble remained well watered. This combination of organic magnificence, architectural craftsmanship and technological innovation lent the Hanging Gardens status as one of the Seven Wonders of the World.

The rich city of Babel (in which the Hanging Gardens stood) attested to the wealth and sophistication of King Nebuchadnezzar. Assyrian parkscapes functioned in a similar fashion. Each park represented an organic status symbol inexorably linked to structures of political power. A frieze from the palace of Nineveh depicts King Ashurbanipal (reigned 669–631 BC) in a park pavilion celebrating victory in battle. Fanned by loyal courtiers, the monarch and his queen recline in their arbour supping from fine goblets. Hunters pursue a lion amidst vines laden with fruit. The Nineveh frieze graphically illuminates the park as a place not only for vigorous hunting endeavours, but also for leisure, entertainment and merriment. Far from offering rude shelter, the park lodge provided comfort, frivolity and luxurious cuisine after the sport of the day. This surfeit of pomp and elegance, in turn, reminded guests of the affluence of the park owner.

Assyrian parks proclaimed control over nature by their artificial lakes and formal tree plantings. Technology remained integral to park making from the outset. In order to construct fantastical oases in arid environments, planners inaugurated massive earth-moving projects and irrigation schemes. By parading an awe-inspiring menagerie of exotic species, parks highlighted tutelage over foreign lands, the flora and fauna demonstrative of power over both nature and other nations. A park created by King Tiglath-Pileser I (*c.*1100 BC) near his palace at Assur featured a collection of spectacular plants and animals such as the dromedary and the elephant. These spoils derived largely from successful military campaigns. As the ruler motioned, 'Cedars and Urkarinu (box), Allakanu-wood have I carried off from the countries I conquered, trees that none of the kings, my forefathers, have possessed, these trees have I taken, and planted them in mine own country, in the parks of Assyria.'[1]

Other Assyrian regents regarded their parks as totems of power. Ashurnasirpal II (*c.*870 BC) embellished his reputation as a fearsome warrior by his park pursuits. During one hunting excursion he boasted of despatching 450 lions, 390 wild bulls, along with ostriches and elephants – the huge cull emblematic of his ferocity on the battlefield. King Sennacherib (reigned 705–681 BC) viewed his parks as projections of personal munificence. Sennacherib granted an attractive, well-watered area in Nineveh to local citizens, thus creating the earliest known example of an urban park.

Military campaigns not only ensured that the Assyrians received stocks of exotic beasts to fill their parks with, but also facilitated the cultural transmission of the park concept. The army served as the chief exporter of the park idea in the ancient world.

The Persians encountered hunting parks for the first time during their conquest of Mesopotamia in 539 BC. Duly impressed with the lands they visited, Persian elites appropriated the park idea. Highlighting firm links between parkscapes and utopian visions, the new parklands of ancient Iran were known as *pairidaeza* – meaning paradise.

The Persian paradise took two forms: royal game park and ornate garden. As enclosed spaces, parks allowed ruling elites to control natural resources and prevent peasants from stealing timber or meat. Small garden parks filled with flowers and fruit trees paid homage to the Egyptian walled garden (the Persians conquered Egypt in 525 BC) and symbolized the reverence paid to water by desert-based civilizations. The park connoted an oasis in an arid region. The Persian paradise – in both park and garden forms – represented a realm of fantasy, a place of ideal nature. As Greek soldier-historian Xenophon remarked of Persia's hunting reserves in the fourth century BC, 'their name is Paradise, and they are full of all things fair and good that the earth can bring forth.'[2] Xenophon also noted hunts led by Cyrus the Great, who 'exterminated the animals in the park by chasing them and striking them with javelins, cutting them down at such a rate that Astyages [his grandfather] was no longer able to collect game'.[3] Aside from their aesthetic qualities, Persian parks facilitated the most vigorous and masculine of sports. Meanwhile, the size and brush cover available in parks made them ideal places to train and conceal armies. Cyrus the Younger (died 401 BC) inspected 130,000 soldiers in his park at Celanae, Central Turkey. In turn, belligerent forces clearly saw parklands as symbols of the ruling class and viewed them as legitimate military targets. Clearly the park represented a landscape of power.

FROM PARADISE TO EDEN

The Garden of Eden signifies the most prominent vision of a park-like landscape in early Western civilization. Despite the absence of the park motif, Eden contained all the elements of a classic park scene: enclosed, stocked with trees, and ranged by all manner of beasts. Adam served as leading horticulturalist as well as 'first man' in this verdant enclave, his custodianship ending only when a smooth-talking serpent tempted Eve to sample an apple from the Tree of Knowledge of Good and Evil. The Eden account offered a story of origins as well as establishing first relations between God and man. It also implied that the park idea might be as old as humanity itself.

Intriguingly, the parks of the ancient Orient might have influenced the Eden narrative. The word 'Eden' derives from both the Hebrew epithet for delight and the Persian word *edina* meaning field or park. Some revisionist-biblical scholars contend that the book of Genesis was written, or at least edited, around the time of the Jewish exile to Babylon (597–538 BC). During their deportation, the Jews likely learned of the parks planted by the Assyrian and Persian nobility. Worlds away from the predominant desert ecosystem, such places must have seemed akin to miniature utopias – ideal templates for descriptions of Eden. The Garden of Eden certainly bore similarities to the royal parks of the ancient Near East. Like the *pairidaeza*, it featured floral wonders and flowing water. Mimicking the Assyrian game park, Eden sported 'every beast of the field and every fowl of the air'. Theologian Evan Eisenberg dubbed Eden 'God's game preserve, stocked with a breeding pair of each kind of animal, humans included'.[4] Eden signified the world's first menagerie in its ecological completeness. Moreover, the preserve was governed by keen management imperatives. In the fashion of Assyrian reserves and Persian paradises, Eden endorsed tamed nature as opposed to unkempt wilderness. Receiving instructions from God to 'dress it and to keep it', Adam held the pruning forks. The Bible thus established environmental codes for humanity to follow. Granted dominion over the beasts of the Earth, Adam, as inaugural taxonomist, set about naming them accordingly. Though it may be incredulous to label Adam 'the first park warden', he was expected to control and manage his earthly domain.

The parks of the ancient Orient and the Garden of Eden diverged in the matter of human–animal relations. In Assyrian and Persian parks, animals existed as hunting trophies. In Eden, man and beast lived together in harmony. Genesis postulated a bucolic realm free from violence. Relations of predator and prey, hunter and hunted, had no place in this bloodless park. Furthermore, Eden was not dedicated to royal pleasure. Only the beguiling serpent threatened the perfect state of nature.

The Genesis account greatly influenced the park idea in regions exposed to Judaeo-Christianity. Eden came to symbolize pre-lapsarian wealth and organic purity in Western culture. The biblical paradise enshrined an antediluvian utopia that was duly venerated by generations of philosophers, writers and artists. This perfect state proposed an ideal for every landscape designer to follow. While the authors of Genesis may have unconsciously evoked the parks of the ancient Near East in their account, countless gardeners and park architects in subsequent years gazed upon Eden as *their* ideal, and duly appropriated it for their own horticultural creations.

GREEK SACRED GROVES AND CITY PARKS

In Greek and Roman civilization, the park idea was associated with spirituality, public recreation and city living. Greek philosophers pondered the meaning of nature, its innermost workings, the relationships between animals and humankind and how matter related to spirit. Aristotle (384–322 BC) advanced the fundamental notion of nature as the embodiment of everything outside culture, an essence opposed to art and artificiality. This sense of nature and culture as binary opposites continues to govern ideas about the environment and society today. Meanwhile, the suggestion of a state of nature, wholesome and pure, defined in opposition to civilized life, found resonance in Aristotle's time through the concept of the Golden Age – a legendary utopia that grew to rival the Garden of Eden in its significance for landscape planning and artistic experiment. Described by Greek poets and playwrights, the Golden Age of Perpetual Spring depicted an era before the adoption of agriculture, when humans embraced nature's wonder and conversed with spirits in sacred woods. In *The Odyssey* (800 BC) Homer described a garden at Alcinous, a place of perennial spring, where 'fruit never fails nor runs short, winter and summer alike . . . so that pear after pear, apple after apple, cluster on cluster of grapes, and fig upon fig are always coming to perfection'.[5]

Greek interest in spirituality and nature manifested itself in the tradition of the sacred grove. Usually comprised of a few trees, a spring or a mountain crag, sacred groves became intensely mystical places by their associations with deities, spirits or celebrated folk heroes. Gnarled trees, sections of old-growth forest and rocky outcrops or caves typically surrounded the naturalistic shrines and altars. As Pliny the Elder motioned, 'Trees were the first temples of the gods, and even now simple country people dedicate a tree of exceptional height to a god with the ritual of olden times, and we . . . worship forests and the very silences they contain.'[6]

The Greeks were not alone in their spiritual veneration of nature. Examples of pantheism and tree adulation permeated many cultures. The Teutonic nations of northern Europe utilized trees as places of worship. In Scandinavian mythology, Yggdrasil held up the world, its branches forming the heavens and its roots stretching into hell. A spring of knowledge bubbled at its base, and an eagle perched amidst its sturdy boughs. The Maori of New Zealand celebrated a tree that separated the sky from the earth, while Buddha reached enlightenment in the shade of the Bo Tree. For many ancient civilizations, trees signified life, permanence and wisdom.

Rather than landscapes of allegory or emulation, as in the Judaeo-Christian tradition, Greek sacred groves operated as the *literal* homes of the gods. Instead of being confined to prehistory or celestial space, spiritual parkscapes sat within the existing cultural terrain. As Seneca mused in his *Epistles*, 'If you come upon a grove of old trees that have lifted up their crowns above the common height and shut out the light of the sky by the darkness of their interlacing bows, you feel that there is a spirit in the place, so lofty is the wood, so lone the spot, so wondrous the thick unbroken shade.'[7]

The spiritual significance of the sacred grove mandated specific preservationist measures. Civil restrictions and environmental codes of practice governed the use of such spaces. Enclosing walls prevented sheep from desecrating sacred sites, while patrolling priests issued spiritual guidance and fines for vandalism. Edicts forbade hunting, fishing or the felling of trees. Those not dissuaded by monetary penalties were threatened with the wrath of resident deities. The huntress Atlanta was reputedly transformed into a lioness for crimes against the shrine of Zeus. Meanwhile, Artemis, the goddess of wild animals and virginal lands, protected her faunal charges from harm and delivered justice to those who contravened the ethics of fair chase.[8]

Such keen environmental stewardship suggested to historian J. Donald Hughes that sacred groves represented 'classical national parks'.[9] By helping to insulate sacred groves from pressures of deforestation, erosion and urbanization, Greek codes protected ecosystems from the axe and the bow. Sacred groves none the less represented imperfect parkscapes. Some encompassed relatively small areas such as a section of hillside or a series of caves. Meanwhile, the fundamental purpose of the grove – the visitation of resident deities – sometimes promoted activities not entirely conducive to modern concepts of conservation. Animals were routinely snatched to serve as sacrifices to the gods. As Artemis reputedly held domestic animals in disdain, local goats represented typical offerings. Many groves witnessed horticultural and architectural improvements. Flowers were planted, copses restocked, trails cut, and statues, fountains and grottoes installed for the benefit of visitors. The grove served as a recreational hub for Greek society, a realm of ritual, performance, feasting and even chariot racing.

Greek citizens recognized the importance of the park as a civic area. Originally a sacred grove to protect the shrine of Academus, Cimon (510– 450 BC) expanded the Academy of Athens to include a gymnasium, then planted additional trees to create a city park. Elm, myrtle and yew, together with strategically placed seats, provided comfort from the sun and inspired contemplation and debate. Setting up his famous seat of learning in a corner of the Academy in 387 BC, Plato himself associated fruitful intellectual discourse with shady climes. Rather than the hunting preserve of the Assyrians and the Persians, the Greek park served as a place for exercising, talking and thinking.

Yet, the Grecian park still perpetuated elitism. Eager to avoid the bustle of the public venues, wealthy citizens established private parks and pleasure gardens. Plato moved study to his own garden after the Academy lost its air of quietude. This burgeoning interest in exclusive green spaces bespoke a desire for solitude in the urban landscape. The private park also drew inspiration from Persia, where advancing Greek armies encountered the grand estates of Cyrus and his countrymen. Alexander the Great (356–323 BC) applauded Bazisda Park, near the city of Samarkand (in today's Uzbekistan). Alexander reputedly killed 4,000 animals in the preserve, but so appreciated the park idea that he announced plans to perpetuate the tradition.

ROMAN PARKS, COUNTRYSIDE RETREATS AND THE VENATIO

Honouring their Empire as founded in the soil (as well as by the mother wolf of Romulus and Remus fame), the Romans idealized pastoral landscapes as part of their national birthright. Roman cosmology promoted a theory of natural order, a system of classification that established spheres of action for all creation. Natural order endowed humans, as second in the species hierarchy after the gods, with the ability (and the right) to transform nature. At the same time, the Great Chain of Being could be upset if powerful earth spirits were not shown certain courtesies. Prayers and sacrifices preceded the cutting down of trees. Impetus for protecting green spaces also derived from concerns about environmental despoliation due to urban overcrowding.

It was in this context that the civic leaders of Rome realized the value of open green areas. Nature was invoked as a foil to the contaminants of civilization. Wealthy magnates contributed to the greening of Rome by dedicating public parks as signs of paternal authority. In 55 BC, Pompey the Great opened the first public park, the *Porticus Pompeiana,* in the capital. The park featured covered walkways, paintings, water features and trees dedicated to Jove, Apollo, Venus and Hercules. The *Porticus* stood adjacent to a collection of important civic buildings known as the *Opera Pompeiana*, highlighting a common association between open spaces and cultured recreation in the classical world. Green areas were typically constructed around existing amenities and memorials (such as mausoleums, bathhouses and libraries) to enable patrons to assemble and talk. Exported throughout the Roman Empire, the park served as a verdant adjunct to the temple or theatre, an aesthetic complement to urban living.

The Roman park was eminently practical. The *Porticus Pompeiana* offered shelter for theatre-goers during rainstorms, afforded green space for exercise, and provided a stock of firewood in the event of a martial siege. This marriage of aesthetics and pragmatism, combined with a run of bequests from the likes of Julius Caesar, left Rome with myriad parks. In the first century AD, Martial described the capital as alive with 'the beauty of spring and the charm of fragrant Flora'.[10]

Not all citizens felt drawn to the *Porticus*. Elite countryside parks such as Pliny the Younger's (*c*.60–111 AD) estate at Laurentum, located 17 miles from Rome, could be ridden to 'with ease and safety at the close of day'.[11] Whereas the *Portico* heralded the park as a democratic forum, the Roman country villa adhered to more exclusive design remits. At Nero's Golden Temple, near Rome, and Hadrian's Villa at Tivoli, architects constructed sumptuous houses set in parkland settings. The Roman elite strolled in formal gardens with topiary, terraces, grottoes, vineyards, olive groves and ornamental ponds. Statues of gods, mythical beasts and rustic peasants lurked amidst the foliage, amounting to a themed landscape of classical mythology. Diana, the goddess of hunting, and Pan of the woods proved popular as park deities. Stone animals provided inanimate and non-threatening versions of the game beasts that roamed the hunting parks of Assyria and Persia.

Beyond the gardens often lay forested areas dedicated to sporting pursuits. T. Pompeius constructed the largest game park in Italy at 14 square miles. Hunting appealed as a heritage activity that paid homage to an ancient Golden Age of rusticity and allowed the Roman elite to connect with their ancestral past as 'warrior-farmers'.[12]

Pomp and feasting proved *de rigeur* in the Roman park. Guests expected amusement. At Laurentum, Quintus Hortensius created a game reserve called *Therotrophium* enclosed by high walls. At the sound of a horn, tame fauna approached feeding areas. Visitors banqueted on an elevated platform nearby. The animals served as performing beasts, offering animation to the static greenery. Horticultural writer Varro described one visit to the park that could have been taken straight out of a Disney movie:

> There was a wood of more than fifty acres, so our host told us, surrounded by a park wall, which he called not a warren but a chase. There on high ground dinner was laid, and as we were banqueting Hortensius ordered Orpheus to be summoned. He came complete with robe and lute, and was bidden to sing. Thereupon he blew a trumpet, and such a multitude of stags and boars and other four-footed beasts came flooding round us that the sight seemed as beautiful to me as the hunts staged by the aediles in the Circus Maximus.[13]

For Varro, the park operated as a veritable entertainment complex. The tamed and conditioned wildlife represented mealtime cabaret.

The concept of wildlife as entertainment was part of the Roman experience, but human–animal relationships usually lacked the harmony implicit in Varro's chronicle. At a game park owned by the Emperor Domitian (AD 81–96), animals were pursued with impunity towards a specially fabricated arena. As writer Suetonius recounted, 'many people often saw him [Domitian] slay a hundred wild beasts of different kinds.' The Emperor 'would even deliberately plant two arrows in the heads of some of his victims in such a way as to give the effect of horns'.[14] Such actions reflected the common conception that an imperial culture needed to indulge in ferocious activities to prove its martial mettle. Parks testified to Roman conquest of foreign nature, their organic features touted as spoils of war. As Pliny the Elder noted of parades in the capital, 'it is a remarkable fact that ever since the time of Pompey the Great even trees have figured among the captives in our triumphal processions'.[15]

Bloodthirsty pursuits in the park illuminated a Roman fascination with theatre based on animal and human suffering. Gladiatorial arenas that hosted fights to the death pulled vast crowds. In 186 BC, the first *venatio*, or animal show, took place as a prelude to a gladiatorial bout. Exhibitions of bestial brutality soon developed a dedicated fan base. Cognizant of the *venatio*'s low-brow appeal, imperial leaders considered arenas to be valuable venues in which to boost their popularity with plebeians. Organizers searched the far reaches of the Roman Empire to capture charismatic mega-fauna to delight audiences. Elephants, crocodiles, seals, leopards, camels, tigers and bears all featured. As crowd numbers swelled, so did the killing tallies. At a *venatio* to celebrate the opening of the Colosseum, 9,000 animals were despatched in just 100 days. Emperor Augustus orchestrated twenty-six *venationes*, with a body count in excess of 3,500.

NATURE AND DEER PARKS IN THE MIDDLE AGES

After the fall of the Roman Empire, concepts of nature continued to be transmitted between cultures by way of military campaigns, exploration and trade links. The Arab conquest of North Africa, Sicily and Spain (from AD 640), the Crusades (1095–1271), along with the voyages of Marco Polo (1254–1324) along the Silk Road, facilitated an exchange of ideas between East and West.

Visitors to Asia and the Orient brought back tales of fantastical pleasure grounds resonant with spiritual messages. In China, Han Emperor Wu Di (140–89 BC) modelled a grand landscape park after the paradise islands depicted in Buddhist cosmology. Chinese traveller Fa Hian applauded Dshetavana Park, India, used by Buddhist monks, for its 'clear water in the pond, the tall greenery, and the countless flowers of many colours'.[16] In North Africa, the son of Ibn Tulun (who assumed the Egyptian throne in 883) amazed guests with a park stocked with lilies, palms and fountains, along with a menagerie including a rare blue-eyed lion that guarded the ruler in the fashion of a domestic dog. In the seventh century, Arabian forces were so impressed by the vibrant friezes, carpets and parkscapes that graced the royal palaces of Persia that they transplanted the designs to their own parks. Tenets of Islamic horticulture in turn filtered through Europe during the Moorish occupation. In Spain, the mosque of Cordova constructed (785–987) for Abd er-Rahman I included 'the Court of the Oranges', complete with running water, soothing music and shade to promote prayer and meditation. Arranged geometrically, the court signified order and symmetry in the universe.

The construction of castle arbours, monastic cloister gardens and Byzantine courtyards with trees and flowers attested to Western interest in the natural world. Paradise remained synonymous with perfect environments. In Anglo-Saxon, 'paradise' translated as 'meadow' or 'pasture'. Notions of a classical Golden Age, local legends, religion and romantic poetry all perpetuated the concept of nature as a refuge from society. For the nobility, nature signified a retreat for aesthetic pleasure and a venue for spiritual uplift. However, for the average medieval peasant, the organic world meant livestock rearing and crop production.

With the second millennium, the park idea continued to have resonance in elite circles. In Palermo, King Roger of Sicily (died 1154) combined disparate cultural influences to nurture a retreat named the Parco, a 'pleasant and delightful' enclosure stocked with deer, goats and boar. Roger resided at his palace during the summer, finding 'solace at the Parco where, with a little hunting, he would relieve his mind from the cares and worries of state'.[17]

The park of Philopation, Constantinople (built in the ninth century), earned similar accolades as a resort for sport and leisure. As Odo of Deuil, chaplain to Louis VII, noted of his visit in 1147: 'Before the city stood a spacious and impressive ring of walls enclosing various kinds of game and including canals and ponds. Also, inside were certain hollows and caves which, in lieu of forests, furnished lairs for the animals. In that lovely place certain palaces which the emperors had built as their springtime retreat are conspicuous for their splendor.'[18] The park earned kudos as a landscape of hunting, escapism and imperial consumption.

The earliest reference to an English park dates to 1045, in a will noting a 'wood . . . outside the deerhay' in Great Ongar, Essex.[19] Park making expanded throughout Europe with the Normans. From the time of the Domesday Book to the mid-1300s, nobles and clergymen alike engaged in a frenzy of emparkment. An estimated 3,200 parks existed in England by 1300. By 1507, Polydore Vergil, the archdeacon of Wells, exclaimed that one-third of England was either park or forest land, so that 'almost everywhere a man may see clausures and parks paled and enclosed'.[20]

The popularity of park making across medieval Europe reflected elite fascination with hunting. As in prior periods, parks conserved game animals for sport. Owners cultivated deer, hare, boar, pheasants and partridges – all beasts of the chase destined for the royal feast table. The park guaranteed a constant supply of animals. The hunting reserves of Stromovka, near Prague, Bialowieza in Poland, Bakken in Denmark, and Fontainebleau in France served as landscapes of function, huntsmen's larders.

European deer parks were often situated close to royal forests and far from villages. Most featured an irregular or oval perimeter, in order to reduce fencing costs and prevent deer massing in corners during hunts. Parks often included a hunting lodge and a parker's (gamekeeper's) cottage. Many utilized a steep bank topped with pointed stakes known as the pale. The pale allowed wild deer to jump into the park, but not escape from it.

Typically between 75 and 200 acres, British parks encompassed a mixture of woodland, pasture, moor and marsh. As horticultural writers Charles Estienne and Jean Liebault instructed in *Maison Rustique* (1564), 'nor ought the parke to consist of one kind of ground only, as all of wood, all grasse, or all coppice, but of divers'.[21] The Great Park of Abergavenny, Wales, included parts of Sugarloaf Mountain. Although parks were often viewed as untended areas (in stark contrast to surrounding farmland), many were managed intensively to ensure that game animals prospered and predators such as the wolf perished.

Some park owners profited from deer production. Henry III's park at Havering, Essex, boasted an annual yield of forty-four fallow deer between 1234 and 1263. At Christmas in 1250, 200 does were salted and shipped to London for yuletide feasting. Gamekeepers waged a war of attrition on poachers and grappled with environmental problems such as overgrazing, disease and starvation. Only efficient estate management ensured the viability of the park as a landscape of game conservation. One visitor to England in 1549 exclaimed that the country supported more deer than France did people.

Not only deer prospered in medieval parks. Preserves sported fish-ponds, rabbit warrens, falconries and stockades for swine. At Prior Park, Somerset, established in 1090, monks tended grazing land, fish-ponds, vineyards, dove-cotes and a small farm. The medieval deer park operated as a multiple-use landscape, often proving itself integral to the local manorial economy.

Despite its utilitarian remit, ritual and aesthetics still influenced the deer preserve. Park sport was steeped in concepts of chivalry and fair play. Religious imagery, themes of natural abundance and utopian aspirations influenced the design of many parkscapes. As with prior incarnations, the medieval park conveyed an idealized aesthetic. According to *Maison Rustique*, the ideal preserve sat on a rolling landscape of hills and plains, providing scenic vistas as well as amplifying 'the crys of the hounds, the winding of hornes, or the gibetting of the huntsmen passeth through the same, doubling the musicke, and making it tenne times more delightful'.[22] The park served as a venue of sensory delight – a place of adrenalin and stimulation. For the bishop of Coutances, the creation of an appropriate park scene in Normandy demanded nothing short of the importation of English oaks and deer. Other owners installed palisades and mounts for ocular effect.

A society dominated by Christian theology predictably drew parallels between the medieval deer park and the Garden of Eden. Across Europe, architectural and horticultural design bore witness to the confluence of nature and religious allegory. Gothic churches such as Canterbury Cathedral (1175) included imagery of trees in ornate carvings. Aspirations to recapture Adam's horticultural wisdom and to reanimate Eden led to the construction of botanic arboretums at Padua (1545) and Oxford (1657). The association between nature and spirituality made the deer park a paradise landscape in the West. Archbishop Baudry described the estate of the Abbey of Fecamp, Normandy, built in 658, as 'like a garden of Paradise, set in a lovely enclosed valley, between two hills, surrounded by farmland on one side and a charming little wood on the other'.[23] Artists and writers conceptualized biblical landscapes with reference to hunting parks. John Milton in *Paradise Lost* (1667) depicted Eden as a park-like English landscape of rural mounds, tree clumps and glades. In an illustration for *The Historie of the Perfect-Cursed-Blessed Man* (1628) (see fig. 1), Joseph Fletcher framed paradise as rolling meadowland. Behind the figures of Adam and Eve lay a menagerie of exotic creatures, including an elephant, a lion and a camel. An equivalent faunal scene could be found for real at Henry I's Woodstock (1110) with its complement of lion, camel, leopard, lynx and porcupine.

As in earlier centuries, parks operated as symbols of social prestige. To Francis Bacon, parks represented 'the first marks of honour and nobility, and the ornament of a flourishing kingdom'.[24] Fully integrated into aristocratic life, green landscapes bespoke cultural sophistication. With rights to empark-ment usually granted by royal licence, ownership of a hunting preserve was

Figure 1. From Joseph Fletcher, Historie of the Perfect-Cursed-Blessed Man (1628).

fiercely tied to status. Earls, lords, barons, abbots and bishops all expected their own parks. When the fortunes of prominent families waned, rising classes duly appropriated parklands to bolster their own reputations. As Moryson's *Itinerary* (1617) observed, 'Every gentleman of £500–£1000 rent by the year hath a park for them inclosed with payles of wood for two or three myles compass.'[25]

Along with its symbolic value, the deer park played a practical role in asserting royal privilege. Norman law in Britain and France granted the Crown exclusive access to parkland. Elites imposed tolls on grazing and haulage. Wild-roaming deer became royal property. Such measures amounted to sovereignty over ecological resources. For the king, parks served as tools of diplomacy, land to be used to buy off recalcitrant nobles or reward loyal supporters. Park landlords meanwhile demanded tribute. The abbot of Glastonbury required serfs in his eleven manors to work at Pilton Park, Somerset. The array of social obligations embedded in the park idea made it a key power structure in medieval Europe.

Park formation often entailed restrictions on public use. Peasants accustomed to using meadows and woods for grazing, hunting and timber collection suddenly encountered barred landscapes. Those who failed to respect new park boundaries received draconian punishments. For stealing the king's venison, offenders could expect hanging, amputation, castration or transportation. As the Hyde Park Edict of 1536 stated, 'as the King's most royal majesty is desirous to have the games of hare, partridge, pheasant and heron preserved, in and about the honour of his palace of Westminster, for his own disport and pastime, no person on pain of imprisonment of their bodies . . . is to presume to hunt or hawk' in the preserve.[26] The medieval park thereby proclaimed a hierarchy of killing rights stretching from ruler to serf.

For members of the peasantry, hunter-gatherer activities in local woods and meadows embodied part of rural heritage and seasonal custom. Such lands provided vital means of subsistence and serviced community identity. Some villagers proved reluctant to accept park boundaries. As the Statute of Richard II bemoaned, 'Forasmuch as divers artificers, labourers and servants keep for their own use greyhounds and other dogs, and on holy days when good Christian people be at church hearing divine service they go hunting in parks, warrens and coneyries of Lords and others.' The governing class ultimately harboured fears of rebellious peasants cavorting amidst the greenwood in Robin Hood fashion. Aristocrats expected the park to serve as a breeding ground for docile deer herds rather than a restive peasantry. Instead, the Statute of Richard II complained that rabble rousers used park spaces to 'hold their assemblies, conversations and conspiracies to rise together and disobey their allegience'.[27]

During periods of civic unrest, parks and royal forests were targeted for sacking. Angry at enclosures of common land, peasants raided the deer park at Stourton, Wiltshire (emparked in 1427) in 1549 and broke down the pale. Preserves symbolized feudalism and royal excess. Citizens attacked deer parks as a form of gesture politics during the English Civil War (1642–9). Parliamentarian forces categorized parks as legitimate military targets and routinely routed estates belonging to Royalist sympathizers. At Fawley Court, Northamptonshire, Parliamentarians destroyed grain stocks, slaughtered deer and vandalized the pale. In 1642, George Melsam and two accomplices boasted of how they had executed 300 deer in private parks. Charles I met the same fate six years later. The park had joined a national battleground where class, politics and ideological agendas clashed. By the time of the Interregnum, multiple parks were bereft of game. Red deer disappeared from the New Forest entirely. Meanwhile, the government of Oliver Cromwell announced plans to auction off England's parklands to raise revenue. Ninety-three were surveyed and offered for sale.

After the restoration of the monarchy, most of England's deer parks were returned to their former keepers. The halcyon days of sporting pursuits and noble privilege had passed none the less. Elite society turned elsewhere for entertainment. Falling land rents and declining agricultural returns diminished the influence of the old feudal aristocracy. By the seventeenth century, many deer parks were broken up and replaced by farmland. Others reverted to woodland, as management impulses slackened. Medieval Essex had once boasted 160 parks, yet by 1610, only forty-nine remained.

THE PALACE OF THE SUN KING

Parkscapes survived thanks to a developing interest in aesthetics. Fresh ideas about nature as something rational and mechanistic fostered an innovative approach to landscape design that favoured the orderly, the monumental and the geometric. Renaissance humanism, with its promotion of reason and its glorification of classical civilization, influenced the new trend in horticulture. At Boboli Park, Florence (1550), Villa d'Este, Tivoli (1550), and Villandry, France (1532), owners adorned their classical villas and chateaux with formal grounds of clipped hedges and intersecting paths set aside for parade and pageant. The water garden at Tivoli, complete with thrusting jets, still pools and spouting ornaments, featured paths that led to a surrounding hunting park populated by statues, obelisks and pavilions. Louis XIV's lavish estate at Versailles best epitomized this fresh rendition of the park ideal in French-Italianate style.

Much like the early history of the park idea, the story of Versailles owes much to the universality of hunting as a royal pursuit. In 1623, Louis III, a frequent visitor to the forests of Marly and Saint-Germain, decided to construct a hunting lodge. The lodge grew to encompass a nearby park of 117 acres. On assuming the throne in 1661, Louis XIV resolved to update the chateau at Versailles. The new king envisaged a sumptuous palace that would trump Vaux-le-Vicomte, owned by finance minister Nicholas Fouquet, an adversary. The parkland of Versailles promised a rustic enclave for entertainment and ceremony. Versailles also became a locus of royal authority. The royal court and assorted bureaucracy relocated to Versailles between 1678 and 1682. The remodelled residence, complete with formal garden and parkland, initiated a new age under the Bourbon dynasty.

Louis inaugurated the Versailles project in the first year of his reign. The king commissioned architect Louis Le Vau, painter Charles Le Brun and landscape designer André Le Nôtre to together forge a suitably awe-inspiring residence. Le Nôtre transformed the marginal farmland and swampy marshes around Versailles into a grand canvas projecting kingly munificence and natural order. From the nondescript swamp rose a grandiose landscape resonant with structure and symbolism. The French landscape designer believed that beauty emerged through organized space, proposing a vision of Versailles based on a huge half-star shape. The whole ensemble was arranged around a central east–west axis, nearly 10 kilometres long, from which radiated linear avenues and canals, interspaced by terraces, shrubbery, parterres, sculptures and decorative topiary. The symmetrically poised classical garden spanned 250 acres. Outside the formal garden lay the Petit Parc (185 acres), and the old Grand Parc (16,000 acres of wild hunting land, traversed by rides). All this was ringed by a park wall.

Dubbed 'the Sun King', Louis XIV naturally wanted his park to convey power over nature. The sheer scale of the engineering project paid homage to the human ability to dramatically transform the environment. The park took 24 years to complete. Some 36,000 workers toiled on the project. Mounds were levelled, marshes drained, banks created, canals excavated, and lakes dredged. To create the perfect dendron facade, Le Nôtre had old-growth oaks, beech, elm and lime transplanted from France's royal forests. Numerous experiments were attempted in the hope of providing water for the Grand Canal and its thirsty fountains. Pumps, windmills, along with an elaborate scheme to divert the River Eure (50 miles away) by canals and aqueducts, all failed. Engineers solved the dilemma by a system of reservoirs. Hidden hydraulics brought the 1,400 fountains to life. However, due to lack of pressure and flow, the fountains could only be turned on in sequence as Louis walked by. Still, Versailles attested to the power of humans to manipulate nature. Greenhouses allowed the King to serve lettuce, figs and strawberries out of season. Awestruck visitors took a trip along the Grand Canal, serenaded by gondoliers, to observe the collection of exotic beasts, birds and flowers interned in the menagerie. Meanwhile, the sculptures, formal pathways and carefully groomed formal garden lofted nature as first and foremost an artistic property. As Saint-Simon observed, 'The King loved to tyrannise over nature to bring it into subjection with the aid of art and money.'[28]

Versailles reflected regal authority over French society as well as the countryside. From elevated terraces, Louis' estate could be viewed in its entirety. The king's domain extended to the horizon, the palace and its environs a symbol of boundless royal power. Versailles proved an intensely symbolic landscape in which horticultural features were employed to project royal omnificence. The ordered landscape mirrored the centralized nature of the French state, with Louis set at its head as absolute ruler. The vastness of the park underscored the vision of authority by virtue of land assimilation – what historian Keith Thomas has dubbed 'planting for ownership'.[29] The avenues of Versailles fanned out into the surrounding areas, placing the park at the geographical heart of French life. Its roads, like arteries, distributed resources, symbolic authority, and even army units to the far reaches of the province.

Versailles might also be seen as a themed landscape. Between 1689 and 1705, the King himself penned six guidebooks so that staff could lead visitors around the park attractions in a regimented manner.[30] On navigating the vast grounds, tourists observed regal idolatry in the form of clipped topiary, thrusting fountains and chiselled stone. The grotto of Tethys synthesized classical legend with the sun and Louis XIV as king. As one guidebook noted, 'Because in the same way that the poets have pretended that the Sun . . . goes for rest in the palace of Tethys and relaxes from his daily work, it was thought that that ingenious fiction could serve as an agreeable subject for a grotto at Versailles, where the King goes from time to time to take some relaxation and to rest from his great and illustrious toils.'[31]

Versailles was certainly the place to be seen in. Separated from the working landscape, the park represented a fantasy realm, an aristocratic pleasure ground where the elite could indulge in leisure far away from the rigours of economy and society. As Frederick II ventured, 'A young man passed for an imbecile if he had not stayed for some time at Versailles.'[32] Louis XIV routinely held fetes at the park. Guests invited to the 'Pleasures of the Enchanted Isle' fete, held 6–14 May 1664, immersed themselves in carnival, parades, feasting, games, fireworks, theatre and dancing. Huge painted canvases adorned the grounds, providing a grand backdrop to the human performance. Nature and theatrics combined to forge a fantastical and frivolous illusion. A glowing commentary on the 1674 fete by André Felibien hailed Versailles as a magic kingdom facilitated by an army of hidden stagehands:

One thing specifically remarkable about the king's fetes is the great speed with which all this glory appeared. His commands were so carefully and diligently carried out that it seemed like enchantment; almost in one moment, before you observe it, you are amazed to find theatres erected, groves with fountains and figures, refreshments carried about, and thousands of things going on that it would seem impossible to get done without a great many workmen and in a long time.[33]

Arguably, Versailles amounted to a prototype Disney World.

As with many innovative parkscapes, Versailles spawned a plethora of imitations. Myriad park owners desired the artistry, regality and plaudits associated with the Palace of the Sun King. The French-Italianate style, stressing an amalgam of art and nature, giganticism and intricacies, water features and terracing, was adapted to various locales. At Hampton Court, Charles II ordered the placement of avenues and canals on the rustic landscape, while later rulers William and Mary remodelled the court in Franco-Dutch style, with semicircular gardens, canals, walkways, parterres and elaborate topiary. Three huge avenues fanned out from the central house across the horizon. By 1700, 4,000 trees had been planted. At the same time, the old roots of the park idea remained detectable in the landscape – vestiges of Hampton Court's days as a hunting reserve visible in the semi-wild Bushey Park area. Across continental Europe too, elites replanted their parks in the French style. Designed for Duke Friedrich, Herrenhausen, Hanover (1666), offered a geometric garden of well-clipped hedges and intersecting gravel paths with a fountain at its centre, while the castle of Schonbrunn, Vienna (1696), featured a formal landscape with linear paths, fountains, parterres and a menagerie. Further afield, Chinese Emperor Quinlong hired two Jesuit priests to fashion a French pleasure park in Beijing. The remodelled summer palace of Yuan–ming–yuan (1747–59) included an encircling canal, cascades and a water-clock. The fascination with formal gardening grew and grew. As naturalist John Aubrey noted in 1691, 'I may affirm that there is now . . . ten times as much gardening about London as there was in 1660.'[34]

2 The English Landscape Park

On 25 June 1712, social commentator and philosopher Joseph Addison published a landmark essay in *The Spectator* magazine. In it, Addison issued a vitriolic attack on the formal nature and artificiality of French garden design:

instead of humouring Nature, [gardeners] love to deviate from it as much as possible. Our Trees rise in Cones, Globes, and Pyramids. We see the Marks of the Scissars upon every Plant and Bush. I do not know whether I am singular in my Opinion, but, for my own part, I would rather look upon a Tree in all its Luxuriancy and Diffusion of Boughs and Branches, than when it is thus cut and trimmed into a Mathematical Figure.[1]

Addison was seizing on a fresh design aesthetic that promoted the sublime qualities of unkempt and rural nature. Dispensing with formalism and symmetry, a new and distinctive park template took hold in the eighteenth century. The park idea motioned soft curves and rustic disunity over terracing and straight lines. Acres of turf ran right up to houses, with ornamental lakes, rolling meadowland, winding drives and irregular tree cover beyond.

THE ENGLISH LANDSCAPE PARK EMERGES

The new horticultural style drew on a number of influences, an interest in the Orient being one of them. Eighteenth-century Cathay traders and Jesuit missionaries captivated Western audiences with tales of lavish pleasure gardens and intimate mountain retreats. In 1743, Brother Attiret described the palace and adjoining park of Emperor Ch'ien Lung near Peking as a fantastical, haphazard landscape of grottoes, streams, bridges, pagodas and crags. Exotic visions of chaotic wildness spurred emotions of fear among some. None the less, British gardeners gravitated towards Chinese landscape design, mesmerized by its application of flowing water and rocky charms. Colonial landscape theorists borrowed classic Oriental designs such as the pagoda and water feature, in the process reinventing them as intrinsic parts of the English park.

The Italian Campagna proved another inspirational locale for the British gentry. Sojourning elites in the 1700s took 'Grand Tours' across the Alpine terrain. Such scenery reminded them of the Arcadian ideal. Paeans to this lost Golden Age of antiquity, with its rustic shepherds, browsing flocks and ancient ruins, found artistic expression in works by Salvator Rosa, Claude Lorrain and Gaspar Poussin, who popularized a natural aesthetic based on pastoralism. English tourists returned home eager to make their own estates resemble Arcadian art. This fertile connection between horticultural design and painter's canvas found literal form in a new English word – *landskip* – a term first employed by Dutch artists to describe the scene on a freshly brushed canvas now appropriated to describe a pleasing geographic vista.

Theorists pondered the constitution of nature in the park. *A Philosophical Enquiry into the Origin of Our Ideas of the Sublime and Beautiful* (1757) by Edmund Burke and *The Analysis of Beauty* (1753) by William Hogarth exemplified a new scholarly discourse on the meaning of nature. Social commentators envisioned unkempt land as a venue for moral and intellectual uplift rather than a dangerous and fearsome locality. Previously defined in opposition to the countryside, planned landscapes of parks and gardens took on a fresh rustic and informal countenance. Nature no longer required art for beautification according to critics such as Jean Jacques Rousseau. Rousseau much preferred rolling landscapes of meadows and woods to the French-Italian style marked by its statues and urns. Alexander Pope (1688–1744) offered similar advice: 'In all, let *Nature* never be forgot. Consult the *Genius* of the *Place* in all.'[2] Instead of geometry and contrivance, Pope advocated irregularity, variety and emotional connection. Criticism from British quarters assumed a distinctly patriotic countenance. Dosing the park ideal with a potent strain of nationalism, Horace Walpole, in *The History of the Modern Taste in Gardening* (1771), termed the new aesthetic akin to an English revolution triumphing over French formalism. The park depicted political liberalism in organic form.

The reframing of the park idea required significant investment. Fortunately, a period of economic prosperity had set in after the Glorious Revolution of 1688, leaving the British aristocracy and landed gentry with the necessary funds. The continuing process of land enclosure assisted elite control of political life and ecological resources. Between 1761 and 1844, some 2,500 Acts of Parliament facilitated the fencing in and cultivation of more than 4,000,000 acres of common and open land. Buoyed by industrial and consumer revolutions, a rising class of merchants and businessmen sought to enter polite society by buying parkscapes.

Interest in park aesthetics gave rise to a new brand of literature. In 1718, Stephen Switzer produced the first instructive guidebook, *The Ichnographia Rustica*, on transforming country seats into fashionable parks. A dedicated profession of landscape designer emerged. Exponents included Charles Bridgeman (1690–1738), William Kent (1685–1748), Lancelot 'Capability' Brown (1715–83) and Humphrey Repton (1752–1818). Brown designed more than 170 parks, while Repton remodelled 220. Many parkscapes matured long after the deaths of their principal architects. Innovation led to imitation, with professional and amateur gardeners carrying the new schematics to provincial parks and towns. A cadre of gardeners – William Emes in the

Midlands, Nathaniel Richmond in Hertfordshire and Buckinghamshire – crafted informal parks for the minor gentry, while urban-based imitators attempted to create rural vistas in microcosm.

The English landscape park enshrined naturalism as its creed. Landscape designers received lofty praise for their adherence to 'the Genius of the Place' and their ability to apprehend the environment 'with Poet's feeling and with Painter's Eye'.[3] Nevertheless, the English park remained a constructed scene. The new style rejected regimented topiary and straight paths in favour of natural growth and irregularity, but park landscapes still represented contrived scenes designed to leave a particular impression on guests. Naturalness never equated with the preservation of representative scenery, nor did it extol unkempt wilderness. Instead, the English park ideal touted a specific version of naturalism based on the medieval deer park template subtly refined with classical iconography. The task of the architect lay in bringing this vision to fruition by the ample planting of trees and taming of banks and pastures. As 'Capability' Brown admitted in a letter to the Reverend Thomas Dyer in 1772, his mandate involved 'hideing what is disagreeable and shewing what is beautifull'.[4] Travel writer William Gilpin concurred: 'We expect, that all offensive trumpery, and all the rough luxuriance of undergrowth, should be removed; unless where it is necessary to thicken, or connect a scene; or hide some staring boundary.'[5] Conjuring the appropriate scene demanded attention to both micro and macro aspects. Designers paid heed to shading effects through individual tree placement, or gently altered the sweep of a bank to remove rights of way, roads and even villages in the attainment of sweeping parkland vistas. Despite the hearty paeans to heeding the infinite variety of nature, the park emerged as a consumer product marked by a checklist of essential features. Excavations of rocky ground, the softening of land contours, tree planting in clumps and on hill crests, along with the digging out of a serpentine lake, proved obligatory. Parks often included the ha-ha – a concealed ditch invented by Charles Bridgeman that prevented deer and sheep from nibbling lawns near the house while preserving the illusion of undulating scenery stretching to the horizon.

READING THE ENGLISH PARK

The English landscape park denoted an island of exclusivity consciously separated from the working countryside: what landscape historian Tom Williamson dubbed 'a landscape of polite exclusion'.[6] The scenery on display conveyed specific messages about society and culture. As the following four examples illustrate, the park operated as a story, a political cartoon, a status symbol and a work of art.

Created by *nouveau riche* banker Henry Hoare (1677–1725) and his son Henry II (1705–85), Stourhead offered a seemingly simple stroll around a tranquil lake (see fig. 2). However, the park functioned as a landscape of allegory and allusion. Stourhead featured an old hunting preserve of 1,000 acres

Figure 2. Stourhead, Wiltshire. Photograph by John Wills.

dating to 1427, complete with pale, deer leaps and hunting lodge. The existence of this medieval park well suited the aesthetic tastes of the age. Major reconstruction of the estate began in 1744. By damming a river, Hoare created a central lake. Beech and conifers were sown on the sides of the valley, and the lawns adorned with temples, grottoes, a pantheon and a Palladian bridge. The classical references and picturesque quality of Stourhead marked it out as a fashionable country seat.

Hoare designed Stourhead as a 'pictorial circuit garden'. The landscape itself told a story.[7] Hoare rendered the classical tale of Aeneas in the underworld in architectural and sylvan form. Guests had to saunter through the Wiltshire countryside to appreciate the full intricacies of the plot. The journey began at the Bristol Cross (brought to the estate from the city in 1765). Across the lake could be spied the Pantheon (or Temple of Hercules), the apparent centre of a grand landscape painting. To reach there, the trail led past the Temple of Flora, a celebration of pagan river-gods, constructed in 1744–6, and a collection of medieval ponds known as Diana's Basin. Visitors passed over a bridge, and through a conifer grove, to the grotto, a collection of caverns home to a bubbling spring. Constructed in 1748, the damp, dark, rocky cave boasted an inscription that read 'Within fresh water and seats in the living rock, the home of the nymphs', taken from Virgil's *Aeneid*. The central chamber featured statues of nymphs. Returning to the sunlit world, a short path led walkers to the Pantheon (1753–4) (recalling the journey that Aeneas himself undertook), an imposing Roman facsimile complete with statues of Bacchus, Diana and Hercules among others. The trail continued across the lake dam, ascended a rock bridge (1762–5), past the Hermitage (1771), before climbing to the Temple of Apollo (1765), which offered a commanding view over the whole story/scene. At Stourhead, a landscape park was akin to a text. Nature served as an allegorical landscape whereby tourists navigated their way to architectural artefacts of classical significance. This approach to park making marked Stourhead as an early theme park. However, to comprehend the full significance of the park required a classical education, something not required at Disney's themed kingdom.

Stowe, Lord Cobham's family seat in Buckinghamshire, featured a seventeenth-century house and a formal garden spanning 28 acres. In 1713, Stowe grew to incorporate a softly contoured park encompassing 500 acres. Like Stourhead, Stowe proffered a landscape to be read as a text, but whereas Hoare favoured classical allegory, Cobham chose contemporary political commentary.

Stowe Park paid homage to ancient civilizations by its obelisks and its statues, but it also depicted a contemporary Whiggish philosophy that elevated Britain as the new Rome and its landscape as one of liberty. Not just a celebration of antiquity and of perfect nature, Stowe highlighted the park as a cartoon. Its environment consciously delivered savvy political satire. The landscape echoed the ideology of its powerful owner. Cobham's pleasure grounds, in all their splendour, bespoke national confidence and British imperial grandeur. Through its irregular and informal presentation, Stowe's nature praised English liberty at the expense of French absolutism and formality. Moreover, the specific features of the park proclaimed a vision of Whiggish progress, parliamentarianism and humanism. At the Elysian Fields, an open piece of greensward in the east of the estate, resided the Temple of British Worthies (1735). Inside the structure stood statues of dignitaries, including Alfred the Great (who was also celebrated at Stourhead by a tower), Queen Elizabeth I, Walter Raleigh, Francis Drake, Francis Bacon, Isaac Newton, Alexander Pope and John Locke, all honoured as 'gallant countrymen; Heroes, Patriots and Wits'.[8] Across a narrow stretch of water dubbed the River Styx lay the Temple of Ancient Virtue (1734), representing classical morality juxtaposed with a decrepit Temple of Modern Virtue, complete with a headless statue deemed to be Tory politician Horace Walpole. Such temples linked the park to political commentary. Nature and national identity intertwined. For Cobham, the park served as an organic tool of social criticism, a landscape designed to impart a message. Beneath its pleasing veneer of classical beauty and soft contours, the park signified a powerful ideological weapon.

Stowe proved a remarkably popular visitor destination during the eighteenth century. To Williamson, Cobham's seat amounted to a 'theme park'.[9] Hundreds of people journeyed to the park to experience its design innovations. Some stayed a day, others a few weeks. Touring landscape parks emerged as a popular pastime in high society. The park was the chosen milieu for the privileged, *the* place in which to be seen. Estate owners duly responded to the craze by providing accommodation for guests (the Spread Eagle public house at Stourhead being one), while enterprising landlords even took to issuing admission tickets.

Prior Park, Somerset, revealed the value of the park as a marketing tool and advertising motif. At Ralph Allen's estate, perched on the hillside above the spa town of Bath, the park glorified antiquity, social convention and the status of its illustrious owner. Bought as part of the Combe Down estate by the wealthy Cornish stone merchant and entrepreneur in 1726–8, the medieval deer park of Prior Park underwent radical transformation in the 1730s. For members of the rising commercial classes such as Allen, the acquisition of a landscape park offered a fast track to polite society. Like Henry Hoare, Allen regarded his estate as an 'enchanted paradise' that manifested personal ingenuity, enterprise and power.[10] His Palladian mansion stood at 50 metres wide, the widest in the country at that time. From the windows of the house could be viewed the whole of the city, as if part of Allen's own kingdom. An engraving by Anthony Walker in 1752 adroitly depicted the grandeur of the mansion, its environmental situation and imposing aspect (see fig. 3). Alongside the perimeter wall ran Allen's revolutionary haulage tramway. The palatial house hugged the skyline authoritatively.

Though on a much smaller scale than Stourhead or Stowe, the landscape of Prior Park paid homage to fashions in design and aestheticism. Situated in a steep valley, the park offered a triangular lawn leading to a pond and a retaining wall. To the east lay hedges and urns laid out in a formal style, and to the

Figure 3. Prior Park in 1752. Engraving by Anthony Walker. Reproduced by kind permission of Bath Central Library. ©Bath Central Library.

west a 'wilderness' with twisting paths, a serpentine lake, a grotto, a cascade and a green glade, all located amidst dense woodland. Inspired by Alexander Pope – himself a regular visitor to the park – the 'wilderness' took chaos and drama as its governing themes. Rocks, trees, light and shade were consciously employed to incite terror and awe in visitors as they navigated its sylvan depths. This was an environment designed to stir the emotions, a 'direct attempt to produce a thrill'.[11] Reintroduced in the 1740s, deer roamed the south lawn, their presence fermenting a vision of an ancient aristocratic game preserve. Visitors praised the apparently unmodified character of Prior Park. As *Universal Magazine* (May 1754) noted:

Instead of forcing nature to bend to art, he [Allen] has pursued only what the natural situation has pointed out to him. . . . [Allen] levelled no hills, but enjoys the beauty of the prospects they afford; he has cut down no woods but struck through them fine walks, and has, by that means, a delightful grove always filled with birds, which afford the rural ear a music transcending all others.[12]

Prior Park offered a secluded realm for relaxation. However, Allen also saw in Prior Park a country residence to be gazed at by high society. Walker's engraving depicts well-dressed ladies and gentlemen peering over the deliberately low enclosing wall to steal a glimpse of the landscape of leisure and consumption. Allen even took to opening the park to the public every Thursday, so that they might appreciate the floral display and recognize in him a man of taste as well as entrepreneurial acumen. As Philip Thicknesse remarked in 1788, Prior Park provided 'A noble seat which sees all Bath and which was built for all Bath to see'.[13] This mixture of exclusivity and visibility suggested an important role for the park as a status symbol.

Wivenhoe Park, Essex, connected the material landscape with artistry. Purchased by the Rebow family in 1733–4, the Bacon's green estate, as it was originally known, featured a modest country house and park with sixty-four deer. Upon gaining ownership, the Rebows – like Ralph Allen and Henry Hoare – set about remodelling and extending the park to achieve a greater flair. In 1758, Isaac Martin Rebow constructed a new house, while local architect Richard Woods won the contract to redesign the parkland. A 1765 plan by Woods conformed to the traditions of the age in its combination of new carriage roads, tree and lawn plantings, the levelling of contours, the creation of a ha-ha, and the construction of two lakes divided by a rustic bridge. Woods also rebuilt an old deer house on the estate. At the invitation of the owner, artist John Constable resided at the estate, where he compiled sketches that resulted in the canvas *Wivenhoe Park* (1816). Constable presented a typical pastoral idyll that paid homage to the broader English landscape park ideal. With the lake in the foreground, the house behind, and the picture framed by clumps of trees, the artwork exuded a sense of rolling country and open space. Rustic animation came in the guise of swans, a girl on a cart, and men fishing. Constable also widened the lake and steepened its banks for artistic impact and aesthetic aggrandizement. The canvas presented a composite scene of a composite scene. The park itself had already been redesigned to satisfy one aesthetic ideal; Constable took it to another dimension.

Wivenhoe Park proved popular not just with Constable. When visitor D. W. Coller explored the 250 acre site in 1858, he spoke of 'picturesque and diversified views of hill and vale and woodland scenery'. Pertinently, he praised the preserve for its deer, timber resources, and overall 'pleasant rural picture', suggesting an enduring role for the park as a landscape of production.[14] With its herd of cattle munching grass beside the lake, Constable's rendition of the Rebow estate similarly inferred working country rather than a single-use pleasure ground. For all its reputation as a retreat for the upper classes, the English landscape park needed to provide an economic return. Some parks contained enclaves designated for forestry. Others operated as game reserves. With their open meadows and clumps of trees, the aesthetic parameters of the English landscape park suited grazing practices (though nibbled saplings and trampled streambeds presumably detracted from the overall effect). The English landscape park thus combined recreation and functionality, idealism and utility. As 'Capability' Brown observed, the park provided 'all the elegance and *all the comforts* that mankind wants in the Country'.[15]

A LANDSCAPE OF COMPETITION AND EMULATION

The balance of utility and aesthetics helped to enshrine the landscape park as an archetypal feature of the British countryside by the 1800s. During a visit to England in 1828, German Prince Pückler-Muskau exclaimed:

We have made a calculation, dear Julia, that if you were with us . . . you could not, with your aversion to foot exercise, see above a quarter of a park a day, and that it would take you at least four hundred and twenty years to see all the parks in England, of which there are at least a hundred thousand, for they swarm whichever way you turn your steps.[16]

Hyperbole apart, the sentiments of the prince were well-founded. Between 1760 and 1820, the number of parks listed in the English Home Counties increased by 100 per cent. Britain boasted more than 4,000 parks by 1783, the year in which 'Capability' Brown died.

British landowners refashioned old regimented pleasure grounds into rolling vistas with serpentine lakes, open meadows and tree-lined hills. An organic variety of 'cultural capital', each park needed to sport the latest design features to attract distinction.[17] As the contemporary pamphlet *Common Sense* proclaimed, 'Every man now, be his fortune what it will, is to be doing something at his Place . . . One large Room, a Serpentine River, and a Wood are become the absolute Necessities of Life.'[18] Akin to theme park engineers jockeying to build the highest, fastest and longest rollercoaster, landscape park designers strove to craft the ultimate paradise. Park owners and architects nervously paid heed to features being constructed elsewhere. Henry Hoare saw park making, like banking, as a 95 cut-throat venture in which only the strongest prevailed: 'Whether at pleasure or business let us be in earnest, and ever active to be outdone or exceeded by none, that is the way to thrive.'[19] Desires to elicit the ultimate landscape park sometimes produced eclectic and flamboyant canvases. Alton Towers (1812), a fantasy kingdom fashioned from 500 acres of scrubby forest in Staffordshire for Charles Talbot, the fifteenth earl of Shrewsbury, included eight lakes, a 90-foot Chinese pagoda fountain, a cast-iron Gothic temple and a Swiss cottage complete with resident Welsh harp player. At the entrance to the fairytale landscape stood a facsimile of the Choragic Temple of Lysicrates in ancient Athens, inside of which stood a bust of the earl adorned with the enigmatic words 'he made the desert smile'.

Competition extended far beyond British shores. Fervent spates of building and remodelling occurred across eighteenth-century Europe as landowners re-engineered their estates in the modish English style. In 1782, horticultural designers laid out 482 acres at the palace of Catherine the Great and Pavlovsk Park according to the English blueprint, complete with hermitage, agate pavilion, serpentine lake and monumental bridge. The park impressed gardening aficionado J. C. Loudon on a visit in 1812 (although he was less enamoured of the surrounding environs, having been reputedly attacked by wolves *en route* to St Petersburg). Further imitations of the English country seat could be found at the medieval hunting park of Bialowieza, Poland, and the impressive Wilhelmshöhe castle and park near Kassel, Germany. Even the palace of Trianon – grand retreat of the French royalty – boasted its own *Jardin Anglais* (1774), where Marie Antoinette played shepherdess in her private theme park. The rustic fantasy landscape comprised of a series of quaint cottages, their rude interiors concealing palatial interiors fit for the queen, a dairy, a windmill and a barn, arranged around a serpentine lake. Bleating animals and toiling peasants completed the rustic idyll.

Across the Atlantic, President Thomas Jefferson elected to create his Monticello estate as an informal park, viewing the English model as 'beauty of the very first order in landscape design'.[20] Jefferson had visited Stowe, Painshill and Blenheim during a tour of Britain with John Adams (then serving as US ambassador to England) in 1786. Jefferson read their template of open meadows, irregular trees and undulating paths – a vision of pure nature over artifice – as highly suitable for transplant to Virginia.[21] Known for his skills as a naturalist, the President compiled copious lists detailing the species of flowers and trees installed at his retreat in the Blue Ridge Mountains. Traditional park hunting pursuits also found their place in the Monticello ensemble, as one of his slaves, Isaac, recalled: 'Mr. Jefferson had a large park at Monticello: built in a sort of a flat on the side of the mountain. When the hunters run the deer down thar, they'd jump into the park & couldn't git out. When old master heard hunters in the park he used to go down thar wid his gun & order em out.'[22] Though Jefferson may have embraced the English landscape park ideal, his political sparring partner, John Adams, remained unconvinced. Left unimpressed by his tour of England's aristocratic seats, Adams regarded parks not as sumptuous nature resorts but as flagrant symbols of Old World decadence, class privilege and autocracy. 'It will be long before Ridings, Parks, Pleasure Grounds, Gardens . . . grow so much in fashion in America,' he surmised.[23] The democratic soil of the New World was not regarded as fertile terrain for the park idea to flourish. Or so Adams thought.

THE CHANGING FORTUNES OF THE ENGLISH LANDSCAPE PARK

The popularity of the English landscape park waned during the latter years of the nineteenth century. Depressed agricultural prices from the 1870s brought diminishing returns on rural estates, while changes to taxation laws – notably the imposition of death duties in Britain in 1894 – further drained aristocratic coffers. Maintenance budgets were slashed, gamekeepers and gardeners made redundant. Buildings crumbled, shrubs grew wild. Pauperized aristocrats auctioned off as much as 25 per cent of the British countryside between 1918 and 1922. With 485 country houses demolished between 1918 and 1945, many parkscapes disappeared entirely. The Forestry Commission (1919) bought up sizeable acreage, bulldozed houses, and put rolling parkland under timber cultivation. Some parks were swallowed up by urbanization or were sold off for property development. Others became golf courses, hospitals, country clubs and hotels.

During World War II government authorities requisitioned remaining parks for barracks, training facilities and storage. Areas of parkland were ploughed up as part of the 'Dig for Victory' drive. Wivenhoe Park garrisoned 3,000 troops in tents and huts between 1939 and 1946. Firearms training and tank exercises in this period ensured the demise of the remaining deer herd. Pavlovsk Park, designed as an English landscape park and reconfigured as a National Museum after the October Revolution of 1917, faced Nazi occupation between 1941 and 1944. Retreating Soviet forces dug tank traps in the park and buried precious sculptures, while occupying forces blew up pavilions and bridges and felled around 70,000 trees.

In the post-war period, private schools increasingly adopted park houses and grounds for their institutions. Ralph Allen's ostentatious mansion at Prior Park first became a Roman Catholic seminary in 1829, at the time of Catholic Emancipation. In 1981, Prior Park College, a co-ed Catholic further education institution, occupied the buildings. New universities and polytechnics acquired parklands throughout the 1960s. Wivenhoe Park settled into a new role as the campus for the University of Essex in 1965. Trent Park, hunting ground of Henry IV, became Middlesex University, while Newton Park, landscaped by 'Capability' Brown, hosted Bath Spa University College.

The recreational function of the landscape park continued in all-purpose leisure complexes for popular consumption. Lord Bath added exotic lions, gorillas and giraffes to his traditional Wiltshire country house, when Longleat opened its doors to the public in 1949. After a period of dereliction (sold off by the Talbot family in 1924 and used in World War II as a cadet training camp), the Alton Towers Company inaugurated a programme of restoration that saw the installation of cable cars and rollercoasters at its Staffordshire property. By the 1990s, Alton Towers signified a premier British tourist attraction. Such popularity stemmed not from its elegant house and well-kept gardens but from its ever-increasing complement of white-knuckle rides.

A select number of British estates retained their identity throughout the twentieth century thanks largely to the conservation efforts of the National Trust (founded in 1895). In 1937 and 1939, Acts of Parliament allowed bankrupt aristocrats to transfer their estates to the Trust with sizeable tax breaks. In return for (sometimes limited) public access, the family received permission to stay on at their ancestral homes. By 1980, the Trust presided over 40,000 acres of property, rendering it one of the largest landowners in the country.[24]

By the end of the twentieth century, the landscape park had become historicized and nationalized as a significant artefact. In Britain, patriotic idealism and rural nostalgia fused with modern conservation. With the power of the landed elite considerably eroded, the British populace discarded class differences and embraced the 'cult of the countryside and of the country house' as a formative part of their collective identity.[25] Such romantic impulses could be seen in the popularity of magazines such as *Country Life* and books including Evelyn Waugh's *Brideshead Revisited* (1945) as well as the preservationist activities of the Trust. Put simply, the park represented a national treasure. From its aristocratic roots, the park was reinvented as common property, an integral part of what Benedict Anderson has labelled 'the imagined community'.[26] The park projected imperial greatness, national pride and pre-industrial simplicity – themes resonant among a post-1945 British public struggling with economic decline and cultural stagnation.[27]

The fresh attraction of the landscape park engendered a new industry in heritage tourism. Membership of the National Trust reached 2,000,000 in 1990, while 8,400,000 people paid visits to its 162 landscape gardens in 1994. For the price of an entrance ticket, voyeuristic commoners navigated a past age of privilege and nobility, peeked into forbidden rooms and wandered across landscapes usually obscured by high walls. This time capsule of stately homes and gardens – presented in all their historical drama, grandeur and gentility – captivated the popular imagination to the extent that Britain in 2000 resembled a 'kind of huge historical theme park', according to landscape historians Taigel and Williamson.[28]

The aristocratic-cum-plebeian park of the twenty-first century reflected an uneasy combination of political ideologies, cultural mores and environmental values. Critics pointed to the lack of relevance of landscape parks to multicultural Britain. Were such places truly for the people, or were they really old relics that perpetuated elite values? Certainly, the cultural meaning of the park remained open to interpretation.

Modern park stewards meanwhile faced the thorny issue of restoration. Taking control of crumbling ruins and rambling gardens, heritage managers pondered what period or style to return each park to. At Stourhead, exotic (and popular) rhododendrons and azaleas planted in the 1920s and 1930s arguably obscured the Arcadian idyll forged in the eighteenth century. At Prior Park, purchased by the National Trust in 1993, an overgrown garden had witnessed three phases of redesign in Ralph Allen's lifetime alone. The necessity of balancing preservationist impulses with visitor appeal further concerned managers. The park had to be popular with visitors (and thus commercially attractive) to compete in the marketplace of leisure tourism. That meant advertising the attractions as exciting prospects through leaflets, interpretative boards, guided walks and performance evenings. It also entailed the provision of up-to-date facilities, gift stores, kiosks and accessible car parking. Although unlikely to introduce lions at Stourhead to compete with nearby Longleat, National Trust stewards still had to meet the demands of public accessibility and recreational competitiveness.

3 The City Park: Bringing the Country to the Metropolis

From the hunting palaces of Assyria to the storybook landscapes of Stourhead and Stowe, the park idea has so far centred on grand rural landscapes. Yet the park idea is also rooted in urban spaces. Like the wily fox or racoon searching alleys for discarded chicken bones, the parkscape adapted to the built environment. From the European capitals of Paris and Berlin to the sprawling metropolises of Los Angeles and Mexico City, the major cities of the world all feature green spaces dedicated to providing relief from the urban grid(lock) of thrusting skyscrapers and buzzing freeways. Marked by distinctive cuisines, cultural traditions and architectural styles, such diverse cityscapes share common ground in the guise of the park.

THE BIRTH OF THE CITY PARK IDEAL

The great urban civilizations of antiquity produced the first city parks. King Sennacherib, who assumed the Assyrian throne in 705 BC, constructed the city of Nineveh as an impressive capital, from which he commanded a vast empire stretching from Palestine to Asia Minor. The mammoth building programme saw the small town beside the Tigris River transformed into a striking landscape of temples, palaces and squares. The largest city in the world by 668 BC, its 40-foot perimeter wall spanned seven and a half miles. Huge stone bulls guarded the fifteen city gates, while the magnificent palaces and wide paved roads radiated kingly magnificence. With tree-lined streets and canal irrigation, nature served a vital role in making the city beautiful. Adjacent to the royal palace, a city park known as 'paradise' contained rare botanical plants and lush orchards. According to the king, all the trees in the allotment were 'planted for my subjects'.[1] Regulations precluded the construction of houses or workshops around the park.

Revering open spaces for their health benefits, both Greek and Roman empires embraced the city park idea. In the fifth century BC, Greek ruler Cimon remodelled the sacred grove of Academus, Athens, into a city park for practising athletes and strolling philosophers. With its open vistas and shady arbours, the Academy became popular with many urbanites, who utilized the park as a meeting place, exercise yard and debating society. The *Porticus Pompeiana* in Rome served a similar purpose as a green oasis amidst the ten-storey tenements and winding streets marked by throngs of people, squealing hogs and careening chariots. Parks were accessible to all free citizens, although prescribed gender roles lent them an overwhelmingly masculine quality. Women tended to visit friends in private homes, leaving the classical urban park a preserve dominated by men.

Emphasis on public access and civic amenity in the urban spaces of Greece and Rome bespoke the principles of early republican democracy. However, in other cultures, city parks attested to authoritarian relationships and rigid class structures. A spectacular green enclave of 168 acres in the Chinese capital, Beihai Park, Beijing, established in the tenth century by the Liao dynasty, contained a palace, a lake and island with water features, rock gardens, willows, lotus leaves and the famous Five Dragons Pavilion. The entire preserve remained the resort of the imperial family and their guests, who ventured from the hallowed echelons of the Forbidden City to an equally private park retreat. Invitee Marco Polo praised the pleasure gardens in 1266. An impressive White Dagoba was constructed to honour the fifth Dalai Lama, who visited the park in 1651. On an artificial mount overlooking the Forbidden City, Jingshan Park provided a further imperial refuge. Established in 1420, the preserve operated according to the principles of Feng Shui and protected the Forbidden City from evil spirits.

Fledgling city parks in Latin America proved equally exclusive. In the legendary city of Tenochtitlan (today's Mexico City), Chapultepec Park offered a hilltop retreat for the Aztec royalty. The fifteenth-century parkscape provided drinking water for the 300,000 residents of Tenochtitlán, but its impressive botanical gardens and wildlife collections were open only to the ruling dynasty. The arrival of Spanish overlords to Mexico resulted in little change. In 1592, Viceroy Luis de Velasco established a park next to Inquisition Square on the site of an old Aztec marketplace. By the seventeenth century, Alameda Park boasted geometric walks and tree-lined avenues that paid homage to the Islamic courtyard garden as well as to European trends. An enclosing wall ensured that only the elite could sample its delights.

The first city parks in Europe began as medieval deer parks. As urban settlements expanded, the sporting preserves became pockets of countryside within a built environment. Originally a hunting park for the dukes of Brabant, the Warande in Brussels became a city park in 1775, set aside for the benefit of those living in a luxury residential development nearby. Joseph II granted Prater Park, an old hunting preserve belonging to the Austrian monarchy, to the residents of Vienna in 1766. On its establishment, the park was a half-hour stroll from the centre of the city.

The city of London featured a plethora of royal parks, including Greenwich (1433), St James's (1532), Hyde (1536) and Richmond (1637). As the English capital expanded (reaching a population of 400,000 by 1650), old hunting parks provided valuable open spaces. Visitors commended such venues for bringing the country to the town. When asked by Charles II to remodel St James's Park after the fashion of Versailles, André Le Nôtre deferred to the 'genius of the place', explaining that the area's 'native beauty, Country Air, and deserts, had something greater in them, than anything he could contrive'.[2]

From grazing pasture to riding parade, landscape garden to gaming venue, London's parklands offered a wide range of functions. During the reign of Henry VIII, Greenwich Park hosted lavish May Day fetes that included bonfire displays, archery, duels, jousts and banquets. In 1661, Charles II threw open the gates of St James's as a 'public park'. With the monarch keen to parade in front of his subjects, the park became less about deer stalking and more about people watching. Every afternoon, London's fashionable set gathered at Pall Mall to exchange society gossip and wander the tended avenues. Assembled groups played *paille maille* – a game popular in France that involved hitting balls through hoops with mallets – in a shady spot nearby. Thirsty revellers queued to fill their glasses from a farm maid tending a tethered cow. This blend of rusticity and social nicety made a visit to the park a regular pastime. The popularity of St James's Park even spawned a new addition to the popular vernacular – 'park time' – a term used by John Dryden in *Marriage à la Mode* (1673).[3]

Despite the populist rhetoric, most parks represented landscapes of exclusion. Kings or queens reserved the right to withdraw park privileges at will. Assassination threats on Charles II and the plague of 1665 temporarily closed the London parks, while Queen Anne hatched a plan to permanently cordon off St James's and Hyde parks for her own use. Even when gates were open, access remained curtailed by class. The affluent deployed a series of regulations to deter unsavoury citizens from using their parks. In the 1800s, the Duke of Cambridge dissuaded the local poor from entering Richmond Park to gather mushrooms by posting a ranger who prevented walking on the grass. Elsewhere, entry to parklands depended on holding a key, showing a ticket, or paying a fee. Gatekeepers and perimeter walls (originally designed to keep game animals in) ensured that the great unwashed remained outside, beyond the pale. Kensington Gardens employed a strict dress code, with gentlemen requested to wear breeches and boots. Like contemporary nightclub bouncers, park keepers assessed the respectability of each prospective punter. The royal park resembled a country estate brought to the city.

The innovative and the brazen none the less tested the impenetrability of park boundaries. In the 1750s, merchants and lower gentry took to the courts to argue for rights of way through Richmond Park. After brewer John Lewis successfully won the right to cross the preserve, locals engaged in a form of mass trespass by employing ladders to breach perimeter fences, and ranged 'at their pleasure over the greensward' much to the consternation of park keepers.[4] Servants barred from entry to Kensington Gardens harassed visitors at the gatehouses. One irate commentator bemoaned: 'Yesterday it was hardly possible to get near the gate leading into the Gardens, for the crowd of servants who gathered round there, and who insulted every person not particularly known to them, going in, or coming out of the Gardens.'[5] Meanwhile, enterprising locksmiths cornered a lucrative market in unofficial keys. Authorities issued 6,500 licensed keys for St James's Park. Twice that number existed. Thieves, muggers and shysters dodged official entrances entirely by climbing perimeter walls. Such practices left some parks with dubious reputations after dark.

EARLY GREEN SPACES IN THE CITY

Urban spaces outside the traditional park diaspora inspired the city park idea. Street markets, shrines, cemeteries and vacant land designed as fire or flood breaks allowed urbanites to convene, converse and recreate. These 'unstructured playgrounds' hosted civic events such as fireworks displays, festivals, organized games and social interaction, thereby serving as informal city parks.[6]

Urban dwellers also escaped the city bustle in private gardens. In the mercantile cities of medieval Europe, burghers, livery companies and guilds established green spaces for the benefit of their members. London's Worshipful Company of Merchant Taylors crafted its own garden in 1415. In Renaissance Italy, prosperous merchants and dignitaries opened city gardens for high society to mingle in. The garden became a place for witty conversation, illustrious organic display, and social climbing. Florence sported 138 gardens by 1470. Similar enclaves marked the cityscape of Paris, the most notable being the Jardin des Plantes, a medicinal garden established by Louis XIII in 1626 and opened to the public 24 years later.

The provision of city gardens won plaudits from philosophers and writers. In *Utopia* (1516), Thomas More conceived of the perfect city as a green one, with wide streets framed by terraced houses, each with a backyard entrance to an enclosed area filled with flowers, fruits and grassy lawns. Inter-street competitions existed for the best gardens. As More enthused, 'Certainly, it would be hard to find any feature of the town more calculated to give pleasure and profits to the community.'[7] However, the gardens of urban Europe differed greatly from the communitarian vision extolled by More. Whereas *Utopia* envisioned a landscape without property ownership, with houses changing hands every 10 years, the green enclaves of Florence and Paris represented private spaces controlled by the power elite. Ownership of a renowned garden bespoke authority in civic affairs, wealth and prestige. Eager to attract an exclusive clientele, owners imposed rigorous entrance requirements on their organic retreats. Entry to the sanctum rested on guild membership, personal standing, city office or contacts. Those who made it on to the hallowed guest list could access the garden only when the owner decided to unlock its gates. The city garden thus represented a private venue in which the rich could commune with nature – a smaller, urbanized version of the landscape park.

If the city garden celebrated elitist nature, the town square emphasized the importance of civic amenity. A landmark of the built environment since antiquity, the square offered a focal point for residents to congregate for gossip, trade, parades, festivals and even executions. As a public space in the heart of the city, the square cemented community identity and brought citizens together literally and mentally. As architectural historian Paul Zucker commented, the square represented a 'psychological parking place within the civic landscape'.[8] Such a realm expressed the animation of city life in all its energy and spectacle.

One of the most famous squares in the world, Venice's Piazza di San Marco, earned acclaim for its crowds, coffee, absence of traffic, and impressive display of open space in the sinking city. Since its establishment in AD 1000, the piazza served as an important place for residents and visitors to wile away their time. However, the piazza reflected the city rather than offering an escape from it. Invaded by the street hubbub, it remained part of the built landscape, with flocks of pigeons the only nature on display.

However, squares in other cities were likened to parks. The Agora in classical Athens encompassed a large, unpaved space interspersed with trees. Created from marshland in 1775, Padua's Prato della Valle, one of the largest squares in Europe, featured trimmed lawns, a canal, radiating paths and sculptures in French-Italian formal design. Eighteenth-century town squares in England subscribed to the same naturalistic aesthetics as found in landscape parks. Designed by architect John Wood, Queen's Square, Bath, melded urban space with organic decoration. A verdant enclave of lawns and shrubbery, the square was separated from surrounding Georgian houses and carriage roads (today a busy interchange) by a low wall. Wood explained his blueprint as a mixture of aesthetics and utility, viewing the presence of nature as conducive to the principal role of the square as a meeting place. As Wood elaborated:

The inclosing, planting, turfing and gravelling this open area, in the manner above described, was a work of much greater expence than the paving the whole surface of it would have been . . . But yet I preferred an inclosed square to an open one, to make this as useful as possible: For the intention of a Square in a City is for people to assemble together; and the spot whereon they meet, ought to be separated from the ground common to Men and Beasts, and even to mankind in general.[9]

Queen's Square enshrined nature as an important aspect of civic space. It suggested that a green city was more amenable to live in – a view held by town planners since Sennacherib's time, and one that exerts a strong impact on the city park idea to this day.

Residents seeking entertainment in the eighteenth-century English city often looked to the commercial pleasure ground rather than the city square. A response to urbanization, the pleasure ground offered a formalized space for activities that had previously occurred in fields and on village greens. Reinventing private gardens as entertainment centres, pleasure grounds boasted concert venues and refreshment stalls. Part city park, part garden and part amusement complex, the pleasure ground advertised a wide range of activities. Fireworks, magic lantern shows, dances and circus performers provided sparkle. Flower-beds, hedges and tree-lined paths – complete with night illuminations and mechanical features – catered to those seeking more genteel recreation. Ice skating and bowling entertained the sporting fraternity, while the mutinous reputedly gathered in lonely corners to hatch anti-government plots. London boasted several hundred such establishments, the most famous being Marylebone (1737), Vauxhall (formerly Spring Gardens, 1661) and Ranelagh (1742).

Former hunting park of Henry VIII and adjunct of the Rose Tavern, Marylebone Gardens opened with the promise of dog fights and archery. Originally a free establishment, the proprietor soon started charging a shilling entrance fee and adopted a dress code in order to attract a suitably exclusive crowd. Vauxhall earned fame for its walks, evening cascade, concert recitals and ham suppers. In Tobias Smollett's *The Expedition of Humphry Clinker* (1771), Matthew Bramble encountered the many festivities on offer:

I no sooner entered, than I was dazzled and confounded with the variety of beauties that rushed all at once upon my eye . . . a spacious garden, part laid out in delightful walks, bounded with high hedges and trees, and paved with gravel; part exhibiting a wonderful assemblage of the most picturesque and striking objects, pavilions, lodges, groves, grottoes, lawns, temples; porticoes, colonnades and rotundoes; adorned with pillars, statues, and paintings; the whole illuminated with an infinite number of lamps, disposed in different figures of suns, stars, and constellations: the place crowded with the gayest company, ranging through those blissful shades, or supping in different lodges on cold collations, enlivened with mirth, freedom, and good humour.[10]

If the pleasure ground presented an avenue for entertainment and recreation within city limits, the common served a similar purpose, albeit in less formal guise, on the urban periphery. Originally designated by medieval lords of the manor for 'commoners' to graze animals or gather timber on, such areas also provided merriment. Travelling shows boasting bear baiting, juggling and fortune telling impressed locals. Goose and sheep fairs comprised vital parts of regional trade networks. The common retained its appeal as a recreational space even with the growth of cities. Ordinary folk continued to look to remnants of open land for leisure and gaming. Moorfields, a swampy piece of wasteland on the edge of London, drew punters with ice skating, fighting contests, archery and fairs. In 1666, refugees set up camp there to escape the Great Fire of London. On occasion, access to common land came by virtue of a philanthropic donation. In 1634, eccentric Anglican cleric William Blackstone (known for wearing his coat inside out and riding a bull) bequeathed his estate to the citizens of Boston, Massachusetts, for 'lawful recreation'. Boston Common was used for grazing, walking, militia drills, washing clothes, and even for the executions of witches and American Indians.

Cemeteries offered a further venue for city dwellers to congregate in. Though designed as cities for the dead, burial grounds were valued by the living as places for strolling and soulful contemplation. In the early 1800s, municipal authorities in Europe and North America established 'garden cemeteries' outside city limits following problems of overcrowding, disease and grave-robbing scandals in town yards. Père Lachaise near Paris (1804), Mount

Auburn near Boston (1831) and Highgate Cemetery, London (1839), swiftly gained currency as recreational spaces that appealed to the public for their peaceful quality. Winding walks, tree clumps and rolling lawns lent burial grounds a picturesque quality not dissimilar to the English landscape park. As the *Builder* magazine remarked of Coventry cemetery, designed by architect Joseph Paxton in 1845, 'the place having much more the air of a gentleman's park than a city for the dead'.[11] Moreover, burgeoning interest in garden cemeteries suggested a buoyant constituency for the city park idea. As New York horticulturalist Andrew Downing mused: 'But does not this general interest, manifested in these cemeteries, prove that public gardens, established in a liberal and suitable manner, near our large cities, would be equally successful?'[12]

The garden, the town square, the pleasure ground, the common and the cemetery all influenced the emergence of the modern city park idea. Together, these spaces emphasized the importance of preserving areas in which residents could connect with nature, participate in civic amenity, be amused, and contemplate their existence. The lines between venues were sometimes blurred – the commercial pleasure ground promoted itself as both horticultural and theatrical spectacle, the public town square occasionally featured trees and lawns – but rarely did one space offer nature, municipal function and entertainment in one package. It was only in the nineteenth century that urban planners created a single entity that satisfied all these criteria: the modern city park.

THE NINETEENTH-CENTURY CITY PARK

Inspiration for the city park came not just from green landscapes but also from economic and social forces. The industrial changes that swept Europe and North America during the nineteenth century provided the impetus for urban parkscapes. New machinery, factory systems and a burgeoning population made the nineteenth century the great age of the city. In 1825, London's population hit 1,350,000. New York boasted 4,250,000 residents by 1900. For the thousands who flocked to urban areas, the city bespoke optimism, prosperity, energy and modernity. Yet it also brought with it pollution, poverty and disorientation. Workers left the country to encounter an urban life characterized by time keeping and laborious routines, many tending machines for up to 15 hours before returning to tenements that lacked adequate sanitation, fire protection or privacy.

The Industrial Revolution produced a new class of factory owners, merchants and bankers, notable for their financial acumen and inventiveness. But while the city served as a landmark to the ingenuity of the entrepreneurial elite, those with the necessary wealth often chose to cement their status by purchasing country estates. For the industrial magnate, purchase of a landscape park offered a guaranteed route to social prestige. Moreover, with opportunities for recreation in the city limited, the country park offered welcome respite from the smog and grime of the urban environment. As one tourist pertinently observed, 'no wonder aristocrats left London for the country to escape its bleak, black foggy atmosphere and smoke of sea coal.'[13]

Within city limits, the park idea found favour among middle-class residents eager for civic authorities to create urban spaces for their benefit. Citing the high price of real estate, the lack of bureaucratic vision, and the intense pace of city growth, newspaper columnists complained of the lack of green spaces in the metropolis. Areas previously used for leisure and entertainment – common land or village greens – had been swallowed up by the urban behemoth, and rudely replaced by a workaday landscape of railroad depots, factories and commercial buildings. Town squares and royal parks were either non-existent or too small to accommodate burgeoning populations. In Britain, the Select Committee on Public Walks (1833) bemoaned the lack of greenery in the industrial towns of Bradford, Hull, Bolton and Sheffield. *Scribner's Monthly* pointed to similar recreational deficiencies in mid-century New York: 'There is actually no stroll possible! The hateful railroad . . . cut off all access to the river shore . . . and, if one climbs the hill to the highway, he finds that fences, walls, hedges and close huddling houses cut him off from all but a few tantalizing glimpses of the landscape he would enjoy.'[14]

At the same time, the middle class considered the park landscape to be a vital source of uplift for the working class. Middle-class reformers saw their role as 'moral entrepreneurs' capable of encouraging the rowdy masses to behave with decorum.[15] The city meanwhile was viewed as the future for the civilized world, but only if its social and environmental deficiencies could be adequately addressed. As Frederick Law Olmsted proclaimed, 'Our country, has entered upon a stage of progress in which its welfare is to depend on the convenience, safety, order and economy of life in its great cities.'[16] Social campaigners demanded the improvement of urban spaces by the provision of welfare assistance, sanitation, building codes and municipal museums, concert halls and libraries. The park comprised a significant part of their agenda. As an all-purpose medicine for staving off inertia, alienation and social discord, the park amounted to a vital prescription for healing the unsettled. A visit to the park offered the working classes a vital escape from the built environment by entry into a world of greenery, leisure and freedom. Reformers hoped that by retreating into the park urban workers would feel not only healthier – by virtue of taking exercise and breathing 'country air' – but also psychologically refreshed. The park offered a place in which to rediscover oneself beyond the machine, to work off the stresses of the week and commune with others in pleasant surroundings. To the nineteenth-century social reformer, the formulation of such a landscape served the higher interests of the city in both environmental and social terms.

Park creation in the nineteenth-century city also drew on notions of regional and national pride. With the growth of the industrial metropolis came myriad celebrations of urban living. Idealistic visions of the city as a modern, technological and utopian space engendered a sense of civic virtue. For wealthy industrialists and municipal leaders, the establishment of a park offered the chance to proclaim the prosperity, beauty and vigour of their urban stomping grounds. Like Sennacherib in Nineveh, nineteenth-century elites viewed the park – along with public buildings, libraries, museums and concert halls – as an emblem of city identity and civic hospitality. Wealthy benefactors spoke a language of payback by forging green spaces for the factory hands that facilitated their grand life-styles. In 1840, industrialist, social reformer and ex-mayor Joseph Strutt ceded Derby Arboretum as a pleasure ground for the citizens of the town. In his dedication, Strutt motioned: 'as the sun has shone brightly on me through life, it would be ungrateful in me not to employ a portion of the fortune which I possess, in promoting the welfare of those amongst whom I live, and by whose industry I have been aided in its acquisition.'[17] For Strutt and his contemporaries, park creation amounted to a form of social duty. A potent combination of philanthropy and municipal pride ensured a keen market for the park idea.

The reason why reformers and planners of the nineteenth century chose the park over playgrounds, town squares and amusement complexes had to do with education. Significantly, the city park stood apart from other venues by dint of its emphasis not just on idle fun, but on embetterment. The park represented a moral landscape. The crucial ingredient that lent the park this hallowed reputation as a site of redemption and emancipation was the presence of nature itself. With its landscape of trees, meadows, lakes and flowers, the city park represented a conscious attempt to re-create the country in the city. It aimed to counter the debilitating influences of urban life by providing a natural space in the city, to paraphrase academic Leo Marx, bringing the garden to the machine.[18] Park popularity pivoted on the concept of nature as a repository of purity, simplicity, harmony and morality – rendering it an ideal foil for the perceived degradation, complexity, tension and corruption of city life. Such a sentiment drew on Romantic sensibilities that bemoaned the loss of untamed land and viewed nature as a venue for aesthetic rapture and spiritual rejuvenation. It also bespoke a long-standing oppositional relationship between nature and culture. From the Greek and Roman philosophers who recalled the Golden Age of Perpetual Spring to Thomas Jefferson's famous pronouncements on the virtues of agrarian republicanism, individuals viewed perfect societies as shaped by 'natural' values. In the nineteenth-century city – a man-made environment governed not by seasons but by shift work, navigated not by contoured hills but by brick buildings – this philosophy translated into a desire for reconnection with the natural. Eager to bring bucolic scenery into the built environment, the American Art Union instructed urbanites to hang landscape paintings on their walls. Nature stood for goodness, order and peaceful living.

CREATING PARKS FOR THE PEOPLE

The formation of city parks in the nineteenth century entailed two basic practices: first, the appropriation of old royal parks for public use, and second, the building of entirely new parkscapes.

Across Europe, royal parks were reconfigured for popular use. Parisians gained access to the Jardin des Plantes and the Tuileries Garden courtesy of the National Revolutionary Convention. In 1828, city authorities dedicated the Parc de Sceaux (the seventeenth-century country seat of minister Jean-Baptiste Colbert) as an urban recreational space. Further east, residents of Prague enjoyed the delights of Petrin Park, a private garden opened to the public in 1800, along with Chotkovy Sady Park, given over to public access in 1833. Inspired by Enlightenment philosophy together with academic discussion of the merits of parks as social and moral spaces, Friedrich Wilhelm III remodelled the famous Tiergarten hunting preserve in Berlin as a public park. The Tiergarten, or 'garden of beasts', was officially opened in 1840, complete with new lake and zoo.

In 1824, park designer Peter Joseph Lenné berated English parks 'kept for the nourishment of game instead of human beings' compared to the 'liberality of his king and other German princes who generously throw open their gardens to their public at every hour of the day'. British park advocates such as the writer J. C. Loudon agreed that the English capital compared unfavourably with continental Europe in its provision of green spaces. 'The present time seems to be favourable for improving our public parks and gardens which foreigners justly observe are inferior to those of every other great city of Europe,' Loudon railed. Created in 1811 by architect John Nash, Regent's Park received criticism for its closed entry system. As the Select Committee on Public Walks explained, 'It is an absurdity to think of it as a place of recreation and use by the public. It is not a public park, but a place set apart for the use of the wealthy only.' In 1834, 88 acres of Regent's Park were duly opened to public access. Similar measures followed at other parks. In 1827, new regulations at St James's Park mandated 'the whole of the space . . . now laid out in grass, and from which the Public are excluded, will be thrown open'. In Hyde Park, imposing perimeter walls gave way to a less fortified look of painted iron railings. With most entrance requirements to London's parks broadened by the mid-1800s, the city park became a place for the people.[19]

The drive for city parks in the nineteenth century involved the formation of new public spaces. Residents of Bath paid a subscription fund to create Victoria Park, opened by the Queen in 1830. Sponsors viewed the park as a way to bolster the credentials of Bath as a tourist resort and to aid the urban poor. In 1843, civic authorities established the world's first publicly funded park for use by all at Birkenhead. Local dignitaries lobbied for a municipal park to cater for the growing working population. Commissioners bought 185 acres of marshy land notorious for gambling and dog fighting from F. R. Price, with the intention of making a public park. Park establishment represented an opportunity to improve both the area and the lives of the local working class.

Joseph Paxton, railway engineer, MP and landscape architect, produced an £800 blueprint for Birkenhead Park, based on plantings of beech, cypress, weeping willow and silver pear, the excavation of two lakes, and the construction of lodges, boathouses, sports fields and winding drives. Some 10,000 people attended the formal opening of the park in April 1847. Birkenhead earned acclaim as the 'people's park' due to its democratic genesis. *The Stranger's Guide through Birkenhead* (*c.*1851) pondered the egalitarian and aesthetic qualities of the new reserve thus:

When the important advantages to the poorer classes, of such an extensive and delightful pleasure ground, are taken into consideration, no one will be inclined to say that such an expenditure does not merit the most unbounded success, and the deepest public gratitude. Here nature may be viewed in her loveliest garb, the most obdurate heart may be softened, and the mind gently led to pursuits which refine, purify, and alleviate the humblest of the toil-worn.[20]

FREDERICK LAW OLMSTED AND CENTRAL PARK

For many Americans in the mid-1800s, the word 'park' connoted aristocratic Old World decadence. No US city maintained sizeable parks for public recreation.[21] Boston had its common and Philadelphia its town squares, but most urban centres were bereft of green areas for ordinary folk to relax in. However, the creation of Central Park in New York during the 1850s and 1860s demonstrated the applicability of the park idea to New World shores.

Impetus for the creation of Central Park came from a cadre of New York literati, journalists and social critics (including garden designer Andrew Jackson Downing and editor of the *New York Evening Post* William Cullen Bryant), who lobbied intently for the designation of green space in a burgeoning city of 654,000 residents. Existing public spaces were either inadequate – Battery Park spanned 10 acres and earned a reputation for rowdy immigrants and idlers – or were accessible only to wealthy property owners. Campaigners argued that a park would elevate the reputation of New York as a cosmopolitan and cultured space, as well as improving the health of its inhabitants. More mercenary supporters pointed to its potential for raising real estate values.

Cultural nationalism informed desires for emparkment among the wealthy fraternity. Urban greenery signalled American power, prosperity and cultural maturity. The setting aside of parks for the public good responded directly to those who derided American society as crass and materialistic. As Downing noted, 'The true policy of republics, is to foster the taste for great public libraries, sculpture and picture galleries, parks, and gardens, which *all* may enjoy.'[22] Such pronouncements paid homage to the United States as an egalitarian and democratic society, in contrast to old Europe. The park, in its New World incarnation, symbolized the opportunities of republican democracy. It hoisted New York as a natural wonder and a social utopia combined.

At the same time, advocates looked to European precedent for the specifics of park design. American tourists praised parks in both Paris and London as 'lungs for the city'. Writing in the *Horticulturalist*, Andrew Downing noted 'every American who visits London . . . feels mortified that no city in the

United States has a public park'.[23] Frederick Law Olmsted, who toured Britain in 1850, paid particular attention to the merits of Birkenhead after a proud local baker suggested a visit. While Olmsted complained about the ostentatious classical gateway – depicting 'a sort of grandeur . . . that the English are fond of' – he applauded Paxton's transformation of the 'flat, sterile, clay farm' into an immense parkscape. 'Five minutes of admiration, and a few more spent in studying the manner in which art had been employed to obtain from nature so much beauty, and I was ready to admit that in democratic America, there was nothing to be thought of as comparable with this People's Garden,' he confessed. The democratic theme of the park particularly impressed Olmsted: 'All this magnificent pleasure-ground is entirely, unreservedly, and forever the People's own. The poorest British peasant is as free to enjoy it in all its parts, as the British Queen. More than that, the baker of Birkenhead had the pride of an Owner in it. Is it not a grand good thing?'[24] The lack of such a democratic space in New York smacked of neglect. As writer Caroline Kirkland bemoaned, 'Nothing we saw in London made our own dear city of New York seem so poor in comparison as these parks . . . After seeing these oases in the wilderness of streets, one can never be content with the scanty patches of verdure . . . that [in New York] form the only places of afternoon recreation for the weary, the sad, the invalid, the playful.'[25]

Mayor Ambrose Kingsland recommended the establishment of a public park before the New York Council in April 1851. The Council legislated in favour of a 773-acre site in Manhattan in July 1853. The Central Park decision showed the broadening of governmental responsibilities to include civic health and the willingness of authorities to purchase real estate for public recreation. In 1857, commissioners announced a competition for the design of Central Park, with the promise of a cash prize for the winner. Thirty-five entries were submitted. The winning Greensward plan was the brainchild of British architect Calvert Vaux and Connecticut landscape designer Frederick Law Olmsted.

The Greensward Plan lived up to its name – Greensward meaning unbroken stretches of turf or lawn in old English (see fig.4). Olmsted and Vaux envisaged Central Park as a rural idyll between 59th and 106th streets, where urbanites could escape from city life to immerse themselves in pastoral scenery. The crafting of an illusion of rolling countryside dominated planning considerations. At the time of construction, Manhattan had encroached only as far as 38th Street, but Olmsted and Vaux foresaw a time when Central Park would 'be in the centre of a population of two millions hemmed in by water at a short distance on all sides'.[26] Preserving a fantasy of sylvan peace, the designers planted a tree belt around the park to screen off the urban world. So as not to disturb the tranquil unity of the park space, the four roads that bisected the landscape were sunk into the ground and walled, akin to the ha-ha. The park featured an upper region of undulating meadows and a lower wooded region. Visitors navigated the entire two and a half mile long preserve via a series of winding footpaths, bridleways and carriage drives. An open square at the

Figure 4. Aerial view of Central Park, New York, 1973. US National Archives, photo number 412-DA-5908.

centre of the park – the Mall – served as a focal point for citizens to meet, stroll and converse. Close by, the Bethesda Terrace led down to a vast lake and the Ramble, a mysterious area of dense woodland with twisting walks, waterfalls, rocky outcrops and an Indian cave in the fashion of the eighteenth-century landscape park's 'wilderness'.

The Olmsted–Vaux design promised both contemplation and fulfilment. Central Park was consciously crafted in opposition to the city – pastoral nature versus industry. As Olmsted motioned in 'Public Parks and the Enlargement of Towns' (1870): 'We want, especially, the greatest possible contrast with the streets and the shops and the rooms of the town. . . . We want depth of wood enough about it not only for comfort in hot weather, but to completely shut out the city from our landscapes. These are the distinguishing elements of what is properly called a park.'[27]

Although residents sought escape from urban confines through the park template, its fundamental remit lay in making the metropolis liveable. The park was designed to remedy the problems of city life, to make urban denizens feel happier, healthier and work harder. The park thereby civilized the city by naturalizing it. Behind the organic designs of Greensward lay ideologies of social paternalism, civic reformism and democracy. Central Park was steeped in egalitarian imperatives – the landscape itself was to provide a conduit for community expression, civic mingling and cultural uplift. For Olmsted and Vaux, the natural aesthetics of the city park serviced physical health, psychological refreshment and communitarian ideals.

As soon as city commissioners decided on the location of Central Park, surveyors were sent in to assess the area and recommend purchase orders. The designated site was far from vacant. No blank canvas existed on Manhattan Island on which to forge a fantastic rural retreat. Instead, the area slated for park purchase featured shanty towns, hog farms and squatter camps housing poor Irish, German and African-American families. Some 1,600 residents were evicted prior to Central Park taking shape. City plans for a park thus involved schemes of slum removal and gentrification. New York administrators perceived park creation as a programme of social and environmental improvement, establishing an enclave of aesthetic beauty and leisure pursuits in a neighbourhood notorious for its 'vagabonds and scoundrels of every description'.[28] Newspaper columnists and social critics derided the residents of the site as savages who lived off the refuse of the city, built their own tumbledown homes, spread disease, and indulged in violence and criminality. The area was renowned for its illegal liquor distilleries, rowdy dance halls and odious bone-boiling plants. Planners believed that establishing a park in the vicinity would effectively rid them of a 'problem' neighbourhood.

In making this judgement, city officials demonstrated both their ignorance of local communities and their prejudice against immigrants and minorities. Records show that 'pre-parkites' lived in stable, and cohesive settlements.[29] Many worked as unskilled labourers and servants, while one in ten owned a business. The largest of the communities, Seneca Village, comprised a vibrant African-American centre complete with schoolhouse and Methodist and Episcopal churches. In 1853, a judicial commission began its survey of property in the area – ruling to offer compensation payments of an average $700 per lot. Following protracted jockeying and legal appeals, Albany Judge Ira Harris upheld the Commission's Report in February 1856, and the bailiffs moved in. Though disgusted at the paltry compensation they received, residents vacated their homes without incident. Many New Yorkers baulked at the $5,000,000 cost of acquiring park land.

When Olmsted took charge of the cleared site in 1858 as architect-in-chief, the Central Park lot comprised mostly boggy swampland and salt marshes. Its poor soil, ravines and rocky outcrops of granite hardly fitted the Greensward Plan of undulating meadowland. Sceptics contended that this was the reason why the park site was selected from the outset. Its rugged terrain arguably rendered it too expensive for commercial development. Between 1858 and 1861, Olmsted presided over a huge construction site. Some 4,000 workers sweated up to 10 hours a day excavating, draining and levelling the area; 166 tonnes of gunpowder were used to blast the bedrock. Fertile topsoil had to be shipped in from New Jersey. Behind the rural vision lay a comprehensive engineering infrastructure. Olmsted and Vaux utilized new technology to bring their park design to fruition – from tarmac road paving to a network of pipes that filled the 20 acre reservoir and controlled run-off. Gardeners planted a total of 270,000 trees and bushes.

Central Park was gradually opened to New York's citizenry as new features took shape. By the end of 1863, visitors had the run of the grounds, carriage drives and footpaths below 102nd Street. The Lake and the Ramble proved particularly popular. The *New York Herald* enthused: 'there was never perhaps an institution established for public enjoyment which has grown popular and available so rapidly.'[30] With distinctly nationalistic overtones, Vaux celebrated the creation as 'the big art work of the Republic', a public space where all could convene to appreciate American nature.[31] By 1865, attendance reached 7,600,000 per year. The city park was hailed as a paragon of civic pride, moral purpose and democratic wisdom.

The authors of the Greensward Plan received notable plaudits. In 1861, Henry Bellows described Olmsted as a 'Capability' Brown for the nineteenth century:

The Union of prosaic sense with poetical feeling, of democratic sympathies with refined and scholarly tastes, of punctilious respect for facts with tender hospitality for ideas, has enabled him to appreciate and embody, both in conception and execution of the Park, the beau-ideal of a people's pleasure ground.[32]

City planners clamoured for Olmsted and Vaux — now cemented as the principal landscape architects in North America — to create green spaces in their neighbourhoods. Olmsted, Vaux & Co. went on to design parks and parkways in Buffalo, Brooklyn, Boston, Detroit, Chicago and Montreal. They also expanded the city park idea. Convinced of its character as a restorative landscape, Olmsted and Vaux appropriated the park concept for living spaces. Their blueprints for a suburban community in Riverside, Illinois, set houses and winding streets within an undulating park-like space of 'refined sylvan beauty' along the Des Plaines River.[33] The educational benefits of green space underlay similar spatial designs for the university campuses of Berkeley and Stanford in California.

The urban park emerged as a standard feature of the modern North American city during the latter years of the 1800s. In 1869, the *San Diego Union* claimed: 'Every considerable city in Europe and the United States . . . has its vast tract of land reserved and beautified as a park.'[34] San Diego itself boasted Balboa Park, 1,400 acres of desert chaparral ceded as a public recreation area in 1868. City officials in San Francisco reached an agreement with land owners and squatters to establish Golden Gate Park the same year. In Butte, Montana, residents enjoyed the facilities at the Columbia Gardens pleasure ground from 1888 onwards, a park space which the local *Miner* newspaper described as 'a resort worthy of the Great Metropolis of Montana'.[35] North of the 49th parallel, the fledgling City Council of Vancouver established 1,000 acre Stanley Park as one of its inaugural acts in 1886. In Europe, Napoleon III opened the Parc des Buttes-Chaumont to Parisians in 1867. Parks proliferated in British industrial towns burdened by pollution, overcrowding and disease. Presiding over a city judged the third most unhealthy in England, authorities in Bristol created Eastville, Greville Smyth, St Agnes and Victoria parks for public relief in the 1880s. The urban park was read as a social, environmental and moral necessity.

AN EGALITARIAN SPACE?

The nineteenth-century city park revolutionized the park idea. Formerly an enclave for aristocratic sport and entertainment, the park now represented a public landscape. The *New York Herald* presented a utopian picture of class harmony and camaraderie at the skating rink in Central Park: 'Masters Richard and William from Fifth Avenue, in their furs, and plain Dick and Bill from avenues nearer the river . . . mingled in joyful unity, forgetting the distinction of home in their enjoyment of a common patrimony – free air and free water.'[36]

However, the city park rarely achieved perfect democratic function. Often behind talk of civic harmony lay a quiet code of social control and segregation. While pronouncements for park establishment stressed community action, tutelage over the city park regularly rested with the elite. Although serving as public spaces for leisure, health and urban renewal, parks were ordered by racial, gender and class-based strictures.

The middle class saw in the park a means to elevate real estate prices and eradicate 'unsavoury' working-class neighbourhoods. Sentiments of environmental improvement and social control were evinced at Mousehold Heath, Norwich, in 1884, where church landowners bequeathed land for a 'People's Park' to circumscribe fights, fairs and mining activities. In turn, the construction process offered gainful employment for potentially restive segments of the urban populace, thereby diffusing working-class dissidence. Once open to the public, civic leaders read the city park as a tool of socialization, a way of counteracting deviance in urban society, of instilling the working classes with respectable values. Social reformers deemed the park an effective tonic for urban *angst*, a salubrious alternative to the saloon, the music hall, the cockfight and the street brawl. The park embodied an outdoor reform school, with morality taught through the innovative medium of leisure.

While the landscape park of the eighteenth century had room for resource management, the city park of the nineteenth century overwhelmingly proclaimed leisure as its mantra. The park represented a pleasure ground for popular consumption, a place for the city populace to let off steam. Its recreational function contrasted with the governing work ethic of the city in the same way that the pastoral lines of the park offered an aesthetic foil to the urban environment. However, the people rarely chose the leisure pursuits provided for their benefit. Instead, the power elite subtly influenced where, how and when the general public recreated. City parks typically traded in genteel pursuits favoured by the middle classes, such as classical music performance, bird watching, walking and reading – all considered passive activities good for morality and intellectualism. Idle fun or boisterous carousing in the form of gambling, vaudeville, dancing or billiards was strictly precluded. Regulations in Halifax People's Park, England (1857), prohibited soccer, dancing, gaming and bathing, while patrons of Central Park found themselves barred from walking on the grass, using obscene language, selling goods or engaging in 'acts of disorder'. Olmsted judged such provisions as vital to preserving the moralism of Greensward. As the designer motioned in his blueprint for Montreal Park, 'If it is to be cut up with roads and walks, spotted with shelters, and streaked with staircases; if it is to be strewn with lunch papers, beer bottles, sardine cans and paper collars; and if thousands of people are to seek their recreation upon it unrestrainedly, each according to his own special tastes, it is likely to lose whatever of natural charm you first saw in it.'[37]

The practicalities of reaching city parks further rendered them 'geographies of exclusion'.[38] Rarely situated close to poor residential districts, the working class found travelling to the park an unwelcome expense. The limited nature of activities further diminished popular interest. Labourers and their families proved a rare sight at Saturday afternoon concerts in Central Park, due to differing cultural tastes, work obligations and social pressures. Some felt intimidated by the elite clientele parading in their lavish fashions and horse-drawn carriages. The *Irish News* lamented: 'New York wants a place to play leap-frog in, not a mere ornamented place to pass through.'[39] Consequently, many working-class families chose to spend their precious leisure time in commercial pleasure grounds that offered more excitement and less moralizing. The bright lights, frivolity and spectacle delivered by amusement complexes such as Coney Island (see chapter 5) lent the city park an austere reputation. As one critic pointed out:

You come upon it, the municipal Seaside Park, at the end of our dirty white street. Within a thick hedge there is a level greensward. Huge trees shade its borders; like all respectable parks it has flowers and rubbish cans. But with us who go to Coney the park is not popular. Not enough jazz. Too quiet. You can see an old park anywhere, but Coney is the place of the hot dogs, the dance pavilions, the African dodger, the ring toss with its prizes of candy and kewpie dolls.[40]

Race as well as class fractured the parkscape. Land clearance schemes typically targeted low-income or minority communities that wielded scant political power. In Central Park, measures to evict local African-American, German and Irish residents played on contemporary xenophobic sentiment as well as stereotypes depicting immigrant groups as indolent, corrupt and debased. Once established, the city park serviced white middle-class values. Concert organizers in Central Park insisted on classical recitals, while frowning on folk music, group picnics or tunes conducive to dancing. Kept out of the park, German immigrants hosted festivals with dancing, lager and frivolity at the Jones Wood pleasure ground, New York, in the 1860s and 1870s. Although racial and ethnic precepts were rarely mentioned officially, judgements as to the propriety of certain leisure norms and practices related an elite bias. As urban planner Galen Crantz explained, 'In theory the pleasure ground brought all different sectors of society, presumably including its racial and ethnic components, together, but the practice of racial segregation was so unquestioned that officials did not need to call attention to it in any way.'[41]

Gender inequalities further moderated the egalitarianism of the city park ideal. In the 1800s, gender roles rested on constructions of biological difference and social functionality. While men operated in a public context, and seemed marked by competitiveness and aggression, women were widely deemed emotional nurturers, and remained confined to the private sphere. According to the Victorian Cult of True Womanhood, the ideal woman exuded piety, purity, domesticity and submissiveness. Such gender stereotypes had broad application for social reformers keen to project women as moral guardians and stabilizing forces in an era of mass industrialization and urban alienation. Park campaigners saw femininity as an integral aspect of a wholesome landscape of leisure. Reformers lionized the family outing to the park as a way of circumscribing undesirable male-oriented leisure activities of saloon drinking, gambling and street fighting. In 1903, Charles Eliot, President of Harvard, lauded the park as a promoter of 'family life', noting that 'the pleasures men share with their wives and children are apt to be safer pleasures than those they take by themselves'.[42]

The city park strove to project itself as a female-friendly venue. Women-only spas, casinos and restaurants wooed New York females to Central Park. In Golden Gate Park, a refreshment centre overlooked a children's playground, allowing mothers to watch over their kids and chat with friends. Women who failed to abide by gender conventions or appropriate social codes proved less welcome. Park administrators singled out prostitutes as particular enemies of the park ideal. Licentiousness and sexual desire were not judged appropriate in the park landscape. Such sentiments also manifested themselves in the sexual segregation of park space. Proscribed gender roles ensured that fathers were barred from looking after their children in the playground, while rocking benches were marked 'mothers only'. Leisure activities proved similarly mediated. Different sports catered to male and female actors, with genteel games of croquet for girls, baseball for a 'more vigorous' male audience. The fun-fair in Golden Gate Park featured side-saddled wooden horses for female riders.

A complex landscape resonant with egalitarian rhetoric yet party to social inequalities, the nineteenth-century city park presented a flawed idea. It reflected contemporary class, racial and gender divisions. At the same time, the city park was not a static landscape. Gradually, the people claimed the city park for their own.

Like rebellious peasants conspiring to steal deer from the royal park, disaffected urbanites took to the city park as a place to challenge authority. The copses of city parks offered a realm beyond the purview of government scrutiny. In 1830, revolutionary forces fired the first shots in the war for Belgian independence in Warande Park, Brussels. Agitators used Berlin's Tiergarten to ferment support for their revolutionary activities in 1848. In Hyde Park, democratic oratory was championed in Speaker's Corner. Legalized by an Act of Parliament permitting legal assembly and the addressing of crowds, the soap-box venue became a hotbed of political discussion, anarchic rabble-rousing and pertinent social comment from the 1870s on. Karl Marx, George Orwell and suffragette Emmeline Pankhurst all enthralled audiences at Speaker's Corner. From its non-sectarian beginnings, the city park quickly emerged as a landscape of protest.

Park activities also challenged conventional gender boundaries. Female activists asserted their independence by organizing initiatives without male input. In San Diego, the Ladies Annex of the Chamber of Commerce led a programme of park beautification in 1889–90. Arguing that the green space of Balboa Park served as 'the lungs of the city', and emphasizing the necessity of shady spaces for pleasant recreation, the group raised an impressive $514 for tree plantings. Assumed to favour child-rearing pursuits and docile strolls, many women engaged in energetic sports. Women learned to row, skated on park lakes in all-female parties, and cycled roads *without* male assistance. In 1891, one New York paper bemoaned 'the somewhat dangerous nature of the driving of women in Central Park' – a testament both to female empowerment and mainstream gender bias.[43]

The public voice was heard in the park on other, more frivolous issues. While activists challenged political authority and gender conventions, everyday citizens confronted park officers over the issue of recreation. Elite visions of the park as a venue of passive leisure activities came under fire in the latter years of the 1800s by an audacious and vocal citizenry that demanded a broad range of services. Community groups petitioned park officers for refreshment stands, organized sports and lively entertainments. In the 1870s, patrons of Central Park took the law into their own hands by picnicking on the hallowed grass. The working classes expected the park to serve as a multi-purpose recreational landscape, including a social club, sports arena and fairground. Academic Dorceta Taylor elaborated: 'After endless hours of brutal, mind-numbing work, some people wanted to engage in compensatory, active leisure pursuits. The working class had no place at home to exercise and no access to college gyms or country clubs. Therefore, the parks became the premier location for exercising, playing games and sports, organizing social gatherings, courting, and resting.'[44]

Civic authorities responded to popular demands by remodelling the city park into a flexible recreational landscape in the late 1800s. The city park slowly became a democratic landscape of play. New preserves catered specifically to working-class neighbourhoods – among them the Sarphati in Amsterdam, Bolton's Queens Park and San Francisco's Mission Dolores Park – while amenities at existing parks expanded to include organized games, animal attractions and lively amusements. Additions included children's playgrounds, circus shows, tennis courts, athletic tracks, petting zoos, carousels and skating rinks. Amidst the new frivolity, administrators still hoped to maintain the moral purpose of the park. Parks were compartmentalized for different activities. Visitor behaviour was moderated, and facilities such as zoos and galleries advanced an educational function. In the 1880s, old-school park designer Frederick Law Olmsted embraced the new creed by integrating areas for organized sports into schematics for the Boston park system. His blueprints for Buffalo incorporated a baseball diamond, a sport popular among US park visitors.

THE BASEBALL PARK

Baseball facilitated the rise of another popular park form in cities across the United States during the latter years of the 1800s. While the recreation grounds of the city park serviced the ball-hitting desires of amateur players and enthusiasts, across town the ball park provided structured play for professionals and spectator sport for local fans. By the late 1800s, the baseball park had become an important part of the leisure landscape in the USA, highlighting associations of the park with recreation and urban identity.

Devised by New Yorker Alexander Cartwright in the 1840s, baseball gained prominence in the United States during Reconstruction. With gambling common among both fans and players, early games proved rowdy affairs. However, baseball had more to offer than simple vices. Baseball player John Montgomery Ward considered the game eminently 'suited to the national temperament. It requires strength, courage and skill; it is full of dash and excitement, and though a most difficult game in which to excel, it is yet extremely simple in its first principles and easily understood by every one.' During the 1890s, managers at Baker Bowl, Philadelphia, attracted 'respectable and refined classes', by serving notice of park rules forbidding 'gambling, betting, profanity, obscenity and disorderly conduct, as well as Sunday ball playing'. By the end of the nineteenth century, baseball had emerged as America's favourite national pastime.[45]

Baseball fields found fertile soil in bustling cities. The first urban baseball parks emerged in recreational fields, old race tracks, or on deserted exposition and fairground land. Until City Hall intervened with traffic plans in 1889, the New York Giants played at a baseball field on the north-east corner of Central Park. Like amusement parks, baseball grounds were often located at the end of trolley lines to foster tram use. Rarely enclosed or well managed, early baseball parks were concerned with the sheer spectacle of the game rather than the beautification of the urban landscape. Wooden stands offered simple comforts to watching crowds. Just like the city park, the baseball diamond became associated with sound recreation, healthy exercise and democratic gathering. Welcoming venues such as Chicago's Comiskey Park provided the working class with a valuable escape from everyday industrial life.

Beginning in 1909 with the construction of Shibe Park in Philadelphia, steel and concrete baseball parks replaced their wooden counterparts. The use of fireproof materials testified to American industrial might and the common belief that baseball was there to stay. New parks emerged as grand celebrations of city, team and team owner (the most powerful industrial magnates finding in baseball an outlet for their accumulated currency). With a floor of Italian marble and featuring a baseball stitching pattern, the rotunda inside the main entrance to Ebbet's Field, built in 1913 as a venue for the Brooklyn Dodgers, exuded architectural glamour. A chandelier with its arms shaped as wooden bats hung from the ceiling. Parks represented landscapes of popular power and mass cultural significance. In 1910, at the start of the baseball season, President William Howard Taft threw the first ball at National Park, home of the appropriately named Washington Senators. Later Presidents John F. Kennedy and George W. Bush kept up the tradition.

Caught within thriving urban environments, baseball parks varied in shape and size as a direct response to existing road networks and buildings. Fenway Park in Boston resembled a giant footprint due to city restraints. Backed up against Landsdowne Street, its 10-foot-high left field embankment (Duffy's Cliff) stood only 315 feet from the home plate and within reach of many big hitters. In 1934, owners constructed a new wall nicknamed the Green Monster due to its paint hue. The wall reached 37 feet into the sky to dissuade visiting teams from knocking balls outside the park. An even higher screen protected windows in Landsdowne Street from being smashed by home runs.

Rather than compromise play action, the distinctiveness of each park assured an element of chance in team encounters. As baseball writer Philip Lowry commented, 'geometrical variety' proved 'healthy for the game'. Distinct pitch configurations suited pitchers, fielders and batters. Home teams moved and raised fences and walls in order to assist with point scoring, hoping to perfect a home-field advantage or at the very least make the game more entertaining. Huge advertising boards offered rewards to big hitters. At Ebbet's Field, Abe Stark, 'Brooklyn's Leading Clothier', promised a suit to whoever hit his sign. Natural contours also determined entertainment parameters. At Crosley Field, home to the Cincinnati Reds, the sloping nature of the park meant that outfielders ran up a hill to catch flying balls. At Braves Field, Boston, manager Casey Stengel nicknamed the gusts blowing from the nearby Charles River, 'Old Joe Wind, my fourth outfielder'. The idiosyncrasies of each park made each game different, and set turn-of-the-century baseball apart from other sports, where standardization ruled.[46]

Squeezed between outside streets and outfield, grandstands in steel and concrete parks typically allowed spectators an intimate view of the game, and helped fuel baseball as a cherished recreational pastime. City dwellers identified not just with their local team, but with their own unique home field and even its peculiar grandstand layout. Individual parks enriched the baseball experience, the venue itself contributing to the charm of the game. Diamonds such as Wrigley Field in Chicago and Ebbet's Field in Brooklyn thereby assumed the status of mythical landscapes. Baseball commissioner Bart Giamatti considered Fenway Park 'on the level of Mount Olympus, the Pyramid at Giza, the nation's capital, the czar's Winter Palace, and the Louvre – except, or course, that it's better than all those inconsequential places'.[47]

THE CITY PARK IN THE TWENTIETH CENTURY

As with any park landscape, the city park evolved during the twentieth century to meet shifting social dictates, economic pressures, political rubrics and environmental preferences. Old parks were remodelled, and new ones created. Design parameters changed as parks adapted to the cultures that they served.

Concepts of social reform continued to influence park design in the early years of the twentieth century. The park increasingly facilitated goals of cultural assimilation and national identity formation. US planners lauded parkscapes as spatial melting-pots where immigrants could learn the cultural mores and leisure norms of mainstream America. The Stadtpark in Hamburg (1914), forerunner of the Volkspark system, espoused German nationalism in its sports activities. Authorities saw organized play as a valuable medium for cultivating good citizenship and assuaging anti-social behaviour. Structured sports activities, fetes, arts and crafts displays, and gardening allotments all found their place in the park landscape as means to bring people together. The coterie of athletics championships, children's playgrounds and cultural festivals lent the modern city park a far more functional flavour than its forebears. In the early 1900s, planners were more likely to see swimming pools as appropriate park water features, rather than serpentine lakes. Leisure assumed primacy over nature, action superseded ideas of contemplation. Designer of the Stadtpark, Fritz Schumacher, explained that productive use of the park lay 'not in the sense of a passive enjoyment of the scenery, but in an active participation to be practiced in the open air: playing, taking part in sports, lying on the grass, paddling in the water, riding on horseback, dancing; going far beyond the appreciation of music, of art, of flowers and of physical pleasure'.[48]

Significantly, designers working within this new recreational mandate attached less importance to shutting out the city. Views of the city skyline became commonplace. Cars entered Golden Gate Park for the first time in 1900. Formal design schematics reflected the increasingly functional role of the park. Paths were straightened to provide additional space for gaming, and buildings were constructed for changing rooms and as venues for cultural events. Landscapers favoured level ground for the ease of ball players. Designed by Jean-Claude-Nicolas Forestier in 1911, the Parque de María-Luisa, Seville, featured a grid of tree avenues, shady plazas and garden compartments to cater for intensive visitation. Landscape architect Alan Tate applauded the design for its 'sensitivity to context. It explored Moorish garden design traditions at the same time as responding to existing site characteristics, to climatic imperatives and to the emerging functionalist paradigm of recreational utility'.[49]

The parks of the early 1900s provided recreation for the masses in a way that their nineteenth-century precursors failed to do. A wide range of cultural and entertainment pastimes attracted a diverse audience. Nevertheless, racial and sexual divisions remained. In US parks, women were assigned their own gyms, separated from male areas, and screened by trees to prevent peeking. Swimming baths hosted 'men only' and 'women only' nights. Separate park zones existed for African Americans, although poor recreational provisions for black communities belied the 'separate but equal' rhetoric of racial segregation. As of 1919, only 3 per cent of the nation's playground facilities were accessible to children of colour. In Lexington, Kentucky, authorities created a separate network of parks, governed by a dedicated Parks Board, to service African Americans. Frederick Douglass Park (1916), along with ten other parks, catered to the African-American community in Lexington and surrounding areas. As well as a refuge from city life, the park offered a brief escape from social alienation. Frederick Douglass Park gave geographical expression to a cohesive community which gained identity and empowerment by participating in organized events. Groups gathered in the park for sporting competitions, picnics and fondly remembered Fourth of July parades. On one sultry August day in 1932, 20,000 people visited the area.

In the inter-war period, the city park underwent a further evolution. The urban parkscape shed its inclination for social reform and fully embraced recreation as its defining mandate. Authorities no longer couched the value of parklands in terms of social goals. As Galen Cranz noted, 'park facilities were an expected feature of urban life. Park officials around the country adopted this attitude, repeating the claim that they no longer had to justify parks and that recreation had been accepted as an essential of life.'[50] Gorky Park, established along the Moskva River in 1928, offered a range of leisure pursuits for Muscovites. Designed as the 'First Park of Culture and Rest', in it citizens navigated 300 acres of ornamental grounds, a skating rink, playgrounds, amusement arcades and a rollercoaster ride. Architects praised Bos Park in Holland, built during the 1930s, for its functional approach to spatial design. In North America, the focus on recreational provision altered the character of landmark urban spaces. Under the stewardship of Robert Moses, Central Park expanded its amenities. In the 1920s, only the Heckscher Playground existed there. By 1941, Central Park featured twenty dedicated kids' play areas, each covered in asphalt for easy maintenance. As part of Moses' rubric of order and efficiency, the car received a hearty welcome. Car parks were created, roads widened, and features demolished to accommodate automobile usage.

World War II posed new challenges. Many park authorities found their budgets severely curtailed. Staff shortages abounded due to funding cuts and call-up cards. The park none the less continued to contribute to civic culture. Administrators held patriotic drives in parks and volunteered buildings for billeting troops. US GIs learned canoe drills in swimming pools, while British park authorities tore up iron railings to melt down for the war effort. Civil defence priorities also demanded the creation of air raid shelters in green spaces, with the park seen as a refuge from wartime targets. However, due to their placement in towns and cities, many parks were damaged during bombing runs. Used as a military depot, Hamburg's Stadtpark was subject to bomb blasts that destroyed its restaurant and dairy. Across the English Channel, Birkenhead Park lost Palm House and its gate pillars to incendiaries.

In the post-1945 period, increased leisure time and greater affluence renewed the stature of the city park. The park served as a multiple-use leisure area fit for walking, cycling, roller skating, kite flying, softball and soccer leagues, music festivals and cultural events. It also operated as a libertarian space. In the USA, 'loveins' and anti-war rallies appropriated the park as a protest landscape for alternative life-styles and political rebellion. The psychedelic 'Itchycoo Park', sung by the Small Faces in 1967, co-opted the park as a venue for drug taking, duck feeding, sun soaking and personal reflection. In 1989, 1,500,000 million people gathered in Letna Park, Prague, to listen to oratory from Vaclav Havel and Alexander Dubček during the Velvet Revolution.

The environmental revolution also made its mark on the city park idea. Park staff offered ecology tours highlighting the nature on display. Authorities incorporated butterfly zones, bog gardens and wild grass meadows in order to satisfy consumer taste for exploring functioning ecosystems and representative biota. Interpretive programmes emphasized the value of city parks as filters for hydrocarbons, airborne contaminants and noise pollution. In Seattle during the 1970s, Freeway Park greened the roof of Interstate I-5. Workers employed trees and water features to eliminate vehicular noise.

Significantly, the ideas of Frederick Olmsted gained new currency with a generation of urbanites eager to connect with nature. Once more, the park was celebrated as a natural retreat for the city dweller, an ecological enclave. Like Olmsted, environmentally inclined urbanites saw access to green space as a means towards successful city living. In 1991, Toronto City Council announced a park design competition hoping to 'create a new *natural oasis* [and] re-establish a foothold for nature in this vibrant neighbourhood'.[51] The winning template for Yorkville Park featured ten representative Canadian landscapes crossed by pedestrian walks – a nation's ecology depicted in microcosm. Similar impulses governed blueprints for Honmoku Citizens' Public Park in Yokohama, Japan – a city supporting 3,000,000 residents. In 1986, park authorities remodelled a drainage ditch and holding pond to create a wetland ecosystem for twenty-seven species of dragonfly, an endangered insect prized as a symbol of spirituality in Japanese culture.

Modern park designers contended with a range of urban maladies. Not only did the built environment circumscribe the physical limits of the park, but pollutants and toxic soil also dictated botanical choices. The city remained embedded in the park experience. However, unlike the horticulturalists of the 1800s who endeavoured to screen out the urban jungle from the pastoral lines of the park, modern landscape architects appeared far more comfortable with the social and historical impulses affecting park design. By the late twentieth century, the park had earned acceptance as a cultural artefact, part of an evolving and adapting urban cityscape.

In some locales, designers incorporated pieces of industrial archaeology into their schematics. Part of urban regeneration, the post-industrial city park embodied nature, art, technology and manufacturing processes. In El Parc del Clot, Barcelona, established in 1986, an industrial heritage of railroad sidings sat alongside Dali-inspired sculpture and Islamic water pools. Woods, gardens and an aqueduct provided areas for strolling, while asphalt zones (designed around an old railroad engineers' work pit) serviced the needs of rollerbladers and skateboarders. El Parc del Clot celebrated the park as a place of aesthetics and of utility, of the past and the present, of nature and people.

City parks in Paris also celebrated an industrial past. Built on the site of a car factory closed in the 1970s, the Parc André-Citroen opened in 1992 to popular applause. The 35 acre preserve was arranged around a formal rectangular canal and lawn. Adjacent to the central axis stood 'Serial Gardens' based on the themes of artifice, architecture, movement and nature. Parc André-Citroen offered visitors dedicated compartments of sensory delight that combined gardening and contemporary art, although one commentator lambasted the ensemble as 'a kind of horticultural IKEA'.[52]

THE CITY PARK: THE BEST AND THE WORST OF URBAN LIFE

In the 1920s, French architect Le Corbusier envisaged his ideal urban conurbation 'Radiant City' as a vertically arranged landscape of skyscrapers and elevated freeways. The whole city was situated in an expansive parkscape. Like Olmsted, Le Corbusier saw the park as integral to the utopian city. As a valuable place for citizens to rest and gather together, the park stood as an emblem of the modern city at the dawn of the twenty-first century. Urban green spaces attracted a human zoo of joggers, chess players, tai chi experts and picnickers. In Gorky Park, citizens took advantage of chilly winters by skating on the ice-covered pavements. Eager to claim the prized Peter Pan Cup, intrepid swimmers bathed in Hyde Park's Serpentine on Christmas Day for the purposes of vigour and yule-tide exuberance. The park represented a rare public space in an increasingly privatized cityscape. Writing in 1980, sociologist William H. Whyte measured the vitality of the modern city by the presence of well-utilized open spaces with shady seating and attractive vistas. Others heralded the park as vital to urban health. In 2002, Chinese authorities remodelled Heilongjiang Forest Park in Harbin with such a goal in mind. Some 1,200 plants, an artificial lake and garden areas were specifically designed to reduce humidity and city noise. Put simply, the city park was what made the city liveable.[53]

At the same time, the modern city park failed to offer urbanites a perfect Eden. The problems and pressures of the urban jungle frequently filtered into park space. As town planner Jane Jacobs adeptly pointed out, 'Parks are volatile places. They tend to run to extremes of popularity and unpopularity. Their behavior is far from simple. They can be delightful features of city districts, and economic assets to their surroundings as well, but pitifully few are . . . there are dozens of dispirited city vacuums called parks, eaten around with decay, little used, unloved.'[54]

Municipal financing represented a major obstacle to ensuring the sustainability of city parks. As city councils faced spiralling bills, many cut funding to their parks. In the 1970s, Birkenhead and Central Park fell into disrepair due to economic recession and urban unemployment. Dilapidated park buildings invited the attentions of graffiti artists. Piles of trash and rusty railings comparéd unfavourably with the glitzy cleanliness of the theme park, the beach or the shopping mall.

Crime contributed to the declining fortunes of the city park. Anti-social behaviour had always concerned park authorities – Greenwich Park featured a sturdy oak used to incarcerate felons during the 1700s, while Olmsted appointed a police force in Central Park in 1858. In the twentieth century, gangs, rapists, prostitutes, muggers and drug dealers employed the city park for their activities, lending many parks unsavoury reputations after dark. Shootings, assaults and discarded needles provided evidence of urban social decay. Sara Delano Roosevelt Park, New York, hosted pitched battles between rival gangs, the Forsyth Street Boys and the Sportsmen. Reverend Jerry Oniki commented: 'Every sort of vice you can think of goes on in that park.'[55] Also in New York, Bryant Park totalled 150 muggings and thirteen rapes in 1976 and 1977 alone. The city park contained real dangers.

Yet the reputation of criminality in the city park also derived from sensationalist journalism and media spectacle. In 1973, the *New York Times* contained extensive coverage of three murders in Central Park (1,676 occurred elsewhere in the Big Apple, but received less reportage). The dark corners and subtle lighting of the park played on fears of the savage wilderness. Freeway Park, Seattle, despite its bright lights and alarm buttons, still struck visitors as 'a somewhat scary forest [that] still seems forbidding and spooky'.[56]

The democratic structure of the city park made it an ideal venue for marginalized groups, sometimes to the concern of city administrators. With 'love-ins' in Sheep Meadow and pot smoking around the Bethesda Fountain in Central Park, America's counterculture looked to the park as a place to challenge conformity. Those seeking anonymous sexual encounters also took to the park. As a 1995 gay guidebook to Paris motioned, 'Swimming pools, public parks, the quays along the Seine, train stations and major tourist attractions all have potentials never imagined by their builders. Keep your eyes open.'[57] In the 1990s, punters dubbed Hon Lim Park in Singapore 'Jurassic Park' due to its mature homosexual male clientele. Use of the park as a 'cruising ground' spurred criticism from conservatives who objected to its appropriation as a sexual space.

City parks developed vibrant youth subcultures that utilized park steps, benches and pavements for skateboarding, much to the consternation of wardens. Some authorities issued regulations and rendered their parks 'skateproof' by removing opportunities for board stunts, while more progressive councils ceded dedicated land for a new variety of park, the skate park.

The modern city park further served as a refuge for itinerant peoples without jobs or homes, or those suffering from mental problems or substance abuse. For the homeless, the park offered a place to meet others in the same situation, as well as a forum for bartering, reading or sleeping. In Osaka, Japan's second largest conurbation, urban parks supported 2,152 vagrants living in makeshift tent cities. Visitors baulked at homeless usage of the city park, complaining of panhandling, harassment and litter, while authorities attempted to dissuade use of the park by the homeless by installing sprinkler systems and 'bum-proof benches'. In 2001, authorities in Osaka served eviction orders that mandated the removal of Nagai Park residents to a nearby housing shelter. In response, park dwellers established the Association of Poor People of Nagai Park, styling themselves as 'street-sleeper comrades'.

At the end of the twentieth century the city park presented a landscape of duality, hallowed as a healthy leisure resort and manifestation of democratic society, yet derided as a landscape of dereliction and decay. Sentimental peons from Friends of the Park societies sat alongside criticisms of 'Skid Row parks', 'crime parks' and 'pervert parks'. Some landscape architects condemned the city park as a relic irrelevant to the Internet generation, while others pointed to opportunities for urban renewal, cultural festivals and community involvement. At the very least, the park remained a fixture of the modern urban landscape. As the editors of landscape magazine *Topos* noted, 'A city without parks is not a city, at least not a modern one.'[58]

4 Nature and Recreation in the National Park

By the end of the twentieth century, national parks existed throughout the world, encompassing some 4,400,000 square kilometres of land. As of 2004, a staggering 3,881 reserves included such diverse ecosystems as the lakes of Afghanistan's Band-e-Amir (1973) and the Kalahari woodland of Zambezi National Park (1979) in Zimbabwe. Variations in habitat, culture, national policy and economics rendered each park unique, yet a number of common prerogatives joined them together. The International Union for the Conservation of Nature (IUCN) defined a national park as 'a relatively large area where . . . one or several ecosystems are not materially altered by human exploitation and occupation, where plant and animal species, geomorphological sites and habitats are of special scientific, educative and recreative interest or which contains a natural landscape of great beauty'. In this variant of the park idea, the protection of nature appeared paramount. National park ownership entailed careful stewardship of the environment and a valuation of land based not on commercialism but on green aesthetics and ecological worth. A second hallmark of the national park ethos resided in its democratic purpose. Defined as a public domain by government decree, the national park ostensibly provided for all citizens. As the IUCN elaborated, 'the highest competent authority of the country has taken steps to prevent or eliminate as soon as possible exploitation or occupation in the whole area . . . [and] visitors are allowed to enter, under special conditions, for inspirational, educative, cultural and recreative purposes'.[1]

THE BIRTH OF AN IDEAL

The national park is typically understood as an American invention. Widely interpreted as a product of the special relationship between US settlers and New World soil, the national park idea draws on American democracy, generosity of character and national primacy, expressed through natural grandeur. For western writer Wallace Stegner the national park concept signifies 'the best idea we ever had'. Environmental historian Donald Worster situates the conservationist ethos that produced the first national parks as 'one of America's major contributions to world reform movements'. For historian Roderick Nash, national parks are, put simply, as American as basketball and Coca-Cola.[2]

Patriotic testaments aside, assessments of American leadership in the national park story stand up to critical scrutiny. The first person to table the idea of a national park was Pennsylvanian George Catlin. A profligate traveller, sketcher and writer, Catlin hit upon the park idea while touring the Dakotas in the early 1830s. Viewing first-hand the encroachment of Euro-American civilization across what he saw as a pristine continent, Catlin proposed the establishment of a prairie reserve containing free-roaming bison and Indian hunters, a snapshot of pre-Columbian life preserved for all time as a '*nation's park,* containing man and beast, in all the wild and freshness of their nature's beauty!' The nationalistic implications of such a move were far from lost on Catlin. As he expatiated, 'What a beautiful and thrilling specimen for America to preserve and hold up to the view of her refined citizens and the world, in future ages!'[3]

Nothing came of Catlin's plan (in fact the plains that he so admired only achieved protection, as part of Tallgrass Prairie National Preserve, Kansas, in 1996), but his vocalizations were prescient. The same year that Catlin urged the creation of 'a nation's park', 1832, Congress brought Arkansas Hot Springs Reservation under federal jurisdiction for the purposes of public medicinal use. Meanwhile, a cadre of literary and scientific figures gradually echoed the concerns of Catlin about the dangers of American industrialization. Such notable individuals as Ralph Waldo Emerson and Henry David Thoreau saw untamed lands not as their forebears had done – as howling wastes or profitable resources – but as aesthetically pleasing venues worthy of protection. In *The Maine Woods* (1858), New England transcendentalist Thoreau called for the establishment of parks 'in which the bear and panther, and some even of the hunter race, may still exist'. Critical of the private estates of Europe, Thoreau advocated 'national preserves' designed not for regal sport or vacuous amusement but for civic 'inspiration and our own true recreation'.[4]

In 1864, Vermont lawyer and diplomat George Perkins Marsh penned *Man and Nature.* In it, Marsh warned of the capacity of humanity to change the face of the Earth and the fate of great civilizations if environmental limits went ignored. Acting on concerns over the private exploitation of natural resources, the US Congress ceded a slice of rugged scenery in the Sierra Nevada mountains to the state of California for the purposes of 'public use, resort and recreation' the same year. Since their discovery in the 1850s, the cliffs and waterfalls of Yosemite Valley, together with the sequoia trees of Mariposa Grove, had earned plaudits from explorers, writers and artists alike. Viewed as tantamount to unearthing paradise itself – one visitor remarked of Yosemite in 1863, 'If report was true we were going to the original site of the Garden of Eden' – luminaries in California and on the East Coast feared the destruction of the region's wonders by the rampant forces of commercialism.[5] Their solution: safeguard the area as a state park. President Abraham Lincoln duly signed the Yosemite Park Act on 30 June 1864. The grant proved significant by the sheer fact that the government had taken an interest in nature protection. Aside from city parks, Yosemite represented the first public park anywhere in the world.

The realization of the American national park idea came with the establishment of Yellowstone National Park on 1 March 1872. As Roger Kennedy, ex-director of the National Park Service expounded, 'At Yellowstone . . . Lincoln's idea became a fixed national policy.'[6] Impetus for Yellowstone sprang from a desire to protect the mud-pots, mineral deposits and striking scenery of the Rockies from private acquisition (see fig. 5). Arguments from railroad boosters eager to foster tourist traffic, together with the general worthlessness of the land for extractive or agricultural purposes, also aided passage through Congress. The wording of the Yellowstone Act closely resembled the precedent set with Yosemite. The reserve in north-western Wyoming was established as a 'public park or pleasuring-ground for the benefit and enjoyment of the people'. None the less, Yosemite and Yellowstone differed on a number of key aspects. First, the size of the Yellowstone allotment was huge, some 3,300 square miles (Yosemite at the time measured 40 square miles). Secondly, authority for Yellowstone's stewardship came to rest with the federal government rather than any specific state – rendering the park a truly national product. Finally, Yellowstone was the first park to utilize 'national park' nomenclature. Though designated as a 'public' park, the 'national' label was appended to the reserve from the outset. In February 1872, the *Helena Herald* referred to the reserve simply as 'Our National Park', while superintendent Nathaniel Langford favoured this label in his very first annual report.[7]

Figure 5. Mammoth Hot Springs, Yellowstone National Park, 1878. US National Archives, photo number 57-HS-518.

A REVOLUTIONARY IDEA?

Finding the *exact* source of the park idea at Yellowstone proves somewhat elusive. In his 1830s diary, trapper Osborne Russell composed a flowery passage on the glories of the Lamar Valley: 'There is something in the wild romantic scenery of this valley which I cannot . . . describe.' A few decades later, Montana State Governor Francis Meagher reputedly advised that 'the government ought to reserve the territory for a national park'. In 1869, explorers Charles Cook, David Folsom and William Peterson indicated their wish to see the natural features of the region protected from despoliation, though Cook later confessed that 'none of us definitely suggested the idea of a national park'. The most widely quoted 'origin' story involves a conversation between members of the Washburn–Doane expedition over a campfire at Madison Junction on 19 September 1870. As the explorers took to discussing the dollars to be had from land grants adjoining Yellowstone's curious landmarks, one party member, Cornelius Hedges, interjected that the region should not fall to private ownership but be preserved for posterity as a 'great National Park'.[8]

Doubts persist as to the authenticity of the campfire conversation at Madison Junction, not least because Hedges failed to mention it in his own journal. However, the wider significance, along with the revolutionary nature, of the national park idea remains instructive here. The establishment of preserves such as Yosemite and Yellowstone enshrined three decisive tenets: the principle of public access, government responsibility for natural resource management, and a desire to protect nature from the ravages of profligate commercialism in an age when the almighty dollar reigned. Together, these represented innovative directions for the park idea.

From the outset, the American national park concept was situated in opposition to the parks of old. Whereas aristocratic parks existed for the leisure of the landed elite, America's preserves offered public spaces for the 'benefit and enjoyment of the people'. As California conservationist John Muir mused, 'Thousands of tired, nerve-shaken, over-civilized people are beginning to find out that going to the mountains is going home . . . that mountain parks and reservations are useful not only as fountains of timber and irrigating rivers, but as fountains of life.'[9] The national park amounted to a green space for all to enjoy, thereby offering a fresh, egalitarian take on a hoary idea. In 1903, President Theodore Roosevelt (himself responsible for dedicating five national parks) lauded America's parklands for their 'essential democracy' in contrast to the exclusive hunting preserves of Europe.[10]

American preservationists also championed their brand of park making for its ecological superiority. Cultural nationalists interpreted the rugged chasms, soaring peaks and crystal-clear lakes of the American West as a distinguished natural past to rival the constructed cathedrals of Europe. California's Sierra redwoods, saplings at the time of Christ, offered themselves as worthy foundations for the country's Manifest Destiny. As John Muir ruminated,

'No other tree in the world, as far as I know, has looked down on so many centuries as the sequoia or opens so many impressive and suggestive views into history.'[11] Such fervent appeals to history and patriotism saw the park lionized as a place not only for healthy recreation but also as an organic repository for national aggrandizement. Nationalists castigated the Alps as 'mere hills' compared to the Sierra Nevada, and lauded Yellowstone's Lower Geyser Basin as far superior to Iceland's geothermal features. The natural monuments of America's parklands provided ready ammunition to hurl across the Atlantic. In June 1872, the US government purchased Thomas Moran's imposing 7 by 12 foot canvas *The Grand Canyon of the Yellowstone* to hang in the Senate lobby – a pictorial indicator of the fertile connections between nature and nation, park making and American identity.[12]

Advocates also saw the establishment of national parks as a signal of cultural maturity. The park idea proved an indicator of a country willing, and affluent enough, to preserve nature for non-utilitarian reasons. The fires of patriotism were again in evidence. Park making provided a philanthropic retort to Europeans bent on mocking the unbridled materialism of Yankee society. Critics had long pointed to the commercialization of Niagara Falls – a tourist resort since the early 1800s – as an example of shameful American profiteering. With the discovery of Yosemite and Yellowstone came the chance for the United States to make amends. As geologist Ferdinand Hayden expatiated in his 1871 report to the House Committee, preserving Yellowstone would guard against the kind of ruination all too evident at Niagara. The ideology of resource protection and governmental oversight implicit in the national park concept showed the American nation at its most enlightened.

The national park concept clearly reflected New World impulses: the discovery of the West and its scenic wonders, cultural nationalism, democratic philosophy, the industrial development of a continent unprecedented in its speed and scale. The United States seized on the park idea, transplanted it to new soil, and watched it sprout fresh shoots. As historian Alfred Runte rightly pointed out, if the critics of Niagara Falls had convinced *their* government to be proactive in matters of resource conservation, 'England, and not the United States, would now be credited as the inventor of the national park ideal'.[13] At the same time, vestigial links remained between the American idea and European parks. Undoubtedly the national park signified a revolutionary notion in its synthesis of nature preservation and public amenity, but cultural exchanges and shared values ensured that continuity also marked the park story.

Romanticism proved a decisive force in generating the requisite sympathies for new national parks in the USA. A conscious reaction to industrialism, Romanticism fostered an appreciation of wild nature in place of pioneer antipathy. Such reverence for untamed nature can be summed up in the eloquent dictum of Henry David Thoreau: 'In Wildness is the preservation of the World.'[14] Yet, for all its applicability to the New World landscape, Romanticism was *not* an American invention, but rather a product of the

European mind-set exported and adapted by Yankee intellectuals. A plethora of philosophers, writers and artists, including Jean Jacques Rousseau in France, Johann Wolfgang von Goethe in Germany, and William Wordsworth in Britain, shared Thoreau's disdain for industrial encroachment and proffered their own spiritual links to untamed nature. Their musings saw nature elevated as a restorative force and a sublime venue for contemplation in the Old World as well as the New. Such impulses for physical recreation and mental cogitation in a natural setting inspired not just the American park movement, but also the English landscape park of the eighteenth century and the establishment of city parks a century on.

While the national park concept celebrated the nature on display in Yellowstone and Yosemite as specifically *American*, the aesthetic formulations of park campaigners sometimes adopted frames of reference contingent on a longer tradition. John Muir lionized the tumbling waterfalls and glacial cliffs of Yosemite as awe-inspiring wilderness unrivalled across the globe. However, the naturalist equally related his appreciation for pastoral charms. In *The Yosemite* (1912), he described how 'In many places . . . the main canyons widen into spacious valleys or parks diversified like landscape gardens with meadows and groves and thickets of blooming bushes'.[15] For all Muir's attachment to rocky vistas, he still found time to appreciate the meandering river and meadows of the High Sierras. In this regard, Muir championed an environmental aesthetic found in the English landscape park. Moreover, the fact that the esteemed writer used the landscape garden or park moniker as the most appropriate analogy to the wonders of Yosemite suggested that the English park connoted beauty, spirituality and perfection, as well as Old World venality.

Frederick Law Olmsted, a veteran of the park fraternity, ventured a similar duality in his 'Yosemite and the Mariposa Grove: A Preliminary Report, 1865'. Written during his tour of duty as Chair of the Yosemite Park Commission, Olmsted celebrated Yosemite as an American monument to rival the Statue of Liberty or his own Central Park. At the same time, the architect hailed the valley for its pastoral beauty: 'the central and broader part of this chasm is occupied at the bottom by a series of groves of magnificent trees, and meadows of the most varied, luxuriant and exquisite herbage, through which meanders a broad stream of the clearest water.' Olmsted went on to deliver a direct reference to the charms of the British countryside: 'The stream is such a one as Shakespeare delighted in, and brings pleasing reminiscences to the traveller of the Avon or the Upper Thames.'[16]

In terms of culture and aesthetics, the American national park defined itself in opposition to Europe, yet maintained a number of remnant Old World roots. A similar dialectic can be found in its democratic precepts. While the aristocratic estates of the European nobility served as objects of derision for the emerging US conservation lobby, other green spaces in the Old World provided more salubrious templates for park planners. As the previous chapter has elucidated, Yosemite and Yellowstone did not represent the first experiments in 'people's parks'. Public areas designed for outdoor recreation already existed at various urban centres. Cross-fertilization existed between the landscape, city and national park concepts. The writings of Frederick Olmsted, a man whose illustrious career as a landscape architect took him to Europe and all across North America, illuminate such an exchange. In his 1865 report to the Yosemite commissioners, Olmsted decried European landscape parks for their exclusive control of scenery and praised the US government for abiding by its republican 'political duty' and preserving Yosemite for all. Yet, in an address to the Prospect Park Scientific Association (1868), Olmsted firmly situated the park ideal in English soil, while his *Walks and Talks of an American Farmer* (1852) ventured lavish praise of Birkenhead's public 'pleasure ground' – phraseology that would later grace Yellowstone's enabling act.[17]

MAKING THE PARK AS AMERICAN WILDERNESS

The national park represented an experimental landscape. Following the establishment of Yosemite and Yellowstone, administrators faced the question of how best to 'preserve' nature. Inaugural laws offered only limited guidance to greenhorn wardens and superintendents. Stewards faced further problems in terms of financing. Congress legislated in favour of reserves, but proved far less willing to pay for their upkeep. Five years passed before Yellowstone received financial appropriations. In the meantime, hunters shot park fauna for sport, subsistence and the market, while local boosters investigated ways to make a fast buck. Tourists at the fledgling preserve showed scant regard for the sanctity of the natural curiosities on display. Seeking impromptu souvenirs, parties chipped away at the mineral deposits at Mammoth Hot Springs and plugged Old Faithful geyser with trash to ensure a more colourful eruption.

Gradually, however, a consolidated park system emerged. In 1890, General Grant and Sequoia reserves were added to the fold. Yosemite was upgraded to national park status during the same year. The preservation of monumental scenery remained crucial. In 1899, the imposing rock and ice landscape of Mount Rainier in the Northern Cascade Mountains joined the national park contingent – the first American reserve to receive the 'national' park appellation in its enabling law. Grand Canyon achieved protected status in 1908, Glacier, Montana, two years later. By 1916, with fourteen individual units set aside, US government officials recognized the need for a more coherent management framework, and set about establishing a federal bureau to deal with park issues. Under the directorship of Stephen Mather, the new National Park Service proclaimed a dual mandate of preservation and use: 'to conserve the scenery and the natural and historic objects and the wild life therein and to provide for the enjoyment of the same in such manner and by such means as will leave them unimpaired for the enjoyment of future generations'.

An American national park philosophy also took shape during these years. A commitment to protecting the natural features of the preserves while encouraging public visitation shaped the official mind-set. Together, these crystallized into a universal ethos of seeing the national park as American wilderness. This vision invited specific approaches towards natural resource management, Native Americans and tourism.

In the realm of natural resource management, legislation establishing national parks stressed the significance of keeping them in a pristine state. The Yellowstone Act mandated 'the preservation from injury or spoliation, of all timber, mineral deposits, natural curiosities, or wonders and their retention in a natural condition'. The parks stood as paragons to nature's design. As superintendent Nathaniel Langford enthused, Yellowstone amounted to 'a fresh exhibition of the handiwork of the Great architect' rather than a sculpted landscape garden.[18] Such sentiments reflected a 'Cult of the Wilderness' that celebrated the national park as an American Eden untrammelled by man. Hampton Court and Prior Park had their wildernesses, but a vital distinction set apart Old and New World incarnations. For many Europeans, the 'wild' constituted an aesthetic preference and a specific gardening style. Matthew Bramble in *The Expedition of Humphry Clinker* (1771) even described the urban melée of London as an 'immense wilderness'.[19] By contrast, wilderness in the Americas connoted a land entirely devoid of human influence. Consequently, the 'wildernesses' of Yellowstone and Yosemite were seen as entirely different from the contrivances of Versailles or, for that matter, from the constructed urban greenery of Central Park. As Olmsted pointed out, Yosemite represented a 'wild park', a testament to the 'glories of nature' rather than man.[20] Park Service biologists Joseph Grinnell and Tracy Storer ventured a similar comparison: 'A city park is necessarily artificial . . .; but a national park is at its inception entirely natural and is generally thereafter kept fairly immune from human interference.'[21] This was American wilderness: untamed, expansive and iconic.

Things played out a little differently on the ground. Despite the dictum of 'leaving nature to it', managers of Yellowstone and Yosemite prosecuted a regime of environmental tinkering. The 'Cult of the Wilderness' allowed for wilderness by design. Stewards saw nothing amiss in altering park habitats, apparently improving on nature's grandeur by refining the organic canvas. This suggested parallels between the national park and its cultural forebears. In common with landscape designer 'Capability' Brown, America's early park managers favoured a naturalistic aesthetic. Wardens pruned trees to afford a more picturesque vista, and planted exotic flowers to embellish the scenery. Emphasis was placed on the prevention of fire. Charred boughs and smoking meadows were read as unbecoming to the park landscape.

A similar environmental paternalism infused national park wildlife policy. In its medieval manifestation, the park denoted an enclosed piece of ground stocked with beasts of the chase. Although the American national park idea represented a significant evolution from the hunting park, some similitude remained. Despite the general wording of Yellowstone's Act guarding against the 'wanton destruction of fauna', managers operated according to a species hierarchy that privileged certain animals. Wardens nurtured creatures popular with visitors and sportsmen – namely, bison, mule deer and elk – in the general hope of creating a sanctuary for herbivores. When it came to predators, staff traded in a discourse of devilry and bloodlust, viewing wolves, foxes and their ilk as entirely devoid of value. A vitriolic extermination campaign was enacted against such enemies of the 'peaceable kingdom'. Rangers scattered poison around wolf hang-outs, dug out dens and clubbed pups to death, hounded packs with dogs, and raised their rifles at coyotes. The national park operated as a *de facto* game park, with wardens playing the role of gamekeepers in the European tradition. In Banff and Jasper national parks in Canada, staff even entered their predator control 'scores' on a league table.[22]

Moulding the parks into 'American wilderness' also invited the removal of two-legged predators. While George Catlin's original vision mandated a 'nation's park' containing indigenous hunters, the park ideal as manifest in Yosemite and Yellowstone favoured an alternative approach. European landed estates signified obvious landscapes of power, enclaves for elite recreation, where common rights to gather wood or hunt were moribund. Managers of America's democratic preserves proved equally willing to ignore the rights of local communities, disavowing Native American ancestral claims in landscapes designed to appear untouched. According to the 'Cult of the Wilderness', the national park had to present an unsullied Eden. Native hunting and gathering practices were duly prohibited.[23] Yosemite may have been 'a people's park' in the words of John Muir, but local tribes could not hunt, burn vegetation, or collect acorns in their former stomping grounds.[24] Such management practices contradicted the egalitarian rhetoric of the national park idea and also bespoke federal policies aimed at Indian assimilation rife in the same period.

The promotion of tourism assumed early significance in America's national parks. In Yellowstone, cavalry pursuits of local Shoshone, Bannock and Nez Perce tribes (the US Army took control of the preserve in 1886 amidst growing fears of resource despoliation) centred on the need to render the area safe for tourists. Road, trail and hotel building initiatives also resulted from the drive to craft veritable nature resorts. Behind this remit lay a desire to make good on the 'pleasuring grounds for the benefit and enjoyment of the people' rationale embedded in the park ideal. Moreover, officials quickly realized that the future of the national park system depended on winning over the public. The nature lover could be convinced by paeans to natural worth, the mercenary by pointing to potential revenue generation.

The 'See America First' campaign of the 1910s exemplified early tourist promotions by combining an American spirit of mobility, cultural nationalism and an entrepreneurial ethos. As the glossy *National Parks Portfolio* (1917) proclaimed, 'This Nation is richer in natural scenery of the first order than any other nation . . . and it now becomes our happy duty to waken it to so pleasing and profitable a reality.' Implicit in this rationale was accessibility. In the introduction to the *Portfolio*, Secretary of the Interior Franklin Lane articulated official desires to open the parks 'thoroughly by road and trail and give access and accommodation to every degree of income'. Celebrations of scenic wilderness paralleled progress in asphalt mileage and building construction. The government was aided in this regard by railroad companies which advertised the parks with lavish posters, books and exhibitions. Officials also enlisted the automobile in the fight to render the parks popular vacation spots. With the first Model T entering Yellowstone in 1915, and convoys of vehicles soon careening through the specially excavated Wawona redwood in Yosemite, the love affair between the car and the national park was set.[25]

Park advertisements traded in a rudimentary form of theming, with preserves configured as 'playgrounds and pleasure resorts' in the language of the *Portfolio*. Tourists were advised to apprehend famous scenes from specific locales, to heighten their dramatic effect. The national park signified one big landscape portrait to be drunk in. The wonderland tour of Yellowstone promised grotesque rocks, boiling streams and hideous chasms – wild nature writ both as horror and thrill-ride. In this aspect, the freakish nature of the geothermal features edged them a little closer to a circus sideshow or World's Fair than traditional park fare. At the same time, advertisements projected the preserves as wholesome venues, places in which to refresh and rejuvenate, to find in nature an escape from urbanity – a social function not unlike Olmstedian city parks. The national park afforded a place to enjoy America's organic creations, to take to the great outdoors and rekindle the pioneer spirit.

Yet adventure packages in the wilderness rarely promised a complete retreat from civilization. The blankets and tents used by early tourists soon gave way to the comfortable rusticity of the lodge house. Yellowstone's Old Faithful Inn opened for business in 1904, combining rough-hewn architecture with creature comforts and a fireside seat adjacent to the famous spouting geyser. Opportunities for consumption accompanied the visitor experience from early days, with photographer Jay Haynes providing postcards, precious stones and lantern slides of Yellowstone's strange wonders from 1890 onwards.

Entertainment and showmanship proved integral to the park experience from the outset. Blackfeet Indians performed on lawns in Glacier National Park for the benefit of guests, while playful bears licked honey from visitors' hands at Yellowstone's feeding-grounds. Such lively characters represented an animated foreground to a grand mountain backdrop. At Yosemite, the ever resourceful Curry family married nature with pyrotechnics to forge a spectacular entertainment landscape. Visitors gathered expectantly to watch the firefall – an evening stunt which saw embers from a fire catapulted from Glacier Point to the valley below. The national park was packaged as a place of fun and adventure. In 1915, more than 51,000 tourists ventured to northwestern Wyoming to take in the remarkable ensemble of geysers, canyons, resplendent wilderness and wildlife attractions in Yellowstone. As Michael Milstein reflected, 'it might not have been Coney Island, but suddenly Yellowstone had become a cherished part of America's backyard: a popular family playground where the kids, deer and the antelope play'.[26]

SETTLER CULTURES: EXPORTING AND ADAPTING THE PARK IDEAL

Through the late 1800s and early 1900s other countries appropriated the national park idea. Park formation in settler cultures fed from the same sources that inspired the American movement: namely, the disappearance of habitat, a growing connection between nature and national identity, rising demands for public recreation, and an emerging sense of the economic value of park-related tourism. On occasion, the United States exerted a decisive influence on new parks, through a desire to be copied along with its leadership in international scientific discourse. In other cases, planners operated according to national imperatives or took inspiration from other (often imperial) quarters. The American model loomed large, yet, as environmental historian Thomas Dunlap pointed out, 'everywhere local culture was as important as foreign example'.[27] Ultimately, the national park proved a malleable property, adaptable to different life-styles, ecosystems and social mores.

Australian authorities conferred reserve status on the mysterious subterranean wonders of the Jenolan Caves, New South Wales, in 1866. Legislation envisaged the area would act as 'a source of delight and instruction to succeeding generations and excite the admiration of tourists from all parts of the world'.[28] Overseers appointed a keeper, and posted regulations prohibiting vandalism of the stalactites (visitors developed a penchant for breaking off pieces of rock and etching their names on the limestone). The provision of facilities proceeded apace, with the Chifley Cave receiving electric light illumination in 1872. The *Lithgow Mercury* praised the site for its combination of 'rugged grandeur' and 'sylvan beauty', pleasant flowers and 'proper concrete steps built in what were dangerous places'.[29]

In 1879, Australian officials dedicated a preserve 32 kilometres from Sydney as 'the national park' (it was renamed Royal National Park after a visit from Queen Elizabeth II in 1956). The first national park in the world dedicated as such by its enabling legislation, Royal National Park stands as Australia's claim to the original national park concept. Park establishment bespoke various influences – national, American and imperial. A number of Australian park advocates recalled visits to the western reserves of the USA in their pleas for a national park. At the same time, lobbyists couched the primary value of *their* national park as a recreation ground for disaffected city dwellers akin to Birkenhead or Central Park. Environmental aesthetics in the new preserve displayed an Anglo influence. Some 3,700 ornamental trees replaced local bush in order to create an English-style landscape. Staff even took to raising deer and rabbits in the 'people's park' for sport.

In New Zealand, ex-prime minister William Fox recommended a park at Lake Rotomahana on North Island with direct reference to Yellowstone in 1874. His plans came to nothing, but Tongariro (1887), New Zealand's first national park, sprang from concerns over the private exploitation of mountain scenery and fears for the despoliation of geothermal features.

John Ballance, Minister of Lands, anticipated that Tongariro would become 'a source of attraction to tourists from all parts of the world and that in time this will be one of the most famous parks in existence'.[30] The Kiwi preserve ventured an important innovation in terms of sponsorship. Mindful of the encroachment of sheep farmers on to the sacred volcanic slopes of Ruapehu, Tongariro and Mgauruhoe, Maori chief Te Heuheu Tukino IV bequeathed the area to the government to ensure its protection. Tongariro thereby represented the first park in the world to be established at the behest of indigenous peoples. Significantly, at a time when the US cavalry were chasing Native Americans out of Yellowstone, the Maori saw the national park idea as a guarantor of their cultural heritage.

In the 1880s, the Canadian Pacific Railway (CPR) cut across the Canadian Rockies. Enlivened by rumours of mineral riches and fine game, railroad workers spent their spare time hunting and prospecting in the mountains. During one such trip in November 1883, Thomas and William McCardell and Franklin McCabe came across two hot springs – a basin and a cave – in the Bow Valley, Alberta. A sleuth of land claims ensued as the three men, along with all kinds of opportunistic folk, filed title to the steaming pools with a view to developing a financially lucrative spa. The CPR and the Canadian government had other ideas. Fearful of private despoliation of the attraction, authorities in Ottawa ceded 10 square miles around the pool in 1885 as Banff Hot Springs Reserve, due to its 'great sanitary advantage to the public'. National park status was conferred on the region in 1887 following a survey by Dominion land surveyor George Stewart, who categorized the terrain of rugged peaks and gleaming lakes as 'admirably adapted for a national park'.[31] Parliamentary debate on the park issue included heartfelt appeals to patriotism. While cultural nationalists further south heralded the uniquely *American* qualities of Rocky Mountain scenery, for Montreal MP Donald West, 'anyone who has gone to Banff . . . and not found himself elevated and proud . . . cannot be a true Canadian'. Public health incentives and potential tourist revenue also worked in favour of the park. As Premier John MacDonald quipped, the springs would 'recuperate the patients and recoup the Treasury'.[32]

As might be expected, the national park movement in Canada invited a few stolen glances south of the 49th parallel. The USA and Canada shared similar western topographies and land management prerogatives. Sometimes authorities in Canada set out to better their counterparts in the United States, and at other times they sought American guidance. In establishing Banff Hot Springs Reserve, administrators clearly took inspiration from Arkansas. They also planned to trump it – Secretary of the Department of the Interior John Hall returning from an 1886 fact-finding mission to Arkansas bemoaned its poor maintenance, ramshackle plumbing and over-permissive entrance policy. When Banff was upgraded to national park status the following year, enabling legislation paid homage to the Yellowstone Act. Banff became 'a public park and pleasure ground for the benefit, advantage and enjoyment of the people of Canada'. At the same time, Canadian officials seemed more attuned to the potential economic gains locked up in Rocky Mountain scenery than their cohorts in Yellowstone. In its first six years of operation, Banff received $141,254 for roads, hotels and trails, all judged necessary to render the protected 260 square miles 'a creditable national park'.[33] Rather than 'worthless lands', Canadian administrators envisaged their parks as prestigious resorts. Additional national parks sprang up along the Canadian Pacific Railway at Yoho and Glacier (1886) and Waterton Lakes (1895) based on this dual philosophy of nature protection and wildlands tourism.

In Africa, the impetus for national parks centred on animals rather than monumental scenery, a focus which harkened back to the park's ancient roots as a game preserve. With colonization came land clearance, the railroad and the great white hunter. By the early 1900s, British East Africa hosted 150–200 shooting parties a year at the cost of some 10,000 trophy animals. Market hunters facilitated a profitable export trade in ivory, hides and horn, while settlers shot eland and buffalo in fear of such animals spreading the malaria-carrying tsetse fly. This decimation of Africa's wildlife – the poignant symbol being the quagga, the last specimen of which expired in Amsterdam zoo in 1883 – fermented concern among imperial naturalists and sport hunters (often dubbed 'penitent butchers'). In response, they organized the Natal Game Protection Association (1883) and the Society for the Preservation of the Wild Fauna of the Empire (1903).[34] Cognizant of the failure of existing hunting laws, dedicated game reserves emerged in the Cape Colony (1856); the Transvaal states of Pongola (1889), Sabi (1898) and Singwitsi (1903); Kenya (1897); and Northern Rhodesia (1899), to nurture populations of hippopotamus, wildebeest, buffalo, rhino and elephant. These game reserves served as precursors of national parks by virtue of their protection clauses and governmental oversight. At the same time, they made no provision for public access and could be dismantled with relative ease. Emphasis remained on preserving animals for sport, perpetuating a 'hunter's paradise', rather than on offering an inclusive civic venue for non-consumptive recreation.

The national park officially came to Africa in 1925 with the dedication of the Parc Nationale Albert, now Virunga National Park, in the Democratic Republic of the Congo. Inspiration for protecting the monumental volcanic peaks of the Virunga Massif sprang, in part, from Belgian King Albert's tour of US parks in 1919, including a campfire discussion with conservationists John Merriam and Henry Fairfield Osborn at Yellowstone. Suitably impressed by the park idea, yet aware of the lack of wilderness in Belgium, King Albert transplanted an enthusiasm for nature protection to his country's African colony. Additional impetus came from American naturalist Carl Akeley, who campaigned for the protection of Virunga's rare mountain gorillas for the purpose of scientific study. Historian Roderick Nash characterized this process of international conservationist exchange as 'nature importing', whereby Euro-Americans viewed Africa through the filters of imperialist ideology while mindful of the rapid environmental changes occurring in the USA.[35] The park ethos was coloured by a colonial mind-set that apprehended

Africa as an unspoiled Eden untouched by human exigencies (a perception that overlooked the role played by village subsistence activities in shaping the 'natural' landscape). By cordoning off areas as parkland, authorities were able to preserve the myth of Africa as a last wild paradise as well as indulge imperial proclivities for science and government regulation.[36]

In South Africa, advocates of the famous Kruger reserve, the second in the continent (1926), also took a glance at American precedent. Noting that 'it would be a thousand pities to endanger the existence of our South African fauna', Minister of Finance Smuts proposed the upgrading of the Sabi game reserve in 1914 'on the lines of similar institutions which exist in the United States and other parts of the world'.[37] Having read up extensively on the popular appeal and financial success of national parks in the USA, head ranger of the Sabi, James Stevenson-Hamilton, pondered in 1905: 'Would it conceivably be possible to wean the South African public from its present attitude towards the wild animals of its own country?' He went on to venture the following assessment:

It seemed pretty hopeless. The low-veld was wild, dangerous, unhealthy; there were not many scenic attractions; few people had any interest in wild animals unless they were dead. . . . Government in fact, beyond paying the monthly wage bill, left us in the main to shift for ourselves. . . . The American public must surely be very different from ours![38]

Securing a national park for South Africa appeared doubtful, given such a pessimistic verdict. However, the mood in government and among the public altered dramatically in subsequent decades. As modernization, settlement and capitalist farming techniques gathered pace, vanishing nature attracted romantic and aesthetic valuations beyond the standard economic equation. Aware of the disappearance of wild habitat and faunal species, the Report of the Game Reserves Commission (1918) recommended 'a great national park' for the benefit of 'scientists, naturalists and the general public'.[39] The tone of the report reflected traditional imperial interests in botany, science and wildlife protection as well as articulating the nascent idea of nature as a tourist resource.

The drive to create South African national parks further related a rising sense of Afrikaner patriotism. Eager to secure international prestige for the republic as well as to glorify its pioneer heritage, conservationists rallied for the creation of a 'Volkspark' where future generations could see the landscape 'just as the Voortrekkers saw it'. The African savannah with its complement of charismatic mega-fauna symbolized the august of the South African nation, just as Sierra redwoods did for the USA. Behind this nostalgia lay important political considerations. Advocates saw the formation of Kruger National Park as a route towards fostering a collective (white) national identity. Stevenson-Hamilton, privately at least, saw the capital, and the irony, of using the Kruger moniker: 'the "Kruger stunt" is I think of priceless value to us . . . I wonder what the old man, who *never in his life* thought of wild animals except as biltong . . . what he would say could he see himself depicted as the "*Saviour of the South African game*"!!!'[40] Equally, park creation enhanced the authority of the National Party in placing land and natural resources under governmental tutelage. Kruger National Park served as a landscape of power whereby the white elite executed control over indigenous communities. As in the USA, traditional subsistence activities were reframed as illegal poaching, the historic role of hunter-gatherer neglected in favour of forging parks as repositories of white cultural identity and pristine wildness.

THE TWENTIETH CENTURY: PARK PROLIFERATION, ECOLOGICAL SCIENCE AND INTERNATIONAL DISCOURSE

The national park idea proved popular in the late 1800s as part of a process by which settler communities came to terms with their environments and forged distinct spiritual, romantic and patriotic associations with the land. In the twentieth century, concerns about unbridled industrial change and the fragmentation of the countryside saw the park extend its influence further. National parks came to symbolize international prestige in the global community.

Whereas parks in North America, the Antipodes and Africa were idealized as untouched landscapes, Europeans proved far more willing to accept national parks as cultural spaces. In part, this reflected a variance in environmental ideologies – the landscape of Europe had, after all, been consistently (and obviously) modified for thousands of years, leaving the 'Cult of the Wilderness' with far less psychological allure. On a practical level too, park designers were scarcely able to forge large wilderness areas on a continent marked by a high population density and extensive private ownership.

Sweden established Abisko, Stora Sjöfallet, Sarek and Peljekaise national parks by act of the Riksdag in 1909. These preserves, spanning some 1,100 square miles, comprised forbidding landscapes of rock and ice in the Lapp province. Inspiration came from a variety of quarters, including the US example, German forest conservation, and the activism of committed individuals such as explorer A. E. Nordenskiold. Administered by the Swedish Academy of Sciences, the Lapp parks followed a strict remit of scientific research. In 1914, the Swiss government ceded 61 square miles of alpine scenery near Zernez as Engadine (Swiss) National Park with scientific enquiry also in mind. The area had been dedicated as a private nature reserve in 1909, thanks to the efforts of conservancy groups. Meanwhile, the protection of historic landscapes assumed primacy in the dedication of Spain's Covadonga National Park (1918) in the mountainous region of Cantabria – the site where the Moors were vanquished in the twelfth century. As the location for the country's inaugural parliament assembly or 'Althing' (AD 930), the Icelandic park Thingvellir (1928) commemorated a distinguished cultural history as well as a tumultuous geological past. Other reserves in Europe illuminated the park idea as an evolving cultural phenomenon. In Italy, Gran

Paradiso National Park, ex-hunting reserve of the royal elite, was established in 1922, specifically to protect the range of the endangered alpine ibex. In Poland, the old hunting reserve of Bialowieza acquired national park status in 1932. Six years later, the Greek government ceded 15 square miles of the sacred grove of Mount Olympus, craggy home of Zeus, as a national park.

In the Americas, philanthropy and conservationist impulse combined. Mexico inaugurated its national park system with Desierto de Los Leones (1917), an hour's drive west of Mexico City, thanks to conservationist Miguel Ángel de Quevedo and his concerns over deforestation. The park had been demarcated as a forest reserve in 1876 to protect water resources. At its centre-piece lay an impressive Carmelite retreat dating to 1611, the product of the monastic order's desire to worship the deity in the wilderness. In Argentina, park creation came from the philanthropy of Dr Francisco P. Moreno, who gave 10 square miles to the nation. Dedicated as Parque Nacional del Sur in 1903, the park was renamed Nahuel Huapi in 1934.

The presence of British, French and Dutch colonial authorities also fostered a germination of the park idea. In India, Jim Corbett National Park (originally known as Hailey) was established in 1936.[41] In Japan, spiritual reverence for mountain scenery combined with a hiking craze and growing concerns about the disappearance of green spaces to produce the National Parks Law of 1931. Inspiration also came from wilderness aficionado John Muir, who once hosted Japanese naturalist Ryozo Azuma at his California home. By 1936, Japanese authorities had created twelve parks, including Setonaikai, Chubu Sangaku (known as the 'Japan alps'), Unzen-Amakusa and Akan volcanic mountain complexes, and Nikko, famed for its cedars and ancient shrines.

The proliferation of parkscapes in the early twentieth century encouraged a professionalization in the staffing and management of nature reserves. Canada pioneered the first federal agency mandated with park protection in 1911, though the US National Park Service (NPS), created five years later, is more recognized. In South Africa, the National Parks Board of Trustees assumed stewardship over Kruger and other preserves. Training in landscape architecture, engineering, wildlife management and civil service gradually replaced army command and amateur naturalism as prerequisites for employment. Banff hosted its first warden school in 1925. Parks were systemized, extended and furnished with administrative infrastructures. The US National Park Service extended stewardship over state parks and historic buildings in the 1920s and 1930s. New recreational units came in the form of the Blue Ridge Parkway, North Carolina/Virginia (1933), and Cape Hatteras National Seashore, North Carolina (1937).

Authorities reappraised traditional management policies in the inter-war years. Influenced by the emerging discipline of ecological science, a new generation of stewards, most active in the USA, engaged in a critique of existing park practices. Scientists articulated a need for parks to protect both representative landscapes and rare native fauna. Biologists George Wright, Ben

Thompson and Joseph Dixon, all working in the newly established NPS Wildlife Division (1933), endorsed a doctrine of 'total preservation' in their landmark report *The Fauna of the National Parks* (1933).[42] Wright and his cohorts called for parks to be refocused on the protection of habitat and the preservation of wild spaces for scientific and educational purposes. The dedication of Everglades National Park, along with Australia's Tallowa Preserve (both in 1934), reflected this new emphasis on representative habitat in preference to monumental scenery.

Animal programmes were similarly scrutinized. A positive appraisal of predators, due to their rarity and ecological value, emerged. With elk starvation in the Grand Canyon and exotic red deer irruptions in New Zealand, resource managers learnt to recognize the unintended consequences of meddling in biotic systems. As James Stevenson-Hamilton confessed, the removal of carnivores such as mongoose, jackal and wild cats from Sabi had caused an explosion in rodent numbers:

The ideal wild life sanctuary should aim to be fully and accurately representative of the particular area . . . All indigenous species of fauna and flora ought to be represented, but the introduction of exotic types of either should be religiously avoided . . . Only by keeping such a place perfectly natural, may the student acquire true knowledge, and the ordinary visitor a real education in natural history.[43]

Venturing a fierce criticism of sapient environmental transformations, along with an embryonic biocentric philosophy, Stevenson-Hamilton railed: 'If and when Man should ever disappear from Earth, there is no form of nature but would benefit by his departure.'[44] Once read as vermin, predators became 'special charges' of the parks. African wardens refrained from shooting lions. All control policies ended in the continental US parks from 1933. In Canada, commissioner James Harkin insisted that 'predatory animals are of great scientific, educational, recreational and economic value to society'.[45] Such emphasis on ecological conditions equally brought a reassessment of zoos and performing animal shows. Henry Baldwin War, of the University of Illinois, lambasted the NPS for its historic focus on faunal entertainment, advising that visitors should visit fun-fairs rather than national parks for such attractions. Bear shows at Yellowstone smacked of vacuous amusement, anthropomorphism and barbarity, 'all the flavor of a gladiatorial spectacle in Ancient Rome'.[46] Menageries in Yosemite and Banff closed in 1932 and 1938, respectively. Yellowstone's bear-feeding show served its final entrée in 1941.

Conversations proceeded across international lines between governments, scientists and non-government organizations on matters of ecological philosophy and conservation. In North America, US, Canadian and British officials discussed all manner of issues, from the protection of migratory birds to predator control. As Franklin Lane, US Secretary of the Interior, advised NPS director Stephen Mather, 'maintain [a] close working relationship with the Dominion Parks Branch [Canada] . . . and assist in the solution of park problems of an international character.'[47] Canadian officials, in turn, looked

to the USA for advice on resource management, not least because US con-
servation agencies received far better funding before 1945. Conservationist
discourse across the 49th parallel led to the creation of the first international
peace park at Waterton-Glacier in 1932. Similar proposals were ventured by
Miguel Ángel de Quevedo, who led a delegation in 1935 for an International
Park Commission and US–Mexican border preserve. In 1940, the *Daily
Oklahoman* proudly reported, 'While Europe Fights, Mexico and America
Plan Peace Park.'[48] Such plans have yet to reach fruition.

In Europe, such exchanges led to the formation of the International
Congress for the Protection of Nature (1909). Co-founder Paul Sarasin (an
instrumental force in establishing Swiss National Park) characterized the
mission of the organization as 'to extend protection of nature to the whole
world from the north pole to the south pole, covering both continents and
seas'.[49] Moves to foster a formal consultative committee faltered during World
War I, but discussions continued thereafter. In 1933, a number of powers,
including Britain, South Africa, France, Italy, Portugal and Spain, signed the
Convention Relative to the Preservation of Flora and Fauna in their Natural
State, a decree demonstrative of the growing international interest in parks
and conservation. The Convention recommended a 'special regime' for the
protection of endangered fauna, especially in Africa, and advocated national
parks along with more rigorous hunting laws as appropriate remedies for
species decline. Significantly, the Convention offered a common definition of
a national park, one that incorporated preservationist, scientific and populist
tenets:

> The expression 'national park' shall denote an area . . . under public control . . . set
> aside for the propagation, protection and preservation of wild animal life and wild
> vegetation, and for the preservation of objects of aesthetic, geological prehistoric,
> historical, archaeological, or other scientific interest for the benefit, advantage, and
> enjoyment of the general public.[50]

The document drawn up by the Convention was a transitional one. It ventured a traditional image of the national park as a pristine paradise, yet championed new ecological rationales of regional protection and sustainability. The
decree revealed a lingering imperial mind-set in offering no provision for
indigenous hunting – seemingly putting the rights of animals before humans –
yet also signalled an emerging modern discourse on the park as a vital biotic
space as opposed to a mere tourist venue.

THE POST-WAR ERA: NATURE PROTECTION AND AUTO-RECREATION

Conservation funding plummeted during World War II. In the USA, national
park appropriations fell from $21,100,000 in 1940 to $4,600,000 in 1944. In
Sequoia National Park the number of personnel dropped by more than 50 per
cent following enlistment in the wake of Pearl Harbor. Many parks were

appropriated as military camps, hospitals and training grounds. Troop exercises occurred in Mount McKinley and Hawaii. Banff and Jasper housed prisoners of war. The war also raised the spectre of requisitioning. Salt mining was permitted in Death Valley, and NPS staff reluctantly allowed timber cutting in Olympic National Park out of 'critical necessity'.[51] The patriotic *Calgary Herald* even envisioned a wartime role for Banff's beaver population: 'far away from the roads, where tourists delight to see them', the industrious rodents could allegedly be 'trapped and used for war work'.[52]

The demands of conflict dampened the national park movement only temporarily. In 1948, various government bodies and NGOs established the International Union for the Protection of Nature (IUPN, later IUCN) – a supranational organ designed to promote nature preservation, educational outreach and environmental information. The IUCN highlighted a growing interest in global nature by advocating nothing less than the protection of 'the entire world biotic environment' as well as advertising the continuing internationalization of the park idea.[53] In 1958, the IUCN began compiling a definitive list of global reserves. Four years later, it hosted the First World Conference on National Parks in Seattle. At the conference, more than sixty nations debated a range of issues from wildlife protection to wilderness and religion.

While activists and civil servants discussed the merits of the national park as an environmental good, members of the public took to the great outdoors in record numbers. Rising levels of affluence and leisure time saw the parks become favoured destinations for vacationers in Europe and North America. In 1955 alone, Yosemite hosted 1,060,000 people. Yellowstone received 1,408,000 visitors. Banff attracted 1,000,000 annual guests for the first time in 1960–1. That figure had doubled by 1967. During the same year, 2,099 visitors rafted through the Grand Canyon.

Although hinted at for some time, the national park idea finally manifested on British shores in the 1950s. In *A Guide Through the District of the Lakes* (1810) William Wordsworth asked for 'a sort of national property, in which every man has a right and interest who has an eye to perceive and a heart to enjoy'.[54] The Commons, Open Spaces and Footpaths Preservation Society (1865), the oldest citizen environmental group in the world, carried forth Wordsworth's call for public access to the British countryside, as did the National Trust (1895) and the Council for the Protection of Rural England (1926). In 1904, Charles Stewart called for a national park for Scotland, a cause championed by *The Scots Magazine* from the late 1920s.[55] In 1932, protesters exercising their 'right to roam' staged a mass hill-walking trespass of Kinder Scout in England's Peak District. Endorsement came from the government-appointed Addison Committee (1929–31), although the issue remained moribund until after World War II, when civil servants looked to the national park idea as a way of bolstering national unity in the context of wider post-war reconstruction. Conservationists lent their support to the project, raising fears of urbanization and industrial encroachment alongside traditional pleas for democratic access to the countryside. The time for park creation seemed politically appropriate, given the new Labour Administration's public works and social betterment philosophy, its interest in comprehensive town and rural planning, along with its aspirations to rein in landed control of property.

Encompassing 544 square miles of moorland and rocky hills, the Peak District became Britain's first national park in 1951. Ten further parks were created in the 1950s, including the Lake District, Dartmoor, Brecon Beacons, Snowdonia, Exmoor and the Pembrokeshire Coast. Significantly, Scotland was left out of legislation, due to the power of Highland landowners, reticent county councils, and pressure from the Forestry Commission and energy interests who wanted free reign to tap timber and hydroelectric resources in the region.

The British incarnation of the national park idea balanced North American influences with national conservationist impulses. Lord Bledisloe, Parliamentary Secretary to the Minister for Agriculture, visited Yellowstone and Banff in the 1920s. For Bledisloe, national parks served vital aesthetic, conservationist and social functions, providing not only 'beautiful sanctuaries for wild animals and birds, as well as for the wild flowers and ferns', but also 'a most perfect holiday resort for persons of all classes'.[56] A similar philosophy graced the Dower Report (1945), a government paper that clearly paid homage to the Yellowstone proto-type in its call for 'beautiful and relatively wild country' preserved 'for the nation's benefit'.[57]

At the same time, British legislators realized the different social and ecological composition they had to work with. A small, densely populated island, Britain lacked the requisite space to dedicate vast reserves. After all, Yellowstone was the size of Yorkshire. While the US park system comprised large swathes of government property, three-quarters of British reserves remained under the purview of private owners, necessitating a different approach to land management. Britain's landscape told a story of lengthy human occupation, environmental transformation and economic activity – all of which planners had to incorporate into the Anglo park ideal. Snowdonia featured monumental scenery, including the peaks of Snowdon and Cader Idris, but also jet fighter exercises by the Royal Air Force, sheep farming, hydroelectric power facilities, and a plethora of grey stone villages within its 848 square miles.

In 1999, political devolution and the creation of a Scottish Parliament saw the national park idea finally reach fruition in Scotland. In 2002, Loch Lomond and the Trossachs National Park was set aside, (1) to conserve the area's natural and cultural heritage, (2) to encourage wise use of natural resources, (3) to promote public enjoyment of the region's special qualities, and (4) to facilitate the economic and social sustainability of local commu-nities (some 15,600 people lived within the 720 square mile reserve). Such goals harkened back to Yellowstone in 1872, yet ventured a significant caveat. The British national park was not just a place of nature and visitation, but also a home and a workshop.

PARKS AND THE ENVIRONMENTAL REVOLUTION

In the 1960s and 1970s, a new global environmental movement emerged. A response to the insidious spread of nuclear fallout, chemical contamination by toxins such as the pesticide DDT, as well as high-profile disasters such as the sinking of the *Torrey Canyon* and the Santa Barbara oil spill, environmentalism offered a sharp critique of the direction of modern society and its implications for the planet. In April 1970, 20 million Americans participated in Earth Day, a day set aside for environmental protest, festival and grass-roots organizing. 'Ecology' and 'going green' quickly became the buzzwords of the new crusade. Significantly, the environmental revolution is often presented as a decisive shift away from traditional conservation (and with it, park making) in favour of a new concentration on 'the modern industrial threat'. Characterized as a politicized, media-savvy activist, the stereotype of the modern environmentalist suggests concern over not the decline of individual species, or ecosystems, but the survival of humanity itself. This analysis overlooks the enduring impact of the park idea on modern discourses regarding humankind and nature. Its emphasis on industrial contamination and sapient health notwithstanding, the global environmental movement has been influenced by the park idea in several instrumental ways.

Many environmental campaigners acquired their love of the planet as a direct result of contact with park-like landscapes. In her ground-breaking text *Silent Spring* (1962), American naturalist Rachel Carson related the dangers of DDT and other pesticides. Carson gained her sense of natural wonder, moral philosophy and biotic humility through discreet observations of America's coastline, first as a child and later as a marine zoologist. She witnessed the dangers of DDT – a truly modern environmental threat – principally through seeing *nature* at risk. The public impact of *Silent Spring* – it sold 500,000 copies in hardback and was published in fifteen countries in just one year – owed much to its engaging naturalist style situated firmly in the tradition of John Muir's works on Yosemite.

It was precisely the fight to protect parks from industrial despoliation that facilitated the transformation of traditional conservation outfits into modern environmental organizations. Originally formed as a genteel mountaineering fraternity in 1892, the Sierra Club emerged as a radical campaign organization for parks and wilderness areas in the 1960s. A series of exhibit-format books produced in the period illuminated club philosophy as a marriage of old and new concerns. In *My Camera in the National Parks* (1950) photographer Ansel Adams extolled national parks as evidence of an 'enlightened relationship of nature and man' – precisely the ethos highlighted by environmentalists as lacking in modern industrialism.[58] The Sierra Club's *This is the American Earth* (1960) amounted to a spectacular tribute to national parks as vital symbols of human freedom and ecological health *as part* of a modern environmental discourse stressing imminent threats to the Earth from technology and human arrogance. Meanwhile, under the coaxing of executive director David Brower, the Sierra Club cut a new pro-activist trail with a series of high-profile campaigns. Members argued for new national parks in the North Cascade Mountains and California's redwood forests, protested resort development at Mineral King in the Sierra Nevada, and vigorously opposed dam projects within the Grand Canyon. Such actions in defence of the park idea allowed the development of new protest tactics based on media exposure and ardent lobbying. In summer 1966, the Sierra Club purchased a series of full-page advertisements in the *New York Times* to protest dam projects on the Colorado River, one of which touted the seminal line: 'Should we also flood the Sistine Chapel so tourists can get nearer the ceiling?'

Although some veterans disapproved of the new directives, the popularity of the Sierra Club could not be denied. Membership rose threefold between 1966 and 1970. Under the umbrella philosophy of 'environmental survival', traditional concerns for parks and wilderness merged with new issues of energy consumption, industrial pollution and population growth for the first time. Everything seemed relational. Without a sustainable biome free from nuclear fallout and chemical carcinogens, national parks had little hope of survival. Moreover, in the estimation of David Brower, the park idea had its own unique contribution to make to modern environmentalism. For him, an effective remedy to the impending ecological crisis was, quite simply, the creation of 'Earth National Park'. As Brower extrapolated in a January 1969 advertisement for the *New York Times*, the ideas from Yellowstone and Yosemite could be fruitfully applied, and extended to the space race generation: 'It is now the entire planet that must be viewed as a kind of conservation district within the Universe; a wildlife preserve of a sort, except we are the wildlife, together with all other life and environmental conditions that are necessary constituents of our survival and happiness.'[59] Humans were now the endangered species, and thus required their own park refuge. Fellow Sierran Edgar Wayburn ventured similar sentiments in a quieter fashion in the club *Bulletin*. Far from an outdated concept, the park idea brought forward a valuable ethos of appreciation and aesthetics to a modern discourse. As Wayburn explained:

survival is not enough . . . In many places this is being hailed as the emergence of a 'new' conservation as opposed to the 'old'. The 'new' is supposed to be spear-heading the just-discovered 'gut' issues of survival; the 'old' more narrow (and called by some 'elitist') is supposed to be still saving trees and worrying about Wilderness areas and National Parks . . . We can also end up living in a concrete world and subsisting on algae, if survival is our only aim. The earth was meant to be a liveable, beautiful place: none of us must settle for less.[60]

Nor were park-related issues absent from the agendas of newly formed environmental lobbies. Friends of the Earth (FoE), Greenpeace and other groups famous for their protests against nuclear power, oil drilling, climate change and biotechnology also articulated concern for wilderness and parklands. Founded by David Brower in San Francisco in 1969, following his acrimonious departure from the Sierra Club, Friends of the Earth hoisted 'Think globally, act locally' as its mantra. FoE counted affiliates in sixty-nine countries by 1970. Campaigns included whaling protests, the fur trade, dams and wilderness protection, along with fights against the MX nuclear missile, acid rain and the World Bank. In the late 1990s, FoE lobbied for the creation of a South Downs national park in the UK, opposed the Jabiluka uranium mine for its deleterious impact on Kakadu National Park in Australia, and highlighted plans by Shell to drill for gas in Kipthar National Park in Pakistan.

Another bastion of modern environmentalism, Greenpeace, maintained a similar dual-track approach. Founded in 1971 to protest nuclear testing off the Aleutian Islands, Greenpeace engaged in high-profile direct action campaigns to scupper whale and seal culls in the 1970s. Significantly, in the early 1980s the group lobbied for the creation of a 'world park' in Antarctica. Fusing concerns over mineral exploration, marine mammal harvests and global warming, Greenpeace advertised the park idea as a suitable protective device for the world's 'last great wilderness'. Activists established World Park Scientific Station in 1986. In 1998, twenty-six nations ratified the Environmental Protection to the Antarctic Treaty (the Madrid Protocol), rendering the continent off limits for resource exploration for 50 years as a 'natural reserve, devoted to peace and science'. In the view of modern environmentalists and international governments alike, the national park concept represented the most credible system to protect Antarctica from exploitation.

PARADISE THREATENED

By 2004, some 9.5 per cent of the Earth's surface had been set aside as national park land, nature reserve or wilderness area. However, the integrity and security of such spaces was not without challenge.

As more people flocked to the outdoors for recreation, 'loving the parks to death' represented one key problem. Popular nature trails suffered soil erosion and habitat damage. Camera-wielding tourists startled grizzlies in Yellowstone and water buffalo in Kilimanjaro. Meanwhile, tourist infrastructure included hotels, roads, gift shops, gas stations, food outlets, campsites and parking lots. Mass construction consumed core habitat. Floodlit waterholes near hotel lodges in African reserves disturbed the natural behaviour of animals. Grazers concentrated on succulent lawns, while bright lighting kept away predators. In Banff, shopping malls, cinemas, a cable car and a golf course catered to a daily onslaught of 25,000 visitors.

Industrialized tourism represented another problem for park managers. Motor vehicles translated into noise pollution, high carbon monoxide emissions, congestion, habitat degradation and road accidents. In 1955, the *US News and World Report* observed: 'This summer 19 million Americans will visit parks that are equipped to handle only 9 million people. Result: Parks overrun like convention cities. Scenery viewed from bumper to bumper traffic tie ups.'[61] The situation had hardly improved in the 1990s. In Banff, the four-lane Trans-Canada Highway brought upwards of 15,000 vehicles (including freight juggernauts and RVs) through the eastern gateway of the park every day in 1995. Between 1986 and 1995, eleven of Banff's struggling wolf population died on the road. On a hot summer weekend, both Yosemite Valley and Dovedale Falls in the Lake District resembled car parks rather than national parks – all frayed nerves, revving engines, queuing traffic and asphalt haze. Park tourists rarely ventured far from their vehicles, choosing instead to congregate around major attractions, or 'honeypots'. In Britain's national parks, four out of five visitors remained in their cars or walked less than 3 kilometres. Autophilia came to challenge biophilia. Popular fascination with the road trip rendered the national park just a sideshow to be viewed through the windshield. The park became a place to drive through, rather than experience directly. As US conservationist Joseph Wood Krutch complained, 'Instead of valuing the automobile because it may take one to a national park, the park comes to be valued because it is a place the automobile may be used to reach.'[62]

Other forms of technology facilitated a similarly mechanized experience. Airplanes and helicopters buzzed over Grand Canyon, while snowmobiles (some 1,600 a day) careened along the snow-packed trails in Yellowstone during winter. People always looked to the park for recreation – from family vacations to extreme sports – but for some, the activity, the ride or the machine was what mattered most.

As a result, boundaries between the national park and the theme park blurred. Both venues satisfied human desires for automotive excitement. In Yellowstone, the grand loop road offered a slow-motion ride through a frontierland of rugged canyons and bubbling mud-pots, the scenery courtesy of geological design rather than clever engineering. A raft trip through Grand Canyon promised a splash-canyon journey to trump Disneyland, albeit with a longer queue and a higher price tag. In 1972, 16,432 people signed up for this adventure on the Colorado River, the sheer volume of passengers leading one commentator to dub the experience more 'carnival-style thrill ride' than wilderness excursion.[63]

A further peril to the national park emerged in the form of alternative valuations of nature. For developers, the parks symbolized wasted opportunities, locked-up resources whose value lay in their extractive, agricultural, timber or real estate merits. Petroleum companies lobbied for rights to oil reserves near the Great Barrier Reef National Marine Park, the largest World Heritage area on the planet at nearly the size of England. Pharmaceutical corporations ventured plans to delve the fabled geysers of Yellowstone for microbes. Agribusinesses touted intensive farming to offset rural decline in the Brecon Beacons, Wales. During the twentieth century, many park boundaries were whittled away to accommodate economic interests, from the decision to dam Hetch Hetchy Valley in Yosemite (1913) to reductions to Kutai National Park, Indonesia (1982), slashed by 1,300 hectares for industrial projects. Development pressures also encouraged illegal encroachment. In India's Ranthambhore National Park (1981), a 426 square kilometre preserve in

Rajasthan, tiger populations crashed, due to unlawful grazing, poaching and forestry within the reserve.

Threats also came from beyond park borders. As 'ecological islands', small biotic remnants surrounded by landscapes of agriculture, mineral extraction, logging and settlement, parks proved vulnerable to outside economies. Ranthambhore National Park featured twenty-three villages within 5 kilometres of its perimeter. Some 60,000 domestic animals competed with thirty tigers and other wild fauna for territory and forage. As aerial photographs of the border between Yellowstone and the Targhee National Forest starkly illuminated, developers engaged in clear-cutting, strip mining and gas drilling right up to park borders. Meanwhile, the effluents of industrial society impacted on preservationist intentions. In the 1990s, the Florida Everglades fell under threat from a network of canals and levees dumping agricultural run-off into the 'river of grass' and siphoning off fresh water to supply the region's thirsty condominiums and theme park complexes. Reduced water levels and rising salinity from dams upstream jeopardized the future of pink flamingos in the wetlands of Ichkeul, Indonesia, a hunting reserve of the Hafsids since 1240 and a national park since 1980. Airborne pollutants proved equally insidious. Acid rain from industrial sites in the ex-Soviet Union, the so-called black triangle, compromised 60 per cent of tree cover in Krkonose National Park (1963) in Bohemia, while sulphur dioxides from fossil fuel power plants and exhaust emissions in Los Angeles drifted some 240 miles east to reduce visibility in the Grand Canyon.

Shifting political environments also affected national park systems. In January 1996, the entire complement of US reserves shut down following a wrangle between Democrats and Republicans over the federal budget. With funding priorities centred on tax cuts and the War on Terror, many environmentalists in 2004 considered the Bush Administration to be a principal danger to America's parklands. When Homeland Security raised the terror threat level from 'yellow' to 'orange', the Park Service incurred additional overtime costs of $2,000,000 a month. Meanwhile, the opening of Padre Island National Park in Texas (1962) to oil drilling, as well as controversial plans to allow gas exploration in the Arctic National Wildlife Refuge, suggested that officials favoured economics over ecology. The close relationship between government and big business – both George W. Bush and Dick Cheney maintained connections with extractive industry, while Secretary of State Condoleezza Rice boasted an oil tanker bearing her name – provided fuel for a legion of political cartoonists playing on the 'this Bush is not green' motif. On a more serious note, a poll conducted in late 2003 found 84 per cent of 1,361 NPS employees in agreement that the government was 'enacting policies and laws that will destroy the grand legacy of our national parks'.[64]

Elsewhere in the world, limited political resolve left some reserves mere 'paper parks'. According to the Worldwide Fund for Nature, up to a third of Chinese national parks amounted to little more than ecological origami.

Poloniny National Park in Slovakia received protection in 1992, yet its old-growth forests remained victim to extensive clear-cutting due to economic and legal constraints. Other reserves suffered neglect due to bureaucratic corruption, under-funding, staff shortages and deficient infrastructure. Poloniny featured one employee per 2,930 hectares. In Jau National Park in Brazil (1980) a complement of four rangers protected 8,800 square miles of Amazonian rainforest from illegal forestry and the poaching of fish and turtles. Fewer than 600 park staff, with one plane and scant radios, faced off against ivory squads across Zambia's nineteen reserves. National parks further proved vulnerable to political destabilization and military conflict. In 1994, the IUCN placed Virunga National Park on the list of World Heritage Sites in danger following a war in neighbouring Rwanda that led to 1,500,000 Tutsis establishing refugee camps nearby. Large-scale habitat loss ensued as desperate exiles logged the park for fuel and poached its animals for food. In 1996, domestic conflict within Congo led to Virunga itself becoming a battlefield. Infrastructure was destroyed, and wardens fled. Locals appropriated areas of the park for mining, grazing and coffee production, while armed militias put their automatic weapons to use harvesting elephant, gorilla and hippo for the bush meat market. Virunga's hippo population, some 33,000 strong in 1986, numbered a mere 1,300 by 2004.

If 'loving the parks to death' represented a critical problem for parks in the affluent West, perhaps the most pressing matter in the developing world concerned issues of indigenous rights, poverty and economic sovereignty. In Virunga, locals viewed conservation with disdain, as park authorities appropriated valuable resources over which villagers claimed ownership. The national park had little relevance to impoverished communities, who associated the concept with imperialism, resource control and ethnocentrism. By the twenty-first century, many parks had come to represent contested spaces, geographies of dislocation claimed by a plethora of groups each touting different constructions of nature, history and identity. Amboseli National Park in Kenya, a game reserve since 1906 and a national park since 1974, symbolized in the eyes of international conservationists the romance of the African wild. Amboseli represented an iconic paradise roamed by abundant wildebeest, zebra and gazelle before the imposing backdrop of Mount Kilimanjaro. For the local Maasai tribe, however, park establishment in the 1970s encompassed the dismantling of traditional pastoral user rights, an increase in cattle and sheep disease, crop trampling and soil erosion, cultural contamination from illegal tourist photography, and a siphoning of gateway receipts to outside interests. Keen to nurture the park as a safari resort, with wildlife equated to biological dollars, government authorities failed to listen to indigenous demands for grazing access. When financial compensation proved unforthcoming and a water pipeline scheme fell through, the Maasai registered their disapproval by spearing elephant and rhino. Both conservation and regional sustainability appeared imperilled. Without local people as economic stakeholders, the long-term sustainability of national parks remained in jeopardy.

As environmental commentator Erik Eckholm noted, national parks cannot survive 'as fortress islands in a sea of hungry people'.[65]

RESTORING BALANCE: MISSING PEOPLE, MISSING ANIMALS, MISSING HABITAT

The national park tenders a landscape of paradoxes. It is a space defined as 'natural wilderness', but shaped by shifting environmental aesthetics; valued as a refuge from society, yet penetrated by cultural, economic and political exigencies; portrayed as having an altruistic ethos, yet concealing power abuses and ethnic prejudice. Some critics deem the entire concept as beyond redemption. In 1993, African National Congress member Derek Hanekom claimed that national parks offered little to Africans living in poverty and needed to be abolished.[66] Edward Abbey lamented the state of Arches National Park in Utah (1971), seeing it as a cathedral of consumption, all floodlit signs and smiling female attendants, a 'utopian national park: Central Park National Park, Disneyland National Park'.[67] According to disgruntled conservationist Michael Frome, Yellowstone today provides a dystopic experience, an 'urban tourist ghetto' and 'popcorn playground, just another anodine theme park'.[68]

The national park seems caught somewhere between its promotion of pristine nature and competition with Disneyland. The natural eruptions of Old Faithful too easily compare with the nature facsimile situated in Anaheim's Frontierland. However, we need to remember that, though vulnerable to our manipulations, national parks remain *relatively* unspoiled landscapes. A recent study of ninety-three reserves in twenty-two countries discovered a higher level of species and habitat preservation within their confines as compared with outside.[69] National parks advance a number of vital environmental and social functions. They protect global biodiversity by storing relatively intact landscapes and genetic libraries in a wider environment under transformation; they stabilize regional ecosystems; they provide core refuges for rare plants and animals; and they cater to human economic, spiritual, recreational and cultural needs.

At the same time, changes are needed if national parks are to operate effectively in the twenty-first century. Tourist regulation, effective biotic representation, a bioregional perspective and indigenous participation are essential additions to the national park mantra. Some progress is already evident. In the late twentieth century, Costa Rica developed a successful, environmentally sensitive tourist programme combining conservation and local economic benefits in its twenty parks. At Yosemite and Banff, current management plans call for rolling back development. Park stewards and environmentalists anticipate extending the global reserve system to include all ecotypes. Already the restoration of extirpated species includes the Przewalski horse in Hustai National Park, Mongolia (1992–8), and the grey wolf in Yellowstone (1995–6). Bioregionalism has entered official discourse, with conservation agencies updating the 'island reserve' concept to embrace regional planning and inter-agency liaison on issues from grizzly bear management in the Greater Yellowstone Ecosystem to the creation of 'superparks' such as Kgalagadi Transfrontier Park (1999) in South Africa/Botswana.

Indigenous rights are finally being considered. In 1996, the Kenyan Wildlife Service announced the 'Park beyond the Parks' scheme allowing tribes to develop ecotourism in reserve buffer zones. Today, the Maasai are more involved in Amboseli, thanks to a community plan delivering economic incentives from wildlife tourism. In Kakadu and Uluru-Kata Tjuta parks in Australia's Northwest Territories, aboriginal leaders sit on the Parks Board of Managers, locals are employed as rangers, and indigenous communities utilize the park for spiritual and subsistence purposes. Official publications stress the rich natural *and* cultural heritage of Kakadu. From 40,000-year-old cave pictographs to resident saltwater crocodiles, people and reptiles are both presented as integral features of a vibrant ecosystem. Such schemes illustrate that sustainable development and the protection of nature can be compatible and mutually beneficial. If conservation authorities embrace indigenous values as well as international conservation directives, and aid local biodiversity and the regional economy, the national park idea can survive. As Albert Mullet, Koori representative from Victoria, Australia, volunteered: 'We can work together to mend the damage 200 years of inexperience has wrought. We can bring the spirit back to the land. And protect it for another 40,000 years.'[70]

5 Amusement Parks and Theme Parks

As well as serving as forums for contemplation, spiritual uplift, hunting and conservation, parks have provided people with the opportunity to play and have fun. Amusement is one of the park's primary functions. While the amusement park, and its post-1945 offspring, the theme park, may smack of twentieth- and twenty-first-century infatuations with media entertainment and leisure (thus complementing entertainment landscapes such as neon Las Vegas), their roots go back a surprisingly long way. The first roller-coaster is widely acknowledged as Russian in design. In seventeenth-century St Petersburg, toboggan-style rides allowed daring locals to drop down massive snow-packed inclines. In 1804, the first wheeled coaster appeared in Paris under the name 'Russian Mountains'. In 1817, the Promenades Aeriennes, featuring a handy safety rail, made its début in the French capital.

Landscape and city parks themselves provided ideal venues for mass merriment. Lavish fetes at Versailles entailed theatre, parades and dancing. Visitors to Vauxhall Gardens negotiated mazes, gasped at firework displays, and queued for balloon trips. Prater Park in Vienna featured its own amusement zone, the *Wurstelprater*, as early as 1766. Prior to the advent of the modern amusement park, fun and frolics were integral to the park experience.

Bakken Park in Denmark boasts the mantle of the world's first amusement park. Considered therapeutic for common ailments, a spring attracted the first visitors to Bakken Park in the 1580s. Entertainers and artists in time gravitated towards the water spectacle. By the 1870s, wooden booths housed refreshments, while vacationers played skittles, danced in the music hall, and rode one of the earliest symbols of the true amusement park – a steam carousel. Along with Bakken, Tivoli Gardens in Copenhagen brought unbridled fun to the nineteenth-century Danish park landscape. The king of Denmark, Christian VIII, granted permission for an amusement area on the periphery of bustling Copenhagen following the observation by owner George Carstensen that 'When the populace are enjoying themselves they forget about politicking'. The park served the goal of political quietude. Early enjoyments included coconut shies, a test-your-strength machine, a horse-drawn carousel and a simple rollercoaster. Gradually the city grew up around the park, while the attraction itself became increasingly spectacular. By the early 1900s, Tivoli boasted fantasy architecture, including a Chinese-styled Pantomime Theatre and Tower, renowned restaurants, and the Bjergrutschebanen (or Mountain) rollercoaster, still favoured by visitors a century on.[1]

The modern amusement park also took its cues from recreational activities outside the traditional park diaspora. Venues other than city parks and gardens naturally involved public shows of play. The provision of recreational facilities in cities, from bathhouses to theatres, fed into the amusement park idea. Seaside resorts such as Brighton, Margate and Bournemouth, so popular with Victorian bathers, brought together amusement staples such as the penny arcade, the gipsy fortune-teller and the sideshow (most notably Punch and Judy). Blackpool in the 1870s featured two piers: the Central Pier, dubbed 'The People's Pier', which drew working-class punters with open-air dancing, and the North Pier, which catered to a 'better class' of visitors with its orchestra and assembly rooms. Half a mile from Blackpool's Promenade, Raikes Hall Park, Gardens and Aquarium opened in 1871, featuring fireworks, dancing and an aviary. Likened to Vauxhall Gardens, Raikes served as a precursor to the amusement park, as well as indicating the direction that Blackpool would soon be taking in its rub with public entertainment.

Circuses and freak shows also informed the amusement park idea. Circuses in the 1800s exhibited myriad forms of entertainment, many of them soon to be replicated in amusement parks. The typical show involved jugglers, trapeze artists and gymnasts, trained animals, human clowns, freaks and sideshows. The 'Big Top' generated outrageous visual spectacle. Tents and outbuildings boasted a full complement of unusual species, as well as 'nature's mistakes', including bearded ladies and two-headed calves. Entertainers honed their skills for the mass production of mirth. As early as 1827, St Petersburg supported a stationary circus, although many circus masters chose to remain nomadic. The arrival of a travelling circus, with its long procession of entertainers and props, brought revelry to rural villages. Impatient and inquisitive crowds gathered to welcome the itinerant performers. 'Lord' George Sanger's circus traversed England in the late nineteenth century to popular acclaim. However, it was American showman *extraordinaire* Phineas Taylor (P. T.) Barnum who claimed 'The Greatest Show on Earth'. Barnum's circus entertained a young Queen Victoria in the 1840s at Buckingham Palace. Barnum's General Tom Thumb, a young boy less than 2 feet in height, impersonated Napoleon with aplomb, thereby making a great impression on the royal entourage. Victoria called Thumb 'the greatest curiosity I, or indeed anybody, ever saw'. Barnum's American Museum in New York City, housing all manner of attractions from 'industrious fleas' to knitting machines, proved one of the Big Apple's premier popular attractions until the building burnt down in 1868.[2]

Combining otherworldly allure and spectacular energy, circuses and freak shows evidently stuck in the minds of audiences. Early amusement park owners recognized the mass appeal of said attractions, and sought to capture the same carnival-like atmosphere in their own enclosed worlds. On opening in 1903 at Coney Island, New York, the Luna amusement park included an outdoor circus as one of its features, with elephants a common sight on the promenade. Meanwhile, the 'Congress of Curious People' featured 'the world's tiniest people', along with Zip, 'the most remarkable curiosity ever seen by man – A Freak of Giant Strength – Eats and Enjoys Humans', who was in fact an African American by the less beguiling name of William Henry Johnson. Writing in the 1900s, Frederic Thompson defined the emergent amusement park industry as predominantly about 'child's play' and 'frankly devoted to fun, the fantastic, the gay, the grotesque'.[3]

In 1851, Crystal Palace in London hosted the first World's Fair, a dazzling showcase of technology and science from around the world. Its 13,000 exhibits included the new electric telegraph and machinery from the American Industrial Revolution. Subsequent World's Fairs and Expositions (popularly known as Expos) generated many of the ideas that later became associated with amusement and theme parks. Fairs and Expos typically included 'foreign villages' – sections giving a taste of 'exotic' civilizations – akin to distinct worlds found at many of today's theme parks. Notions of technological progress and inventiveness predominated. One event in particular, the World's Columbian Exposition held in Chicago in 1893, exacted lasting influence on the amusement industry. Dubbed the 'white city' for its futuristic urban utopianism, Chicago's Expo was awash with fantastical architectural projects. The world's best designers, including Frederick Law Olmsted, contributed to the layout of the Exposition, their efforts giving rise to a wondrous creation that duly impressed the thousands of visitors who passed through it. 'Courtiers in the garden alleys of Versailles or Fontainebleau could not have been more deferential and observant of the decorum of place,' noted John J. Ingalls, admiring the orderly behaviour of guests. Attempting to distinguish high culture from base pursuits aimed at titillation, the Chicago exhibition featured a specific zone set aside for amusement activities. The 'Midway Plaisance' amusement area included the Hagenbeck Circus, jugglers, an International Beauty Show, foreign villages, a popular belly dancer by the name of Little Egypt, and the original Ferris Wheel. Inspired by the industrial water wheel, George W. Ferris designed a revolving contraption that rose 264 feet into the air and carried up to 2,000 passengers. The colossal edifice, an engineering marvel, dominated the immediate skyline. For American Studies Professor Russel Nye, Chicago signified 'the germ of the modern amusement park'. Versions of the Midway and the Ferris Wheel became *de rigueur* at amusement parks in subsequent years. One crucial difference none the less set the World's Fair and the amusement park apart. Unlike the permanent provision of fun offered by amusement parks, World's Fairs existed purely as temporary spectacles. Many attendees felt sorry to see the attractions dismantled. Despite operating for four months, a riot followed the final ride of Chicago's beloved Ferris Wheel. The public demanded that such a wonderful amusement stay with them longer. In 1905, White City Amusement Park opened in Chicago with its own Ferris-like Observation Wheel, promising to capture some of the excitement found within the Columbian Expo in 1893.[4]

CONEY ISLAND: ELECTRICITY, SEA AND SPECTACLE

A seaside resort since the 1840s, Coney Island, New York, had already established itself as an amusement centre by the time of the Chicago Expo. Railroad links in the late 1870s aided Coney's development. Officially, Coney catered for everyone. Unofficially, beaches were segregated by class. For the richest New Yorkers, Manhattan Beach beckoned, with its deluxe hotels and an explosive display by James Pain, self-professed 'pyrotechnist of Her Majesty the Queen'. Pain's shows included a dramatic take on 'The Defeat of the Spanish Armada' that would likely have pleased royalty on the beaches of England. Equally entertaining (and historically themed), but perhaps less urbane, Buffalo Bill's Wild West Show entertained the middling classes on Brighton Beach in 1883. At the West End (Norton's Point), less affluent visitors made do with watching prize-fights and examining the curiosities of a dime museum. Although regulated by class and taste, amusements were spread widely, with no common theme or governing narrative. A gaudy collection of jugglers, peddlers, ball-toss games and tent shows competed for tourist revenue. The evolution of a distinct amusement district in west Brighton promised to bring more structured entertainment, and, at the same time, pull divergent crowds together. In 1884, James V. Lafferty erected the Elephantine Colossus, a huge tin-covered elephant that reached 150 feet into the air and gazed down on spectators through 4-foot-wide glass eyes. A cigar store nestled inside one of the elephant's legs, a museum in its left lung, with hotel rooms in the animal's trunk and cheeks. The same year, the Switchback Gravity Railway, known as Thompson's Coaster (after its designer LaMarcus A. Thompson), opened for business, offering riders their first taste of a rollercoaster. Newspaper critics responded with fears over the safety of this early coaster, scared by travelling at such a 'frightful rate of speed' – up to 6 miles per hour. The whiff of hot dogs, invented at Coney by a German immigrant, completed the basic amusement complex.[5]

Named after its forty juggling sea lions, Captain Paul Boyton opened the world's first enclosed amusement park, Sea Lion Park, at Coney Island on 4 July 1895. The simple notion of the 'amusement park' emerged from the decision of Boyton to erect a barrier around a group of his attractions and charge an entrance fee – thus Boyton appropriated the park label for his distinct brand of recreation. Boyton's Shoot the Chutes ride, tagged 'The King of All Amusements', tantalized visitors by sending them on a toboggan run into water beneath. Cages of wild wolves scared the squeamish.

Sea Lion Park inspired other amusement operators to advertise their rides under one banner. In 1897, George Tilyou opened Steeplechase Park at Coney, further establishing the resort as a leader in popular entertainment. Replacing the real horses of olden parks with crude mechanical beasts, the Steeplechase Gravity Ride (hence the park name) provided horse-racing enthusiasts with their own race to the finish, courtesy of wood-carved equines on wheels. Tilyou constantly added new rides to his roster. With the entrance ride 'Barrel of Love' throwing strangers' bodies against one another, the Human Whirlpool (a rotating polished wooden disc) leaving guests scrambling and disoriented, not to mention air blow-holes lifting women's skirts in Marilyn Monroe fashion, the park arguably pandered most to those looking for sexual titillation. The huge, grotesque Funny Face insignia greeting park guests outside Steeplechase warned of possible lewd happenings within. Tilyou prohibited the use of liquor inside his amusement empire to prevent things turning too rowdy.

Hoping to lure a white-collar clientele, Fred Thompson and Elmer 'Skip' Dundy opened Luna Park in 1903 with the promise of offering respectable entertainment based on exotic cultures and places rather than the razzle-dazzle of impromptu bodily contortions. In contrast to Steeplechase's adult (and adulterous) feel, Luna aimed to be 'the place for your mother, your sister, and your sweetheart'. The press named it a 'Realm of Fairy Romance' – a comment now directed at Disney parks. A fantastical midway complete with ethnic villages, Roman chariots as box offices, and some 250,000 lights, the ambience of Luna both resembled the Chicago Expo and presaged the feel of a modern-day theme park. Dubbed 'Baghdad by the Sea' thanks to its Arabian architecture, Luna exuded the exotic and wooed thousands of visitors. The flair of inventor-capitalist Fred Thompson for fantasy, consumption and movement proved unrivalled at that time. However, in 1904, a new park, Dreamland, opened with the mandate of trumping the fantasy of Luna. Dreamland boasted one million lights, a simulation of the biblical story of Creation, and a gondola trip through the 'Canals of Venice'. 'Lilliputia', a 'model' village inhabited by 300 dwarves (and a step up from the usual freak show), entertained voyeuristic patrons. Dreamland cost an exorbitant $3,500,000. Perplexingly, for owner Senator William H. Reynolds, visitors remained more enchanted with the garish enticements of Thompson's Luna.[6]

Alongside Coney Island stood the Statue of Liberty. Both landmarks welcomed seafaring immigrants to the USA, attesting to the nation's multifarious cultures and its invocations of progress and opportunity. Yet Coney and Liberty differed in their stances on what it truly meant to be an American. The famed statue stood for a land embracing solemn justice, checks and balances, a thoroughly responsible citizenry, while Coney's coasters shot into the sky as mechanized indices of leisure time and carefree life-styles. The skeletal shapes of Coney park rides imparted notions of a new dynamic country promising greatness. One writer noted how the Elephantine Colossus 'bursts upon the astonished gaze of passengers on the incoming European steamers, it gives them their first idea of the bigness of some things in this country'. Freshly disembarked Europeans and tired city types flocked to such a gleaming (yet tawdry) beacon of entertainment. During the summer of 1909, 20 million people visited Coney Island, an attendance figure greater than Disneyland managed when it opened a half-century later. Coney succeeded because it offered a valuable release for urban workers, a veritable 'people's playground'. However, while nearby Central Park and the Statue of Liberty stood for social improvement, Coney indulged in no such venerable pretences. This was a place where base passions and instincts were released, where thieves, the poverty-stricken and the promiscuous congregated. Coney quickly garnered a reputation for 'sleaze', earning the unofficial epithet of 'Sodom by the Sea'. 'Seeing the elephant' alluded to more than just an intimate encounter with the orifices of a giant mechanical beast – women could be picked up at its feet. Temporarily liberating enslaved industrial workers from their machines and bosses, the amusement park unleashed powerful passions and shocking social freedoms. Sigmund Freud once remarked, 'The only thing about America that interests me is Coney Island.'[7]

The Coney kaleidoscope of fun images fuelled a rising interest in amusement parks across the USA. Trolley car operators in bustling cities recognized the added revenue to be gleaned by encouraging small amusement parks to be set up at the end of tram lines, thus guaranteeing a steady use of electricity. The Great Lakes beach resort of Cedar Point, Ohio, primarily reached by train and steamship, included an amusement park in 1897. It soon expanded into a proper midway in 1906, with new arcades and entertainment. By 1920, Cedar Point offered three rollercoasters, an 'authentic' native village, and a movie theatre. With old Greek statues and gargoyles from prior years knocking heads with wooden coaster monsters, Cedar offered a mismatch of themes and time periods, appositely nicknamed a 'big mess of fun'. Meanwhile, even traditional park landscapes felt the entertainment buzz. At Riverview, Chicago, the Schmidt family added a Philadelphia Co. carousel to their recently opened shooting park, giving those not considered manly enough to carry firearms a way to pass their time. By the 1920s, Riverview had expanded into a genuine rollercoaster venture. At the same time, the number of amusement parks in the USA peaked at approximately 2,000.

Far from confined to North America, the amusement park idea also captured the minds (and purse-strings) of Europeans. In 1896, a replica of Columbian Expo's Ferris Wheel, 'The Great Wheel', opened in Blackpool, joining the recently erected facsimile of Paris's Eiffel Tower, the Blackpool Tower. Designed by W. B. Barrett, the Wheel carried up to 1,000 passengers, but rarely reached capacity, as one revolution took a tiresome 35 minutes. Thanks to the notoriety and spectacle of Coney, it was relatively easy for the founder of Blackpool Pleasure Beach, Londoner William George Bean, to admit that 'We wanted to found an American-style Amusement Park'. Having spent several years in the United States, Bean returned to the United Kingdom enthusiastic to replicate the success of trolley-park and beachside amusement resorts found on the East Coast. In possession of the British rights to the Hotchkiss Bicycle Railroad, Bean installed an odd-looking bicycle ride along a fixed track at Blackpool, not far from resident gypsies and *ad hoc* fun-fair attractions. Meanwhile, former butcher John William Outhwaite operated a carousel nearby, a gift from his father-in-law, who manufactured amusements in Philadelphia. In 1904, Bean and Outhwaite collaborated to purchase a large strip of the South Shore. A year later, they renamed it Blackpool Pleasure Beach. The Pleasure Beach emerged as an unconventional signature landscape of blooming Anglo–American relations, the 'Great Rapprochement' finding popular guise in the borrowing of technology and the sharing of fun. A popular American import, the 'River Caves of the World', opened in 1905. The River Caves ride, which cost £3,000 and consumed one and a half acres, thrilled boat-riders with a dazzling trip through themed 'underground' caverns, including the 'Mysterious Dripping Well of Arizona' and the 'Cave of Emeralds of Ceylon'. In 1907, Bean's amusement roster included its first wooden rollercoaster. Based on a design by L. A. Thompson, the coaster reached 40 feet into the sky and travelled up to 35 miles per hour. It cost £15,000 to construct. In 1910, the 'Spectatorium' re-created the battle between the *Monitor* and the *Merrimac* in the US Civil War in wonderful panoramic (360°) vision for attentive British vacationers. American amusements magazine *Billboard* applauded the work of Bean: 'This huge open air combination of shows is as near a reproduction of Coney Island as one could imagine in England.' Little wonder that by 1912 the Pleasure Beach had begun advertising itself with the slogan, 'England's Premier American Amusement Park'.[8]

Existing parks such as Prater and Bakken also took on new-fangled entertainments. Prater mirrored American fascination with the Ferris Wheel by adding its own 200-foot model as early as 1897. A Lilliputian railway appeared in 1928. Somewhat slower to adjust, Bakken added a rollercoaster in 1932. As Coney's reputation for sleaze grew, so too did European amusement parks generate their own adult airs. Social mingling at Prater included prostitutes available for much more than waltzing in concert cafés. Mindful of such lowbrow pursuits, the local council at Blackpool enforced regulations that restricted gaming, fortune-telling, tricksters and frauds operating along the beach.

Coney Island designers meanwhile advised on the establishment of Luna Park in Melbourne, Australia, where a 'Mr Moon' face welcomed guests to the cornucopia of amusements. A four-row carousel by the esteemed Philadelphia Toboggan Company, along with a coaster railway, a River Caves boat trip, live entertainment and sideshows as bizarre as a Canadian Log Walk and as questionable as a 'Negro stunt' wooed local Aussies. Evidence of the global notoriety of Fred Thompson's vision at Coney, further Luna parks emerged in Berlin, Rome and Buenos Aires.

A DIFFERENT KIND OF PARK?

The amusement park differed from prior park templates by its overt emphasis on fun. Traditional parks certainly pandered to the recreational whims of guests and owners, but amusement existed as a subtle sideshow rather than a centre-stage attraction. Games were brought to the venue as temporary additions to the park scene (such as the Versailles fete), rather than as permanent pieces of architecture. Amusement park designers differed from their precursors by reinventing the park as a place dedicated to thrills. As W. G. Bean elaborated, the amusement park worked on 'the fundamental principle . . . to make adults feel like children again and to inspire gaiety of a primary innocent character'. This 'fundamental principle' seemed remarkably simple, yet resultant parks were awash with ideas and overlapping themes.[9]

While Disneyland is widely acknowledged as the original theme park thanks to its unique medley of fantasy worlds, earlier amusement parks also featured themed areas. In English landscape parks, allusions to Greek and Roman mythologies abounded. In a similar vein, Luna Park at Coney Island brimmed with Renaissance and Oriental influences. Steeplechase included a Palace of Pleasure based on the French Renaissance, complete with a Louis XIV era ballroom. The exotic was made welcome in both park blueprints. However, while hidden statues in landscape parks catered to learned aristocratic parties, turn-of-the-century amusement parks serviced mass culture by drawing on the most recognized of folktales and presenting them in bold and brazen form. The vagaries of classical allegory at Stourhead gave way to sensational re-creations of the fall of Pompeii at Coney. While erudition was necessary to comprehend Virgil's *Aeneid* in a dusky grotto in England, most Americans visiting Knott's Berry Farm amusement park in California from the 1920s could relate to the 'authentic' Wild West gun-fights and stories staged for their benefit. The amusement park played to popular culture. Meanwhile, rather than a classical story (and related imaginative architecture) nestled unobtrusively in a seemingly natural park landscape, fantasy in the amusement park dominated every vista and every stage. Unrestrained fancy marked the amusement park experience.

The invocation of fairytale stories and exotic worlds enabled amusement park owners such as Fred Thompson to draw scattered rides together and present them as one complete entertainment package. At Coney, several amusement parks prospered simultaneously, because each one had a unique atmosphere. While technically much the same from one machine to another, carousels, coasters and water rides differed by virtue of their own park-specific narratives. Amusement parks thus emerged as modern-day amphitheatres, providing guests with interactive stories as striking as Luna's focal ride 'A Trip to the Moon' and as ambitious as Dreamland's 'The Creation' and 'The End of the Earth', which together managed to compress human history into tumultuous spectacle. Such rigorous scene-setting increased the enjoyment factor attached to each thrill: imagination allied to the ride experience raised the fun threshold. Re-creations of the 'Fall of Pompeii' and the 'San Francisco Earthquake' allowed guests to experience pivotal events with such vividness that many were left breathless.

Presenting convincing fantasy worlds within tiny park confines required consummate skill, artistic flair and a penchant for illusion. Steeplechase Park occupied 15 acres, but seemed much larger thanks to its visual spectacle. Visitors were led to believe that the park about them represented a different world from the one outside its boundaries. By immersing guests in a fresh and exciting adventure, fantasy architecture proved a useful tool of deception. Amusement commonly traded in the art of altered perception – of the mirth to be gleaned from funny mirrors, crooked houses and other aesthetic tricks. On exiting the Steeplechase Ride at George Tilyou's park, riders unknowingly ended up as entertainers in the Insanitarium. Entering the stage on all fours, guests found themselves facing a clown with an electric stinger, a farmer and a cowboy. A gleeful audience, many having already undergone such torment, watched as bemused couples received electric shocks and had their clothes rearranged by air blasts. Such pursuits illuminated the amusement park as a gigantic distortion mirror, a venue where guests became part of a screwball spectacle.

With a nod to World's Fairs, fantasy in amusement parks often took the form of technological futurism. In stark contrast to the organic sheen of most city and national parks, amusement parks operated as showcases for man and for modern technology. Dr Martin Arthur Couney's incubator machinery at Coney's Dreamland drew the crowds, and thanks to the financial donations of visitors, saved 7,500 prematurely born babies between 1903 and 1943, including Couney's own daughter. Rollercoasters and carousels demonstrated human inventiveness. The machine became a fixture of the park courtesy of industrial society, but amusement parks revealed a side of technology that the average worker had yet to encounter. Park equipment operated on a different wavelength to normal industrial contraptions. To a degree, the rationality of the factory system was subverted, so that boats got people wet, dodgem cars collided, and technology ran amok. Fecund links between technical progress in the park and in the city led Russel Nye to claim that a day out at an amusement park 'was not a flight from urban life but a journey to an intensified version of it'. It also offered a topsy-turvy take on industrial living.[10]

The growing significance of technology paralleled the declining role of nature in the park. Carousel makers, led by English machinist Frederick Savage, planted exotic animals on their machines, but in wooden or metal incarnations. Horses soon came to decorate every park carousel as the most popular choice of 'steed' with the public. Skilful horse riding in the country park was replaced by a slow circular jaunt in the amusement park. Meanwhile, fantastical, overblown structures replaced sweeping trees as key features on the park skyline. Nature seemed too subtle and slow-growing to keep up with the spectacular motion demanded of fresh amusement parks. Only older parks such as Prater and Bakken mixed together the separate worlds of amusement and nature.

The new amusement park thus offered the visitor little contemplation of nature. Instead, excitement, noise and action dominated in a built environment. Amusement parks operated as highly energized places. Both park atmosphere and park lighting were electric, visitors caught up in an intense and bewildering social experiment. As the seamless move from the Steeplechase Ride to the Insanitarium showed, guests in amusement parks played the role of participants in unfolding dramas (akin to actors on a stage), then switched to curious onlookers as others entertained. Punters gawped at glimpses of flesh as the Human Whirlpool turned, then ventured on to it to forge their own public exposé. Rides such as the Tunnel of Love encouraged physical contact and romantic frolics. Unlike aristocrats strolling in a dignified manner along serpentine walks, uninhibited visitors in the amusement park shouted and misbehaved. Pure pleasure, play and indulgence predominated.

The sense of intimacy and unbridled freedom at such places as Coney had some value in allowing people of different classes and backgrounds to mix. However, the fact that visitors amiably collided in the temporary fantasy of the park rarely translated into a more bohemian society outside. Jim Crow laws infected the democratic aspirations of many American amusement parks, as in the case of 'whites only' Fairyland Amusement Park, opened in 1923 in Kansas City. Park owners banned African Americans from entering the park except for those employed as entertainers. Segregation continued until the Public Accommodations Law forced Fairyland to open its gates to all in 1964. Yet, the first amusement parks did reflect the rise of a new urban mass culture and a leisure industry more attentive to the needs of working citizens. Public commentators duly feared that the unashamedly exotic and erotic nature of some parks threatened to erode Victorian social values.

Appalled by the shenanigans found in the average amusement park, the owners of Kennywood, near Pittsburgh, Pennsylvania, sought to clean up the park idea by announcing strict rules of conduct inside their leisure resort. 'No fakes, no liquor, no gambling, and no disorder' read the park entrance sign. Fearing the lascivious consequences of too much flesh on show, modern one-piece bathing suits were duly banned at the Kennywood swimming pool. However, such regulations seemed somewhat draconian. The owners of Coney Island amusements were hardly guilty of ruining family entertainment in modern America. In 1920, Steeplechase Park opened 'Babyland', a mini-ature amusement park for young children complete with two hobby-horses and a shrunken carousel. Put simply, Coney Island and its ilk met the desires of working- and middle-class families to spend money and have fun while times were good.[11]

LITTLE AMUSEMENT IN THE DEPRESSION

Unsolicited flashes of flesh or sudden outbreaks of petty crime never really compromised the life of the amusement park. The first significant threat instead emerged from nature. Fire shows proved popular at Coney Island, but popular theatre disguised the real risk of conflagration. Steeplechase was rebuilt after a disastrous blaze in 1907, the tourist business kept alive by Tilyou charging 10 cents for access to the 'Burning Ruins'. While 'Fighting the Flames' dazzled audiences at Dreamland, combustion of a more serious nature threatened. On Memorial Day weekend in 1911, Dreamland burnt down. A fire began in Hell Gate, and spread throughout the park. One million lights went out, replaced by fearsome flames and cries for help.

Figure 6. Abandoned Giant Slide at Coney Island, New York, 1973. US National Archives, photo number 412-DA-5415.

In the 1930s, worldwide economic depression precipitated a collapse in the amusement industry and plunged park leisure into crisis. By 1940, the total number of US amusement parks had dropped to below 250. Dirty, dilapidated parks that had once thrived on their novelty suffered from a lack of funds. Melbourne's Luna Park weathered cash loss, an undesirable clientele, and a freak death on its dipper ride in the Thirties. A new 'pretzel ride' in 1936 failed to stimulate interest. Luna's American cousin on Coney Island faltered due to a tumultuous fire and bankruptcy. While the end of World War II implied an increase in leisure time, no guarantee existed that the public would return *en masse* to places such as Coney. Television quickly emerged as the new governing force in entertainment, with the amusement park seemingly consigned to a past era (see fig. 6).

THE APPEAL OF DISNEY'S NEW THEME PARK

Partly responsible for public fascination with celluloid, Walt Disney hardly appeared the most likely candidate to breathe fresh life into a passé entertainment avenue. Walt and his brother Roy established their first cartoon studio in the early 1920s. Attention to detail and shrewd marketing assured that their chief mascot, Mickey Mouse, was recognized around the world by the mid-1930s. In 1937, Walt Disney Studio released its first animated feature film, *Snow White and the Seven Dwarves*, to public raptures. Intrigued by the idea of providing an official tour of Disney's Burbank studios, in the late 1940s

Walt Disney turned his attention to a full-scale amusement park based on in-house characters. Following significant research and planning, Walt Disney Incorporated purchased a 160 acre orange grove in Anaheim, California. Partially financed by credit from American Broadcasting Company (ABC), Walt ploughed $17,000,000 into the scheme. In return for the loan, Disney produced a weekly television programme for ABC called *Disneyland* that served as an advertising platform for all things Disney (including the park). Meanwhile, the material park took shape in Anaheim. From fertile soil and succulent fruit sprang the plastic haven of Disneyland replete with steel mesh trees, vinyl leaves and robotic mice. By opening day on 17 July 1955, Walt's park featured five themed worlds: Frontierland, Adventureland, Fantasyland, Tomorrowland and Main Street USA – distinct locales drawing on American history, Disney cartoons and technological utopianism for stimulation.[12]

Widely credited with the invention of the theme park, Walt Disney succeeded in setting his resort apart from others that preceded it. In his estimation, Disneyland promised 'a new concept in family entertainment'. The cartoon maestro projected a fresh and exciting park look that differentiated Disneyland from other parkscapes. None the less, the idea of Disneyland (and its later iterations in Florida, Paris and Tokyo) still came from public experience of fairs, amusements and parklands.[13]

Walt Disney was clearly responding to what he saw as the failings of extant amusement parks. Under-financed and often slothful, the American amusement industry had failed to take advantage of new media forms (such as television) to advertise. At the same time, amusement parks were trapped in their dingy past. A fabled trip to Coney Island with his daughters led Walt Disney to lambaste amusement parks as 'dirty, phoney places run by tough-looking people'. Coney was no place for families. Although Coney's designers offered advice during the planning stages of the Anaheim Park, Disneyland and Steeplechase remained worlds apart, the brash entertainment of the East Coast attraction antithetical to all that the nascent Californian resort stood for. A visit to Tivoli Gardens in 1950 impressed Disney far more than his brush with 'Sodom by the Sea'. The Copenhagen park exuded cleanliness and family fun, and duly encouraged Walt to contemplate his own American Tivoli. Soon after, a Danish manager made a trip to Burbank Studios. In 1952, Disneyland designer Harper Goff spent time at Knott's Berry Farm in California, admiring its array of restaurants and museum-like shows. A year later, a fact-finding team from Disney visited Blackpool Pleasure Beach. Research into established amusement venues demonstrated the seriousness of the project ahead.[14]

In his plans for Disneyland, Walt Disney recognized the need to learn from the mistakes (and the successes) of past park managers. Where chaos ruled at Coney and Blackpool, Disney sought order at Anaheim. Rather than a ramshackle collection of rides, Disneyland set out meticulously detailed zones (or worlds) of entertainment conveniently accessed by a central hub. As Walt recounted, 'I'm tired of museums and fairs where you have to walk your legs off. I didn't want anybody at Disneyland to get "museum foot".' Accessible attractions and signposts predominated, the aesthetic delights of each themed area diverting attention away from the effort of walking and queuing. The distinctive, themed 'entertainment architecture' of Disney enclaves, based on fairytales and historical romance, continued a penchant in park design for exotic locales (as in Coney's Arabian-themed Luna Park) and narratives (as in Stourhead's myth-making grottoes and temples). Disney simply increased the scale of theming to new levels of immersion. With fantasy figures and ornate structures cloaking commercial opportunity, 'window dressing' disguised the utility of the park landscape. Underneath the nineteenth-century costume, Main Street USA functioned as a 1950s-style shopping mall. Tools of distortion and deception used at US amusement parks were reapplied by Disney to produce a holistic fantasy. Mirrors furnished an aura of depth to single-room houses on Main Street. Tightly twisting queues for rides – designed to alleviate boredom – resembled mazes found in European landscape gardens such as Henry I's Woodstock Park.[15]

Walt Disney re-created trains, arid Western landscapes and even European castles at Anaheim. At the hub of the park, Snow White's castle paid homage to Neuschwanstein in Bavaria. However, central to the Disney park ideal was the reproduction of America itself. While US national parks served as banners for American greatness, cultural nationalism found new energy in simulated landscapes. Disneyland, rather than Yosemite and Yellowstone, served as the new bastion of US patriotism in the 1950s. The Disney Corporation managed this feat by re-creating history with a purity that cleansed away misdemeanours and blights. Main Street USA, Disney's entrance point to the separate worlds of his park, aped a 'typical' main street of the late nineteenth century, but with the sidewalks kept immaculately clean, the people friendly, and the stores full of goods to buy. While his own childhood experiences of rural Marceline, Missouri – the inspiration for Main Street – had hardly been trouble-free, Disney eagerly rewrote the past. In turn, Frontierland romanticized Western conquest, taking off where Buffalo Bill's Wild West Show (itself a feature of the Columbia Expo) left off. By steeping the past in nostalgia, the park both encapsulated and exonerated the classic American Dream.[16]

Given the physical proximity of Disneyland to Los Angeles, Walt's theme park inevitably paid heed to the sprawling metropolis close by. The fake period styles of LA's Mission era, automobile-dictated life-styles, and Hollywood cachet all fed into California's Disneyland. Most important of all, Tinseltown set the tone of park experience. Disney Imagineers (designers) visualized this park as a movie set. Aiming at an authentic re-creation of a Western town in Frontierland, Harper Goff copied his own saloon design for the film *Calamity Jane* (1953), hence taking his inspiration from movie stills rather than history books. The Jungle Cruise of Adventureland borrowed heavily from *The African Queen* (1951). Hollywood set designers crafted Wild West ghost towns using one-dimensional timber frames. Disney similarly made Main Street a whimsical façade. Shops went back only one room, with buildings reduced in scale on higher levels. Perspective was everything. Like a Hollywood film set, Main Street represented a sham, a mass deception. Rides operated as interactive movie reels, fast-moving spectacles rolling forward like a series of moving images. Park worlds, and their visitors, paid respect to Disney's celluloid heritage.

Like a fastidious film director, Walt Disney demanded absolute control over his creation. Like a landscape park designer, he displayed a penchant for meticulous planning and systematic thought. Akin to French-Italian styled estates, Disneyland functioned according to rationality and logic. Random or unpredictable forces were rarely tolerated. Rejecting the spontaneous, carnival-like atmosphere of Coney, Walt envisaged Disneyland as a perfectly marshalled environment, a toy train set that operated according to schedule or a garden that always bloomed on time. A modern-day Louis XIV planning his royal retreat, Walt Disney laid out Disneyland according to his own personal preferences. The park was indulgent, idiosyncratic and costly. Hence, Disney drew easy comparison with park monarchs before him. In 1973, critic Christopher Finch related how 'Walt Disney has built a Versailles of the twentieth century', despite Disneyland being designed 'for the pleasure of the people', and not just the king. However, Disney moulded the park in such a way that it inevitably suited some clientele more than others. As Karal Ann Marling described it, the park operated as a 'Versailles for middle-class Americans in plaid Bermuda shorts'.[17]

Parks have always represented the cultures responsible for their formation. Disney's master-stroke lay in modernizing the turn-of-the-century amusement park so that it perfectly matched the interests of post-war US society. The central appeal of Disneyland rested on its attention to the American heartland and the expanding white middle class. The conservative, consumerist, leisure-driven families of the 1950s found in Disneyland a symbol of their rise to power. Disneyland offered a consumer paradise for post-war suburbanites. Disney's Wienies, vertical markers serving as visual 'treats' positioned around the park, showed at a microcosmic level how citizens navigated both park landscapes and social situations by searching for rewards. Main Street offered a shopping mall dressed in frontier garb. On a macro level, Disneyland itself existed as one giant Wienie for the middle class – a premier icon of what life could offer them. Abundance, security, idealism and conservatism thrived inside the park. With Disney, the perfect day out was never left to chance. Safety and harmony derived from conformity and control. Disneyland stood in stark contrast to the wildly liberating atmosphere of Coney, where pecking and participation seemed mandatory. Rather than circus-style freaks and untrustworthy promenade peddlers, Disney's entertainers were a homogeneous, polite and well-behaved crowd (albeit dressed in a variety of animal costumes). In the conservative-minded 1950s, nobody appeared to mind the emphasis on order, or the fundamental shift in amusement park design from uncontrolled adult carnival to curtailed family fun. A different kind of community – one founded on enforced likeness rather than chaotic lewdness – could be found at Disney. And it suited the contemporary mood perfectly.

Disneyland comforted mainstream US society. With its otherworldly ambiance and calming sensibilities, the park provided temporary refuge from anxieties over the escalating nuclear arms race, a plutonium-tipped thorn in the side of baby boomer optimism. California's Disneyland served as a huge psychological bomb shelter for its guests, protecting the nuclear family from the perils of the new atomic age. Utopianism, Disney's faith in the future, soothed social stresses. As Disney's John Hench reminded, 'what we're selling throughout the Park is reassurance'.[18]

The opening of Disneyland attracted remarkable attention, not all of it complimentary. Early critics found the park to be a safe, clean but overly com-mercial environment. Neither was the grand opening without its problems: sticky asphalt, paltry drinking fountains and a gas leak. The 'feel good' comfort architecture employed by Disney Imagineers meanwhile won few plaudits from art critics – the park was simply too anodyne. Disney responded to calls for more public amenities, yet resisted pandering to every fancy. While cater-ing to the contemporary boom in automobile sales by arranging a huge car lot outside the entrance, Disney enforced the sequestering of automobiles *outside* park boundaries, forcing visitors to navigate his fantasy world on foot. With some irony, wilderness aficionados drove through national parks on weekends hardly pausing to catch the breeze, yet theme park junkies walked the artificial world of Disney admiring each vinyl leaf and plastic tree.

For the majority of visitors, however, Disneyland was nothing less than majestic. By its 10-year anniversary in 1965, Disneyland had hosted 50 million guests. The happy hues of Main Street and 'Disney smiles' of park entertain-ers worked wonders. Sightseers felt uplifted. Children indulged in the fantasy world around them. Adults reverted to a childlike state on entering the park. Overwhelmingly, visitors responded to the park in an emotional rather than rational way. Disney 'magic' served up escapism, nostalgia and fantasy inter-twined. The Disney universe captured inside the park exuded holism, comfort and innocence – all concepts with mass appeal.

The success of Disneyland spawned facsimiles in Florida, Paris and Tokyo. Counting Disneyland as a 'first generation' park, Disney Imagineers inter-preted their second project in Florida as an opportunity to craft a superior attraction unimpeded by land restrictions and corporate cash-ins, to render a landscape truer to the original ideas of beloved Walt. In the 1960s, Disney estate managers successfully purchased a total of 27,400 acres of swampland near Orlando, at roughly $200 an acre, using pseudonyms to avoid a Disney-label hike in real estate prices. In response to the encirclement of the original Anaheim site by motels, freeways and burger joints, planners in Florida secured a huge land mass to ensure that the Disney park ideal remained intact and uncontaminated. Walt Disney World, or the Magic Kingdom as it came to be known, promised a totally immersive vacation wonderland brimming with hotels, restaurants, rides and shopping opportunities. Disney World opened in October 1971, 5 years after Walt died, but the Disney vision had never been stronger. Viewed as the ultimate rendition of Disney Imagineering, the Magic Kingdom amounted to a plastic park paradise. Nothing was allowed to intrude on the formulation of fantasy. Subterranean engineering allowed computers from below to control the park on top. Trash shot down tubes to underground refuse collectors, while maintenance shifts ran throughout the night so not to disturb the fun. Special quick-drying paint ensured that Disney World sparkled every morning as if brand new.

In 1982, the EPCOT (Experimental Prototype Community of Tomorrow) Center opened at the Magic Kingdom. At a cost of $900,000,000, EPCOT furnished visitors with a glimpse of different countries and an insight into the future of urban living. A hybrid of a World's Fair and a Disneyized city of tomorrow, EPCOT tantalized and enthralled its punters. The appeal of Disney seemed limitless. By the early 1990s, 70 per cent of Americans had visited one of the two vacation hotspots. In 1998, Walt Disney World recorded its 600,000,000th visitor, underlining the status of the park as 'by far the most important entertainment centre in the world'. Disney's attendance figures far surpassed those of Yellowstone. Disney was universally loved. Dying children made it their last wish to see Mickey Mouse in his home park.[19]

In 1999, scholar Aviad Raz described Disney as 'closer to a secular religion than a producer of entertainment. It is America's national baby-sitter, mythmaker, and re-creator of history.' In recent decades Disney has arguably moved beyond its entertainment boundaries to influence American, and global, sensibilities on topics as diverse as technology, commodities, animals and child rearing. As a primary vehicle for Disney ideas, the park has been stretched to meet the demands of an ever expanding cartoon universe and encompassing corporate vision. Disney Imagineers have made the park idea their own, shaping it to fit their world-view. Walt best explained the Disneyland concept in 1955: 'The idea of Disneyland is a simple one. It will be a place for people to find happiness and knowledge . . . Disneyland will be something of a fair, an exhibition, a playground, a community centre, a museum of living facts, and a showplace of beauty and magic.' Since its beginnings in the Garden of Eden, never has the park ideal proved so ambitious.[20]

MCDONALD'S AND DISNEY

In retrospect, all that the original Disneyland lacked was a McDonald's. With Ronald McDonald as culturally significant as Mickey Mouse, the two lovable exports of Americana might have complemented one another in such a park. Ray Kroc, original franchiser of McDonald's, actually contacted Disney to propose such a collaborative venture in the early 1950s. Kroc had served alongside Disney in World War I. Both men proved shrewd and ruthless marketeers, valued cleanliness and order, and held conservative political opinions. However, still in its infancy (and minus the Ronald character), McDonald's lacked big name kudos, and was duly passed over in favour of other food concessionaries. A decade later, the ever ambitious Kroc envisioned his own amusement park near Los Angeles, but corporate advisers ruled against it.

How McDonald's intersects with Disney is of interest here not just because of the similar paths taken by the two men and their corporations – as Cameron and Bordessa remarked in 1981, Disney theme parks share with McDonald's restaurants several organizing principles, including standardized layouts, an emphasis on family fun, and regular updates to their product lines (in McDonald's case, burgers, in Disney's case, park attractions). Staff members attend either Disneyland or Hamburger 'Universities' (the latter offering its own 'degree in Hamburgerology'). Such similarities might be explained by what one sociologist, George Ritzer, describes as McDonaldization – 'the process by which the principles of the fast-food restaurant are coming to dominate more and more sectors of American society as well as the rest of the world'. Influenced by Max Weber's theories of bureaucracy and rationalization, Ritzer identified four chief ingredients in the McDonaldization process (a process best demonstrated by, but not unique to, McDonald's itself). The four ingredients were efficiency, 'the quickest route from hungry to full'; control, over the customer by a set menu and queuing, over the employee by technology and oversight; predictability, that every restaurant offers the same food and standards of care; and calculability, a focus on size as quality, the Big Mac being a prime example. Given their similarities to Kroc's restaurants, Disney theme parks (and for that matter theme parks in general) might be usefully considered as geographical vignettes of McDonaldized tourism, a process that, in turn, raises the spectre of parks becoming 'packaged' entertainment deals akin to the ubiquitous Happy Meal.[21]

The four ingredients of McDonaldization are all evident within Disneyland. Efficiency thrives in Disney parks, examples being organized parking, all-inclusive tickets, high-speed rides and advanced queuing methods to maximize custom, and fast-food restaurants designed to reduce hunger inefficiencies. Control is exercised over visitors by carefully dictated routes through each world as well as behavioural rules (no litter, height restrictions, etc.). Disney employees serve as entertainers and park guides but also as regulators. Staff members themselves work according to strict guidelines, including restrictions on facial hair and earrings and the maintenance of a cordial Disney smile at all times. All entertainers face automatic dismissal if they remove their cartoon masks in public. Such an emphasis on control assures that the Disney fantasy remains perfectly realized. Predictability revolves around public knowledge of the Disney label and its associated universe. Visitors to Disney theme parks expect to witness certain characters and certain rides, and assume that the park will be clean, safe and family-friendly. Calculability entails an emphasis on park size, value for money, and ride statistics. Ritzer also mentioned in his theory of McDonaldization an implicit 'irrationality of the rational' that tests the limits of the system. In the case of Disney parks, the irrational emerges in *over*-popular rides leading to inescapably long queues and public irritation – a microcosmic example of 'loving parks to death', of the hidden costs of being too successful. The notion of a *Mc*Disney theme park may yet grant Kroc some recompense. Despite his failure to secure a concessionary contract back in 1955, fast-food systems associated with the McDonald's brand now permeate the Disney landscape.

The distinctiveness of Disney meanwhile encouraged another sociologist, Alan Bryman, to borrow the phraseology of Ritzer in forwarding his own theory: 'Disneyization' or 'the process by which *the principles* of the Disney theme parks are coming to dominate more and more sectors of American society as well as the rest of the world'. To Bryman, Disney parks operated according to several principles: successful theming, de–differentiation (or loss of distinctiveness) of consumption, merchandising, and emotional labour.[22]

As mentioned earlier, Walt Disney employed theming as a way to give structure to his parks. Themed areas directed attention away from Coney-style white-knuckle entertainment, and toward more family-oriented fun. According to Bryman, the theming process at Disney had spread to other commercial settings, from the restaurant (take Planet Hollywood) and the shopping mall (for example, West Edmonton Mall, Canada, with its Parisian boulevards, discussed in chapter 7) to the gaudy themed hotel strip of Las Vegas. By de-differentiation of consumption, Bryman referred to the collapse of traditional boundaries of purchasing, noting that in Disney theme parks the whole experience of consumption effortlessly linked one area to the next, from Main Street shops to corporate-sponsored rides, ride shops to eateries. Outside park perimeters, this de-differentiation manifested itself in airport malls and casino hotels. Traditional, single-purpose definitions of hotels, shops and other services no longer held sway. Merchandising meanwhile highlighted the organization of Disney parks (as well as Disney movies such as *Toy Story*) around commercial points of sale. Disney parks flaunted T-shirts of myriad in-house characters, as well as plastic mementos of the park experience itself. Finally, emotional labour described the process whereby corporate employees adopted Disney-style courtesies and were seen to be having 'fun at work'. 'Have a Nice Day' and 'You're Welcome' culture has since become emblematic of the modern service sector.

Disneyization as a theory none the less sports a number of drawbacks. As with Ritzer's McDonaldization, one caveat with Bryman's theory is that while Disney best embodies such trends as emotional labour in society, his focus on Walt plays into the Disney myth of seeing itself as a point of origin, a genesis. If Disney parks are situated in relation to other theme parks, then Bryman has arguably identified the pervasive influence of the modern park idea in today's society, rather than just a Disney motif. As McDonaldization purports to show how the processes of the fast-food industry (not just McDonald's) can be applied elsewhere, Disneyization surely encapsulates the processes of the (theme) park industry and its global dissemination. Acknowledging the influence of Coney Island and Blackpool alongside Disney's creation seems pertinent, in the same way that Colonel Sanders of Kentucky Fried Chicken fame has been left out in the cold by McDonaldization. As mentioned throughout this book, theming has proved a popular tactic for many park designers. Instances of de-differentiation of consumption, merchandising and emotional labour can be located in many modern theme parks. McDonaldization is meant to encapsulate modern systems of food production and explain how they apply to the society. Likewise, Disneyization might be usefully extended to translate as the modern 'parkization' of society. In this regard, the work of Ritzer and Bryman may have aided in our task of systematically identifying at least a few of the influences of the modern park idea.

Bryman chose Disney for good reason. In terms of revenue, recognition and organizing principles, Disney parks lead the field. In 1955, Disneyland set down a template for theme parks that has since been universally copied. McDonald's similarly reigns supreme in the fast-food industry, albeit by a narrowing margin. Both Disney and McDonald's carry a cachet that surpasses regional geographies. While some of the world's parks remain primarily local attractions, the Disney Corporation, through its advertising budgets, animated movies and media industry links, has acquired a truly global market for its creative landscapes.

THE GRIM REALITIES AND POSTMODERN FICTIONS OF DISNEY

For eighteenth-century European landscape park designers, keeping their parks in flawless condition entailed constant pruning. With the clipping of Disney's vinyl leaves unnecessary, the problem 'weeds' of the modern theme park arrive in the form of computer glitches and human fallibility. The Disney Corporation rarely admits problems with its technology, but keeping control over staff and visitors proves taxing. For the Disney fantasy to remain coherent, employees are expected to perform their routines without deviation. The first-name basis of staff contact belies the formality of working conditions at Disney. In interviews (or 'casting') situations, potential employees are judged by their aesthetic adherence to the standard Disney 'look'. Disney University teaches the Disney way, where workers learn not to fraternize with one another, not to improvise, and not to refer to accidents *as* accidents. The phrase 'amusement park' is likewise considered taboo, underlining the enforced separation between Disneyland and its predecessors. For some, the rewards on offer, including fake degrees by the names of Mousters and Ductorates, along with uncompetitive wages, are simply not enough. However, other Disney employees remain 'in love' with Walt's vision and gain genuine satisfaction from greeting visitors with a Disney smile and watching them grin.

Critics of Disney have argued that the park experience reduces visitors to passive consumers unable to think independently or resist corporate merchandise. The opportunities for imagination and play are curtailed inside park boundaries by excessive control, a barrage of images (similar to those produced by television), and an emphasis on individualized experience rather than social interaction. In 1999, author Henry Giroux tentatively compared Disneyland with Auschwitz, both landscapes encouraging a loss of resistance and self-reflection among their 'prisoners'. Disney's world has also been derided as sexist, homophobic, racist and repressive, a vehicle of the far right rather than the freedom-inspiring American dream. For Susan Willis and fellow contributors to *Inside the Mouse* (1995), behind the innocent world of Disney lurks a monster of a mouse. The cute colonial racism of Disney's seminal Jungle Cruise, where native stereotypes abound, underlines governing visions of white superiority. Entry to the park therefore means buying into a questionable philosophy. Certainly, attendance statistics for Disney World indicate that the resort appeals most to white customers. Out of every hundred guests to Disney World, only three are black and two Hispanic. With its idealizations of white suburban middle-class heterosexual living, the park fantasy remains resolutely caught in the 1950s. Disneyland is imprisoned in the past.[23]

This monolithic vision is nevertheless unlikely to change in any fundamental sense. That Disney keeps the park façade static and predictable enables visitors to forget the grim realities of their daily lives. Mickey Mouse wandering the park is, for them, just that: a fun cartoon figure, not a downtrodden employee under the animal fur or a potent symbol of corporate power. The fantasy seems so real, so captivating and so pure that social problems outside park boundaries fade from view, or are brightly glossed over with Disney paint. In his trips to Tokyo Disneyland, Aviad Raz discovered that 'An ongoing hyperreality of pleasure captures the visitor's attention, deflecting it away from sustained critical thought about the "real world"'. The fantasy is all that matters.[24]

While Disney parks draw on a tradition of deception common to all amusement parks, postmodernists take great interest in Disney's relationship with the 'real' and the 'unreal' in contemporary society. The Disney universe complements, and contributes to, modern fixations with fantasy in the form of simulation and 'hyperreality'. Postmodern rhetoric highlights current human proclivities for jumping between places and times so that traditional boundaries scarcely matter anymore. Signifier and signified are no longer separate or distinguishable, and result in the fusion of the unreal and the real. Such ideas appear particularly relevant to Disney's theme parks, where visitors pass between different 'ages' and 'worlds'. As distance and difference collapse, fantasy and reality collide. The Disney canon is also relevant because, on the whole, its parks recreate 'worlds' and 'scenes' that never actually existed. In Disney's Fantasyland, animated cartoons come to 'life', while even Frontierland, meant to pay homage to nineteenth-century American history, instead replicates a generic, idealistic and inaccurate West first invented by celluloid. Such an intriguing interface between movie, park and image ably fits Jean Baudrillard's sense of America as a cinematic, simulated country where the authentic becomes the screened and 'the real becomes a theme park'.[25]

For Umberto Eco, the process of 'theming' abets a sense of geographical and temporal collapse and fosters collective dislocation. With Disneyland's 'New Orleans' close by, why travel to Louisiana, especially when it may fail to match the wonder of the fake? Baudrillard goes further, arguing that 'Disneyland is presented as imaginary in order to make us believe that the rest is real, when in fact all of Los Angeles and America surrounding it are no longer real, but of the order of the hyperreal and simulation'. Theorizing on what's inside the park compared to what's outside presents an ingenious line of enquiry, not least as parks have always reflected the whims of society, with all boundary lines contestable on some level. America, as Disney writ large, has become the home of illusion, inauthenticity and anodyne emptiness. To Baudrillard, hallucinatory Disney parks are quintessentially American and arguably better signifiers of the United States than 'natural' parks such as Yellowstone or Yosemite.

Postmodern criticism of Disney equally applies to the wider theme park genre. Do such parks actively contribute to a global culture fixated on cheap thrills and fantasy-bound escapism, one unfazed by a lack of historical or temporal consistency? Despite their unrealities, the overwhelming success of theme parks might indicate the extent to which consumers crave merchandise and white-knuckle fixes – that fantasy and simulation are important aspects of modern living. Meanwhile, the intersection of park, celluloid and social design is directly revealed by the success of Universal Studios' theme park, Hollywood, where guests clamour to enjoy life (or reality) as movie fiction for a day.

Yet can parks accurately reflect the broader desires of society when most serve only as weekend, and thus temporary, retreats? Has the power of Disneyland to alter public perception been overestimated? Postmodern criticism of Disney certainly makes the mistake of reducing park visitors to simple drones unable to differentiate fantasy from reality, while aggrandizing intellectuals for their supposed ability to objectify theme park experiences without the need to visit. As French writer André Glucksmann proposed, 'The visitor himself does not confuse the dream and reality; buying his admission ticket, he knows well that he who laughs on Sunday, works on Monday.' For many guests, the gloomy reality of existence quickly returns on exiting theme park gates.[26]

MODERN THEME PARKS

The advent of Disney theme parks showed the possibilities for revitalizing a flagging US amusement park industry. Surviving parks aimed to replicate the success of Disney resorts by providing their own themed areas and attractions. At Cedar Point on Lake Erie, park boosters used the tag 'Ohio Disneyland' to attract investment and boost attendance. A $16,000,000 injection of cash, along with help from Marco, a Los Angeles firm with Disney experience, made sure the venture worked out. By 1968, Cedar offered two new car rides, a new coaster, and a new 'Frontiertown' themed area. The park was reinvented as clean, family-oriented and wholesome. In reference to Disney's own Ford-inspired management strategies, Cedar officials boasted, 'We run Cedar point like General Motors.' However, Cedar was never going to be Ohio's Disney. For one thing, shaping a theme park out of an existing amusement park meant compromises over planning – unless razed to the ground, designers had to work with existing rides, buildings and land boundaries. Rather than completely 'Disneyfy' the park, Cedar officials restored older buildings and chose to keep remnants of Cedar's own amusement history such as its garden statues and midway. New parks followed the theming principle more closely. In 1961, Six Flags opened its first park in Arlington, Texas, with areas themed around Spain, France, Mexico, the Republic of Texas, the Confederacy and the USA. The successful park chain soon expanded to Georgia (1967) and St Louis (1971). By 2003, Six Flags owned thirty-nine theme parks across Europe and North America.

Replicating the Disney magic none the less proved difficult. Themed worlds did not always guarantee success. Seeking to exploit the romance of the old West, Frontier Village Amusement Park in San Jose (1961–80) offered burro rides, Indian Jim's Canoes, a mine adventure and a 'Last Chance Casino'. The park's last chance expired when Marriot's Great America, a larger theme park, tapped local business. In 1980, the Frontier Village metamorphosed into Edenvale Garden Park, one park variegation giving way to another. At Magic Harbor, South Carolina, another park based on the Wild, Wild West (so entitled) ended its life in the 1960s when a real-life gun shooting cut short old Western mystique. The re-creation of the Wild, Wild West then became, somewhat bizarrely, a facsimile landscape of Britain. Thanks to investment by the Blackpool Pleasure Beach Company, the British Amusement Park opened in South Carolina for a short period. An accident on its Black Witch coaster led to the closure of the park in the 1990s.

In Britain, an American-style amusement spectacle sprang from a traditional park landscape. In 1980, the stately home of Alton Towers in Staffordshire, England, opened to guests for the first time in the guise of a theme park. Fireworks and fetes had entertained nineteenth-century visitors on park grounds. In the late twentieth century, guests instead took rides on a new-fangled Corkscrew double-looping coaster. A magic carpet ride, log flume, Cine 360° and Circus Show followed soon after. The theme park soon overwhelmed the stately home, the multiple rollercoasters and Alton Ghost House turning the historic gardens and mansion into sideshows, remnants of the past. Although Disney inspired the rise of many modern entertainment landscapes, at Alton, the provision of stomach-churning thrill rides took precedence. Despite park designers experimenting with themed zones in the Eighties and Nineties, it was the white-knuckle rides that drew the crowds.

A similar leisure boom in Japan during the 1980s and 1990s gave rise to a number of ventures. Korakuen Amusement Park, positioned next to Japan's first professional baseball park in Tokyo City, opened in the 1950s. In 1988, Tokyo Dome Corporation rebuilt the baseball stadium, turning the whole area into a successful entertainment complex (known affectionately as the Big EGG). In 1990, Nippon Steel transformed a steel mill into a futuristic space-travel park (Space World), shifting focus from the Industrial Revolution to the manufacture of a high-technology leisure complex. Owners of Tobu World Square (1993) invited guests to wander around a model village of 102 structures reflecting the planet's architectural wonders, from the Egyptian sphinx to the Great Wall of China. Following the terrorist attack on the Twin Towers of New York in September 2001, staff placed a donation box next to Tobu's 1/25th scale model of the World Trade Center. Where Tobu gazed outwards for inspiration, Sanrio Pierrotland (1990) in Tama City favoured introspection. Sanrio theme park served as a native fantasyland, or Japanese Disneyland, where Sanrio cartoon characters including Hello Kitty resided. Hence, Japanese parks captured all kinds of monuments, cultures and fantasies within their boundaries.

Ultimately, modern theme parks appropriated both Disney and Coney entertainment models. Theming, merchandising, family-oriented activities and high-quality services meshed with thrill rides, adult entertainment and traditional garish amusements. The Disney smile was tacked on to the front of the Coney carnival – the result being that most parks lacked the control, conformity and coherence found at Disney, but at the same time, benefited from a malleable design template suited to fun and recreation. Park designs at best paid homage to the freedom of old amusement parks, but with safe family values attached, or at worst served as instantly disposable pastiches of Disneyland without Walt's detail or ingenuity. The enduring presence of high technology and futurism gave the parks some historical continuity, as did their consistent aim to please. The following sections elaborate on key facets of modern theme park design.

THEME PARKS AS CONSUMER LANDSCAPES

Consumption remains a primary feature of contemporary theme parks. In contrast to public parks, where the wallet is rarely a necessity, theme parks are unequivocally about monetary exchange. They require substantial investment to establish and maintain, and also depend on visitor expenditure for survival. Since General Electric sponsored the Carousel of Progress at Disneyland in the 1960s, corporate sponsorship of rides has increased. Shrewd marketing deals enable park expansion, but also transform each themed landscape into a corporate tool, a world of Coca-Cola, Pepsi and Kodak. For the visitor, the notion that money buys pleasure represents a fundamental, albeit undisclosed, lesson of the theme park. Although the single-fee entrance ticket guarantees a basic fun quotient for all guests, park designers fashion additional attractions (or concessions) to offer more to those with more to spend. Meticulous planning facilitates financial success. Designers foster an unrivalled consumer landscape by placing ice-cream parlours and snack-food stalls at regular points on the park circuit. Automated cameras capture hair-raising moments on thrill rides – with the pictures available for purchase within seconds. Neon arcades invite gamers to exchange their loose change for 5-minute stints on coin-ops.

By the process of theming, each park sports several identities that can be packaged into affordable mementos – thus guests exit a generic 'dinosaur' park ride through a gift store bedecked with reptilian merchandise from toy figurines to T-shirts claiming 'I tamed T-Rex'. The park systematically directs the attention of the visitor/consumer, highlighting where and what to buy as part of a pre-set tour around each world. Impulse buying and consumer excess resound. With so many products for sale, few boundaries remain between life inside the theme park and the modern consumer society outside.

In 1981, Cameron and Bordessa controversially claimed that 'materialism is the religion of the US . . . theme parks are its newest shrines'. In fact, the religion of consumption signifies a global phenomenon, with theme park outlets spread across the planet. Thrill parks may be brazen and bold capitalist temples, with rollercoasters worshipped as mechanical gods of GNP, but the subtleties of park franchising defy simple categorization. One of the most intriguing aspects regarding theme parks is the selling of fantasy for cash. Emotions are bought, not free – guests purchase 'bouts' of fun. Yet, visitors rarely recognize the barter that each trip entails. The innocence and frivolity of the park captured in its bright colours and childlike motifs disguises the regimented consumer landscape beneath. Theme parks deceive by making consumption itself part of a greater fantasy. As Umberto Eco found on his trip to Berry Farm, spending time in frontier shops 'blends the reality of trade with the play of fiction' – real dollar bills reduced to Monopoly-style paper currency in a role-playing game. At Disney too, Eco recognized in Main Street 'a disguised supermarket, where you buy obsessively, believing that you are still playing'. Even guides seem misled by their duties at times. One Disneyland job orientation quiz asked, 'We Tokyo Disneyland cast members provide — to all the guests,' the options being 'service', 'happiness' or 'Disney goods'. The right answer was 'happiness', although fresh initiates might have chosen otherwise. Theme parks encourage indulgent behaviour, carefree attitudes, immersion in fantasy, and desperation for mementos to remember the fun by. On-site cash registers duly ring with glee. [27]

THE VISITOR EXPERIENCE: FAKE THRILLS AND REAL DANGERS

Along with consumption, excitement is another primary function of the modern theme park. Providing adrenalin-pumping rides remains imperative to park success. Rather than a convention introduced by Walt Disney, provision of the thrill ride hails back to pioneer amusement parks such as Steeplechase that experimented with rollercoasters and visitor emotions. People have been frightened in parks for a long time, with 'wilderness' zones appended to European landscape gardens to enthral and disturb in equal measure. Turn-of-the-century amusement parks merely packaged fear into minute-long rides and freak show performances. In the 1950s, Disney set out to steer parks away from scary machines and towards more benign family fun.

However, with the success of 'thrill parks' such as Alton Towers and Six Flags, even the Disney Corporation has recognized the significance of the fear factor in park design.

By furnishing the illusion of danger within a safe environment, theme parks flourish on the edge of paradox. Visitors expect to be scared, but never practically endangered. Fear is carefully packaged and impeccably controlled. Danger is inculcated by the devilish names attached to rides, the pitch of attendant noise, the dark scenery of attractions, how far up they travel and how quickly they drop (encouraging vertigo), the rickety, unstable façade of wooden coasters, together with the mass hysteria induced by sharing the experience with others. Peril in the park is masterfully forged, and coaster enthusiasts recognize this. Visitors none the less respond to the simulation with genuine emotion. Like interactive horror films, rides such as Alton's Nemesis and Oblivion invite impromptu wows and screams. Understanding the psychology of wanting to be frightened is beyond the remit of this study. Nevertheless, in terms of the park idea, it reveals parks as places designed not just for comfort or emotional retreat.

On rare occasions, the distance between simulated and real disaster collapses. Technological breakdown or human error interferes with the mediated and controlled facsimile of fear. In 1997, at Port Aventura Park in Spain, a frontier-themed coaster called Stampida threw a rider to his death. The ride closed before being retrofitted with modified safety bars. In September 2000, a train carrying passengers on the Pepsi Max Big One rollercoaster at Blackpool failed to stop, careening into another train parked in the station. Fourteen people were injured. Real accidents take lives and damage reputations. Trust erodes between rider and ride owner. To avoid bad publicity, Disney downplays accidents within its parks, and, for some time, collected victims in discreet Disney First Aid Vans rather than instantly identifiable ambulances. Ironically, Disney's assured presentation of a perfectly safe world has prompted several urban legends, including the implausible tale of the first Mickey Mouse actor who contracted skin cancer from his costume.[28]

A PLACE FOR TECHNOLOGY?

In Disney folklore, technology offers human betterment. The EPCOT Center located within the Magic Kingdom, Florida, represents a technological utopia where machines manage urban and leisure space. The epitome of the rational, computers and machines at EPCOT nevertheless foster emotional responses from guests. The park inspires and enthrals because it projects technological fixes to some social problems (living space, health and hygiene) while ignoring others (poverty, slums). Disney presents the future as a wonderfully organized and opulent 'white city', an aesthetic antithesis to the dastardly war of the machines popularized in *Terminator* and *Matrix* movies. Disney teaches that joy comes through the conduit of technology. Myriad rides provide a surfeit of supporting evidence.

Visitors stand in awe before technology because the presence of machines indicates cheap thrills. In the manufacture of fear, technology remains king. Rollercoasters in early amusement parks used chains and hand-pulled breakers. Contemporary theme parks signify highly technological and automated landscapes. Rides are computer-designed and controlled. Technology is itself a significant crowd puller. Parks entice visitors with their record-breaking coasters – the highest, the quickest, the most contortions. In 1979, Blackpool Pleasure Beach unveiled the first looping rollercoaster in Europe. 'Revolution' cost £1,000,000, but positioned Blackpool as a frontrunner in theme park technology. Vacationers happily paid the 60 pence ride fee. In 1994, Blackpool unleashed the Pepsi Max Big One, a coaster capable of processing 1,700 passengers per hour, each one of them travelling at up to 85 miles per hour with 3.5G force. Dwarfing Blackpool's still operational Big Dipper coaster (1923), the Big One attested to the technological frontiers being conquered at the seaside. Revolution and the Big One helped nudge attendance at Blackpool Pleasure Beach above the 400 million mark on its one hundredth anniversary in 1996.

Theme park aficionados enjoy more than just the 30-second ride experience – they also take interest in the technical statistics of each pleasure machine. The kind of trivia that would embarrass train-spotters is lovingly digested and dissected, in the process aiding comprehension of the monumental structures before them. Owners of Canada's Wonderland advertised how over 900,000 board feet of Canadian wood was used for its coasters, hardly shying away from the fact that a small forest had been cleared for amusement park thrills. The publishing of such information highlights the attention to detail needed to construct amusement machines. Meanwhile, that visitors entertain themselves by reading such trivia adeptly reveals the sheer boredom of life in the queue.

Within the theme park, technology is continually upgraded to meet new challenges. Competition between rival entertainment landscapes often spurs new mechanized endeavours. In May 2000, Cedar Point revealed a rollercoaster by the name of Millennium Force that stood an astounding 310 feet high (with a drop of 300 feet) and reached speeds of 92 miles an hour. In July of the same year, the unveiling of a new Japanese coaster, Steel Dragon at ocean-side Nagashima Spa Land, undermined the reputation of Cedar Point as coaster king. Nagashima's Steel Dragon measured an additional 8 feet in height. It also stole the record for the longest coaster at 8,133 feet (from The Ultimate in Lightwater Valley, UK) and the fastest (reaching 95 miles per hour). In May 2003, Cedar Point responded with Top Thrill Dragster, 420 feet high, with a 120 mile an hour top speed and a price tag of $25,000,000.[29]

Parks also compete by offering fresh slants on established ride forms – such as the first inverted coaster, Nemesis, unveiled at Alton Towers in 1994 to popular acclaim. Recent experiments include the application of magnet motors and hydraulic power. High technology is requisite in the formulation of convention-breaking rides. However, spiralling financial costs of investment, as well as limits to how far visitors will go, imposes finite boundaries on the coaster competition. The Top Thrill Dragster may last only 17 seconds, but for many visitors to Cedar Point, that represents 17 seconds too long. Simply imagining being at the apex of the ride is perhaps frightening enough, without actually experiencing the sensation. While technological licences to thrill seem eminently extendable, a fear barrier may soon be reached whereby spectators watch but dare not board.

A PLACE FOR NATURE?

The continuing rise of technology in theme parks has entailed a concomitant fall in the role of nature. The skyline of the modern theme park is dominated by machinery, not foliage – rollercoasters have outgrown trees. While landscape parks once entertained guests with stone lions and griffins, artificial nature has taken hold in the theme park, uprooting and replacing resident flora and fauna in the process.

Holding up the Swiss Family Island Treehouse at Disney is a mesh and metal tree, featuring thousands of vinyl leaves. The Disney dendron has its own pseudo-scientific taxonomy, *Disneyodendron eximus*, the 'out of the ordinary Disney tree'. On a broader level, theme parks themselves stand out as 'out of the ordinary' experiences by their emphasis on adventure and fear, along with their exotic reproductions. Such places trade in cartoon figures, robots, high technology and simulated danger. Theme parks resonate with visions of fantasy, artifice and escapism. Nature is usually part of this collage – for instance, animal characters make appearances at most parks, and water rides based on Grand Canyon-style rapids remain a theme park staple. However, our collective imaginings dictate what nature should look like. Natural forces in the theme park are so closely controlled, or imitated, that independence and agency are lost. Sites usually feature animals, but in the form of humans inside faunal costumes. Wolves may be anthropomorphized in Yellowstone National Park, but at least their coats don't come off at teatime. In essence, theme park designers offer us cartoon-based, mediated understandings of nature, rather than ecological realities. The natural world in the theme park exists purely for visitor pleasure; thus what we want to see as 'natural' remains paramount. In this equation, nature is often reduced, rendered in plastic and distinctly puerile. As landscape critic Alexander Wilson explained, the natural world is viewed as entertainment alone through such a process of 'whimsification', with Disney as its premier artist.[30]

The Disney Corporation offers nature whimsy writ large on both the big screen and inside its parks. In the early days, Disney cartoonists practised 'nature fakery' in their inaccurate, excited translation of the natural world. The same 'look' was subsequently applied to Disneyland and Disney World. 'Real' nature was 'cast' for parts in rides such as the Jungle Cruise, vegetation chosen to fit the movie-like journey rather than resembling environmental reality.

The production of a fantasy, a 're-created' environment, meant that material nature was more an unpredictable luxury than an absolute necessity. To be fantastical, Disney parks had to look different, to look artificial rather than natural.

Disney's predilection for facsimile might be interpreted as a mistrust of natural forces. The park presents an artificial Garden of Eden, an audio-animatronic Genesis story, with no danger of a plastic apple being stolen or a robotic serpent upsetting human decency. Nature is never allowed to interfere in the greater scheme of things, to put a proverbial (but naturalized) spanner in the works of a technological cartoon utopia. Fake nature behaves, or acts, just as Disney wants it to. The 'audio-animatronic' crocodile on the Jungle Cruise opens its mouth at just the right moment and always hisses on cue. The artificial reptile never threatens guests in a tangible way. Just like rollercoaster rides, the Jungle Cruise emphasizes controlled fear rather than true danger. Tourists instantly recognize the crocodile as a fake, evincing admiration at the skill and ingenuity needed to build such a monster. Others confess disappointment at the lifeless quality of the reptilian mannequin. On its opening, Disney's Jungle Cruise received the playful tag of 'Foamrubbersville'.

For Disney, the fake, the simulation, is nevertheless assumed better than the original (presuming an original exists). The mechanical crocodile performs before an audience, while the real one might be hidden from view, undependable and irrational. As Umberto Eco imparts, 'Disneyland tells us that technology can give us more reality than nature can.' Visitors get to see a snapping reptile (along with several other exotic creatures) on Disney's Jungle Cruise – 5 minutes expended on the Amazon could well prove less rewarding. The message here appears to be that nature, left to its own devices, is simply not entertaining enough to be part of the theme park experience.[31]

The triumph of technology and plastic over flora and fauna implicates America's Disney as a landscape antithetical to America's Yosemite. But does the success of Disneyfied nature pose a threat to places where organic nature is seen to rule? Susan Willis warns how 'the entire natural world is subsumed by the primacy of the artificial' at Disney. Such a statement of intent poses a fundamental affront to the original park ideal – with the grim spectre of all that is natural at some point being lost to simulacra. Walt Disney has already simulated the cultural foundations of the nature park, Disney World replicating a rustic national park-style lodge for its guests. Disney World's Frontierland meanwhile features the Big Thunder Mountain 'wilderness' rollercoaster, complete with constructed volcanic pools mimicking the geysers of Yellowstone. Intriguingly, the two landscapes (the technological fantasy and the natural wonder) are worshipped in equal measure by tourists that traverse both venues. Parks opposed, but valued alike.[32]

Without the 'blank canvas', rigorous theming template or huge financial budget, other theme parks feature far more 'real' nature on display than does Disney. Whereas the Disney Corporation supplanted Floridian swampland to furnish its second entertainment complex, in Britain, theme park designers made use of their inherited garden landscapes. Owners of Alton Towers maintained its nineteenth-century botanic grounds as part of the modern park complement. Although most visitors looked first to the thrill rides, the picturesque setting did offset some of the ennui of queuing as well as serving as an ideal picnic site. Drayton Manor Family Theme Park (formerly Park and Zoo) in Staffordshire, established in 1949 as an 'Inland Pleasure Resort', ambitiously provided visitors with several kinds of experiences. In common with Alton Towers, thrill rides predominated. But a cable-car jaunt across a well-manicured landscape bedecked with strange mechanical contraptions revealed a complex interface between nature and artifice in the modern theme park. Since its inception, the Drayton parkscape has played home to a Jungle Cruise, a Dinosaur Land, a 'Python' looping coaster, and a zoo complete with reptile house. In Europe, both Tivoli and Bakken impress due to their combination of historic rides and impeccable gardens. Nature within the theme park is recognized as a financial asset at such locales, with zoo animals and garden walks appealing to a broader demographic than white-knuckle rides. When pandas stayed at Busch Gardens in Tampa for a 2-year visit, visitors followed the activities of the black and white bears *en masse*. Attendance figures increased thanks to a natural feature, albeit an exotic species in an alien climate. A continuing emphasis on theming meanwhile affords options for park designers to either reduce or increase their range of organic reference points.[33]

THEMING CULTURAL NATIONALISM

Park theming is rarely taken as anything more than innocuous fun. On the surface, dinosaurlands, pirate coves, frontierlands and jungle worlds prompt little offence, and rarely transcend basic folklore. However, what links most themed worlds together is their rendering of the exotic. Theme parks often present the foreign and the unusual in the form of miniaturized countries to stroll through. This trend dates back to turn-of-the-century displays of 'cultural villages' at World's Fairs and Coney Island, yet has found a new outlet in modern theme park landscapes. Cultural villages, however, rarely work. Stereotypes and commercialism prevail to the extent that the exotic becomes whatever the visitor expects to see. Accurate depictions of other societies prove exceptional. The classic Jungle Cruise at Disney, along with countless attractions at other theme parks, provides a singular narrative of romantic colonialism and the taming of savage natives and exotic animals. The story is mass-consumed but rarely questioned.

At Port Aventura, an expansive array of cultural villages highlights the role of the theme park in simulating a new type of 'global village'. Owned by the American entertainment corporation Universal, the Spanish complex features themed worlds from across the globe. Guests find themselves seamlessly crossing between the American Far West, Mediterrania, Polynesia, Mexico and China, without jet lag or feelings of geographic dislocation. While Disney featured 'Around the World in Eighty Days' as a single ride, Port Aventura re-creates global expedition in the form of a day-long jaunt around the park. 'Find yourself at the Great Wall of China one minute and at the ruins of Mayan Mexico the next,' boasts Aventura's promotional literature. Rides borrow natural and cultural resources to simulate the travelogue. Dodgems nicknamed 'Wild Buffaloes' adorn the Far West, a manufactured tropical storm hits Polynesia, while Fumanchu swinging chairs grace the Chinese exhibit. Essentialized within park confines, the whole world seems much smaller.

In turn, theme parks have assumed the role of ambassadors, popular totems of cultural nationalism, and new park envoys to join the nation-promoting wonders of Yosemite and Kruger. In the case of Germany's Europa-Park, the European Union is on offer in all its glory. Europa opened in July 1975, promising 'A trip through all Europe in just one day, from the North Cape to Andalusia'. While featuring its own slice of history with a medieval castle and gardens, Europa also furnished fake versions of a German boulevard, an Italian piazza and a Swiss mountain village. Advertising its vibrant re-creation of Greece, Europa claimed, 'This is where the Gods are on holidays.' The park provided a thrill-seekers' avenue towards understanding 'a true European experience', including a Swiss bob-sleigh ride and simulated fjord rafting. By 2003, park expansion indicated the colonizing of America as Europa's next project. The annexation of North American culture included a Tipi village, reassembled and translated into a European-style camping adventure. 'Feeling like a real Native American in the prairie', campers played Indian in a re-creation of America inside a re-creation of Europe inside Germany.[34]

Attempting to encapsulate the appeal of a continent or a country in a mismatch of collected thrill rides seems inevitably flawed. People, history and events are reduced in size and complexity – national identity plasticized and simplified in a similar way to how theme parks treat the natural world. Cultural stereotypes find safe haven in theme parks, especially given the tourist revenue to be gleaned from foreigners eager to laugh at the 'locals'. The inaccuracy of what is presented seems to matter little, as long as people are enjoying themselves. In May 1981, 'Canada's Wonderland' opened in the town of Vaughan on the outskirts of Toronto. Despite its nationalistic banner, Canada's Wonderland proved anything but. Financed by the American-based Taft Broadcasting Company, the theme park appeared noticeably bereft of Canadiana on its opening. Rather than a popular exponent of Canadian great-ness, Wonderland drew its inspirations from further afield. Themed areas con-sisted of an International Street (based on Mediterranean, Alpine and Scandinavian influences), a re-creation of the World Expo of 1890, a European medieval fair, and 'the Happy Land of Hanna-Barbara' (populated by such characters as Scooby Doo and Popeye). The park was taken as a salient example of American companies doing business in Canada with little respect for cultural differences.

If Canada's Wonderland contained little of Canada, Disney's planned 'inva-sion' of foreign shores in the 1980s and 1990s implied even less representation for local cultures. Theme parks already featured a Western, if not American, *Zeitgeist* by their focus on consumption, leisure and the rewards of capitalism. Writing on Canada's Wonderland, Cameron and Bordessa remarked how 'Theme parks do more than designate, they denote the United States – they are as symbolic of the current success of the American way of life as New York's first cluster of skyscrapers was in its era'. Considered a fundamentally US product, with Mickey Mouse as American as apple pie, the spread of Disney parks to Europe and Asia threatened a new level of Yankee colonialism. While Disney cartoons had already spread across the globe, ceding real estate to the Disney Corporation implied something more serious. Hardly assuaging fears over the worldly power of the cartoon company, Disney chief executive officer Michael Eisner remarked that Mickey helped collapse the Berlin Wall in 1989. At the very least, Disney theme parks threatened cultural shockwaves.[35]

Opened in April 1983, Tokyo Disneyland, positioned on Tokyo Bay, represented a fresh beachhead of American idealism and cultural hegemony in Asia. The eponymous Mickey Mouse seemed poised to usurp traditional Japanese values by drawing the nation into his cartoon park. Tokyo Disneyland symbolized the Americanization of Japan. Japanese employees faced jargon-laden Taylorist work manuals focused on breaking down tasks into separate components. The first park visitors were forced to consume American fast food. However, for Disney scholar Aviad Raz, Tokyo Disneyland entailed the 'active appropriation of Disney by the Japanese', rather than the Disneyization (and Americanization) of Japan. By the 1980s, Japanese society already featured a significant consumer economy as well as a prosperous leisure industry. Disney tapped an existing social need. The park catered to Japanese life-style preferences. Rather than exercise complete control over the project, Disney contracted a Japanese corporation, the Oriental Land Company (OLC), to manage the park. The OLC followed traditional Japanese employment practices for regular staff. Part-timers accepted Disney manuals as processes of economic modernization and the leaving behind of traditional Japanese master/apprentice relations. Disney's emphasis on presentation (the Disney look), conformity and obedience replicated similar practices at other Japanese amusement parks. Besides, script rewrites and new rides catered to an Asian audience. 'Cinderella's Castle Mystery Tour' pandered to Japanese fascinations with ghosts, while 'Meet the World' summarized a few thousand years of Japanese history in a 30-minute film. While the ambitious (yet reductive) scale of the timeline embodied classic Disney, the show remained locally distinctive. Guides wore kimono-style costumes rather than the usual animal attire. Tokyo Disneyland thereby provided a Japanese take on what America was all about – professing a mediated image of the United States courtesy of Disney and the OLC. By 1997, more than 200 million had visited.[36]

Spurred by the success of Tokyo Disneyland, Disney looked to Europe for its next project. That many Europeans proved willing to make a transatlantic pilgrimage to Disney World, Florida, suggested that Europe had potential for its own cartoon park. After surveying over 1,000 potential sites (with Barcelona in Spain an early frontrunner), the Disney Corporation was focusing on Marne-la-Vallée on the outskirts of Paris by August 1985. The lure of Parisian tourists, tax deals, free infrastructure and cheap land figured highly in the decision. Nicknamed 'Mickeyrand' by his critics, Premier François Mitterand made the Mouse welcome in France. Despite locals resisting an American take-over and protestations from the Syndicate of Amusement Parks of France that Disney would bankrupt existing small parks and fairs, Euro Disney gradually moved forward. In March 1987, Premier Jacques Chirac signed a $7.5 billion contract with Disney. Park construction duly followed.

With a media hullabaloo costing some $220,000,000, Euro Disney opened on 12 April 1992. Hollywood actress turned Disney compère Melanie Griffiths exhaled, 'It's just like a fairytale!' before palace fireworks on opening night. However, the Disney experience failed to instil French critics with similarly positive emotional vigour. Despite happily posing with Mickey Mouse before cameras on a courtesy trip to California's Disneyland, Paris theatre director Ariane Mnouchkine expressed distinct discomfort with the Euro-mouse, and famously lambasted the park as 'a cultural Chernobyl'. Intellectuals dubbed the resort 'the fifty-first American state'.[37]

Significant reworking of the theme park to cater to European tastes had failed to guarantee approval. Rather than recognize Mont St Michel church as an inspiration behind Sleeping Beauty's Palace, the presence of French colonialists in Adventureland, or visionary Jules Verne in Tomorrowland, critics saw only an insidious rodent spreading American imperialism, or 'Coca-colonization'. In their estimation, the European way of life needed protection from the Disney smile. During planning stages, local protesters pitch-forked effigies of Mickey Mouse. On the opening of the park, terrorists planted bombs. A time-honoured clash between the Old World and the New World resurfaced, with American culture derided as puerile and unsophisticated in the process. For critics, American theme parks depicted a country without a history, a people fixated with dreams and burdened with a lust for facile recreation. Few noticed the universality of the park format, be it at Versailles or Anaheim. Park designers and visitors alike had always indulged in fantasy. After being wooed to Paris, Disney now seemed a pariah, a plastic blot on the capital's landscape. Eager to highlight the superiority of France's home-grown entertainment industry, marketing director of Parc Asterix (1989), Nicholas Pérrard, chimed: 'Disney is based on fantasies, we are based on realities.' Pérrard conveniently ignored Disney stylistic flourishes in the world of Asterix, preferring to promote his resort as a bastion of French history and synthetic vignette of cultural nationalism. As a later tourist guide reminded, 'You will enjoy this very French leisure park.'[38]

The very 'American' theme park next to Paris initially struggled to meet its targets. Financial losses raised the spectre of closure over Europe's first Disney Park in 1993. The London *Independent* called Euro Disney 'America's cultural Vietnam'. However, an illustrious new ride (Space Mountain), a financial rescue package, fresh marketing and better cost management, along with the new moniker of Disneyland Paris helped re-establish the Parisian theme park as an entertainment hub. By 2000, attendance averaged 12 million a year. In 2002, Euro Disney Studios, a movie-based theme world, joined the park complement.

The way in which parks intersect with societies around them is evidenced by these two Disney case studies. The boundaries that physically separate the park from the outside world only serve to reduce, rather than eliminate, a cross-pollination of ideas. At Tokyo Disneyland and Disneyland Paris cultural exchange remains undeniable. The exotic world outside the park influences the landscape inside – and vice versa. Believing the park to be entirely divorced from local social mores is a flawed assumption. So too is essentializing the controversies surrounding Disneyland Paris and Tokyo Disneyland as part of an ongoing USA versus the world meta-narrative. Even if it purported to represent mainstream America in the 1950s, Disney no longer reflects US culture in its entirety. Today, the Disney Corporation is just as much about corporate power, about forging a vision with universal understanding and appeal, as it is about American values. In this regard, Disney imparts the realities of globalization as much as the perils of Americanization. For Shelton Waldrep from the Project on Disney, the Magic Kingdom truly signals 'a nation-less space (the future) where companies replace countries'. Theme parks bring the micro and the macro together, collapsing boundaries and geographic space in a process of globalization best epitomized by the Disney ride 'It's a Small World'.[39]

HISTORY AND THEME PARKS

Disney theme parks in Europe and Asia promised a convenient 'visit' to America. Perhaps, given the global influence of Mickey Mouse, Disney has helped frame international perspectives on US history, culture and society. Using powerful imagery and convincing environments, theme parks have continually invited select viewpoints on national pasts. History has been part of the amusement experience ever since World's Fairs provided historic exhibits and Coney Island simulated the fall of Pompeii. However, while tourists happily soaked up Disney's take on nineteenth-century Frontierland and Main Street USA, some Americans criticized the theme park for its questionable representation of the past. In 1993, Disney came under attack on home soil when it forwarded plans for a history-based theme park, revealingly dubbed 'Disney's America'.

One of Walt Disney's original ideas for Disneyland had been for the park to offer 'A Miniature Historic America'. When the Walt Disney Company marked out a 3,000 acre site in Virginia's Piedmont in the early 1990s, just 35 miles from the White House, a crowd of community members and educators joined forces to fight off the advances of Mickey Mouse. Along with conventional fears over pollution and congestion, the 'Protect Historic

America' coalition railed against the concept of a 'fun' park dealing with the horrors of the Civil War on a Virginian landscape already rich in history. The United States already had its own official interpreter of historical landscapes – the National Park Service. Fears over the Disneyfication of history – the rendering of the past as a corporate-spun whitewashed fantasy – eventually led to the cancellation of the project two years in. The lesson seemed to be that Disney and America were not synonymous after all.

Elsewhere, amusement and theme parks have increasingly 'played' with history. Stephen Fjellman associates Disney theme parks with the tag 'Distory', whereby Disney transforms the past into an optimistic, false, vacuum-cleaned vessel, a 'crafted amusement'. Not only Disney is guilty of producing 'Mickey Mouse History'. Theme parks continually tap historical episodes as context for rides and tourist environments. Inside the park, designers appropriate history as pure entertainment. Parks provide guests with a whimsical and kitsch take on periods such as the Wild West and medieval Europe. Rather than 'outdoor museums' that aim to evoke the ambiance of the past with some degree of accuracy, modern theme parks filter history through such a restrictive lens that what remains is often little more than popular folklore.[40]

Perhaps history has little place in the modern theme park, a compendium of 'worlds' that deliberately defies conventional logic of time and space. After all, theme parks exist to provide fun, not education. A stab at historic-themed recreation, Freedomland, New York (1960) promised '200 years of the American heritage' within boundaries that mimicked the contours of the continental United States. Yet the park lasted 4 years, and by the time of its closure resembled an atypical amusement park, with history-based shows replaced with bumper cars and rollercoasters. In common with video games and popular television, theme parks are not expected to produce sophisticated forums for intellectualism or historical analysis. Entertainment, not authenticity, matters most. None the less, the themed worlds produced in parks inevitably impart powerful messages. Surprisingly, the landscapes of Coney, Disney, Parc Asterix and Europa all convey similar codes. They bolster our faith in technology, corporations, economic wealth, personal satisfaction and consumption. They invoke history as a celebratory and linear story of progress, and paint the future as bright and fun. For all their frivolity, parks operate as didactic resources for the masses. Where once we looked to classical mythology and Shakespearian prose for instruction, we are now guided by Mickey and Asterix.

Meanwhile, history itself has not always been kind to the amusement and theme park genre. A scattering of defunct venues indicates the slim chance of survival within the amusement industry. Parks have opened and closed in the span of a few short years. Like circuses and fairs, theme parks sometimes proved temporary crowd-pleasers. Upon closure, elaborate park landscapes have been dismantled and removed, their only proof of existence left in city records or local newspapers. A few fan-based websites now exist that highlight this history of lost parks, with <www.defunctparks.com> providing a litany of more than 200 failed ventures in the United States alone.

A few historic park landscapes have nevertheless received protection, even resurrection. In 1975, Coney's Cyclone rollercoaster, first constructed in 1927, gained landmark status courtesy of the New York Parks Department, and joined the ride fraternity of Astroland Amusement Park (opened in 1962, but popularly welcomed as a vestige of Coney's traditional amusement scene). Australia's Luna Park reopened in 1998 thanks to lobbying by the Friends of Luna Park. The restoration project included the park's original carousel (1913), its scenic railway (1912), dodgems building, pretzel ride and fabled Mr Moon entrance. Slowly, it seems, visitors are coming to recognize their intimate love for older parks and the entertainment value contained within wooden coasters and horse carousels.

Parks that have survived the longest trade in the past, the present and the future, selling their history, the latest thrill rides, and visions of 'Tomorrowland'. Park owners innovate and experiment, but also keep token elements of the past, hoping to ensure that their park remains part of the cultural and geographical mind-set. As Karal Ann Marling remarks, 'Disneyland is so much a part of the American landscape that it's hard to imagine a time when the park wasn't there.' That same sense of permanence applies to Bakken, Blackpool and Tivoli, parks that fuse with their locality to become integral to regional distinctiveness. The lesson of the defunct theme park appears to be that, in order to survive, the park needs to reinvent itself. Otherwise 'dinosaurworld' becomes just a pile of old plastic bones, and the fantastical appeal of the park dies out.[41]

6 Trapping Nature in the Animal Park

Nobody quite knows the exact origin of the old American expression 'seeing the elephant'. Folklore has it that news of a travelling circus reached a pioneer agriculturalist with produce to sell. The farmer set off for town in the hope of selling his wares and witnessing an animal show to boot. On meeting the ensemble, the man stood in awe of its lead attraction – an elephant – but his horses bolted, leaving the cart upturned and his vegetables ruined. The farmer nevertheless considered the spectacle worth his tribulations. 'But I don't give a hang for I have seen the elephant,' he reputedly mused. By the time of the California Gold Rush of 1849, a real animal was no longer needed to give meaning to the phrase. Miners spoke of 'seeing the elephant', by which they referred to their Wild Western adventures, their fortunes and their follies. A half-century later, working-class vacationers on the Eastern seaboard talked of 'seeing the elephant' at Coney Island, by which they meant Elephantine Colossus, the themed hotel where all and sundry received a brush with the dangerous and the exotic.

Our love affair with elephants pre-dates the lure of Coney amusement park and the California Gold Rush by some centuries. For generations, people have wanted to see charismatic mammals. Romans put elephants on show (and into battle) in gladiatorial circuses. Ancient Chinese emperors gazed contemplatively at the wondrous beasts in their own private menageries. Alongside lions and tigers, elephants have been cast among the world's most entertaining, unusual and formidable beasts. Eagerness to witness such creatures has spawned the greatest of expeditions and adventures. However, rarely satisfied with watching an animal in its native habitat, successive traders, scientists, dignitaries and conservationists favoured collecting the world's species and displaying them first in menageries, then in zoological parks and, more recently, in wildlife parks. Animals have been captured and brought into the park as premier attractions.

THE FIRST ANIMAL PARKS

Humans have always collected animals. As early as 10000 BC, pre-literate hunter-gatherers trapped wolves and jackals in order to domesticate them. By 7000 BC, communities corralled goats, sheep and wild boar. The first bona fide animal collections emerged in ancient Egypt, China and Mesopotamia approximately 3,000 to 4,000 years ago. In Egypt, pharaohs received storks, baboons and gazelles (among others) as royal tribute. Egyptian royalty tamed their wild animals and kept them under strict guard in elaborate palaces. Some creatures were sacrificed in religious ceremonies, while others were mummified to accompany dignitaries into the afterlife. In 285 BC Alexandria, the Feast of Dionysus featured a spectacular procession, including nearly one hundred elephants, twenty-four lions and sixteen cheetahs. In China, emperors took similar pride in their faunal collections. Wen Wang of the Zhou dynasty founded the 'Park of Intelligence' (or Knowledge) around 1000 BC in the province of Henan (located between Beijing and Nanjing). The walled 900 acre park featured deer and antelope, as well as its own staff of keepers. During the rule of the Han dynasty, Emperor Wu Di set aside a reserve that married wilderness allure with seventy sumptuous palaces. Faunal residents of the park included swans, turtles, rhinos and elephants. Babylonians and Assyrians also kept exotic beasts in their royal parks. Gained through trade and gift-giving, rare animals such as lions found themselves caged or placed in pits. Enslavement bespoke the power and prestige of their owner. Lions, gazelles and birds of prey entertained visiting audiences, and provided exciting hunting opportunities inside vast hunting reserves. Animals undeniably enriched the park scene, granting it an ecological and aesthetic vitality. In 700 BC, Assyrian King Sennacherib (architect of an elaborate city park in Nineveh) carefully populated his 'themed' parks based on the Amanus Mountains in Syria and marshland in south Babylonia with representative flora and fauna.

The ancient civilizations of the Middle East not only maintained some of the earliest animal collections, but also produced one of the first animal stewardship narratives. In the *Epic of Gilgamesh*, the immortal Utnapishtim told of a great flood vented on the city Shuruppah by the gods. Forewarned by the divinity Ea, who commanded that he 'Tear down house, build a ship . . . Aboard the ship take thou the seed of all living things', Utnapishtim spent seven days constructing a boat, which he then filled with silver, gold, family, friends and 'the beasts of the field, the wild creatures of the field'. After both a dove and a swallow failed to find dry land, salvation arrived courtesy of a raven's 'caw' – signalling the finding of food and freedom. The *Epic of Gilgamesh* pre-dated by some centuries the tale of Noah's Ark as recounted in Genesis. In the biblical account, Noah collected two animals of each kind to board his vessel before God purged evil from the world. Both stories remain significant for connecting animal survival with human fortitude. More importantly, both situate humans as environmental stewards, directly responsible for overseeing (and confining) creatures for their better health. While latter-day park keepers rarely followed the precepts of Gilgamesh, the concept of Noah's Ark, with its hybrid ethos of collection and conservation, influenced countless zoological parks, and arguably still influences contemporary practice.

Ancient animal collections belonged mostly to ruling elites, who conceived of each lion and elephant as an acquisition rather than a responsibility. While marvelling at exotic creatures, most privileged citizens conceived the animal as a colourful symbol of regent authority. Rare species served the function of royal jewellery, animated palatial ornaments or fierce playthings. Like Disney's Mickey Mouse, they lived and died to entertain. The rise of the Roman Empire underlined fertile ties between territorial conquest and animal acquisition. Legions captured desirable species for transport directly to the emperor or for holding in stockyards (vivaria) in anticipation of public show. Animal combat regularly preceded gladiatorial bouts in Roman amphitheatres, faunal blood-letting a popular crowd-pleaser prior to the main contest. Engineered massacres at the *Venatio* thrilled audiences. The Circus Maximus in Rome staged mass culls of lions, bears, elephants and leopards. On one occasion, Septimus Severus arranged that a ship break apart in the arena only to unleash 100 animals for target practice. As the Roman Empire reached its zenith, the death toll rose to new heights. Celebrating military success over the Dacians, Emperor Trajan welcomed the killing of 11,000 animals in gladiatorial games that lasted some 3 months. Given dominant martial rituals in the Empire, it is of no surprise that most Romans considered animals primarily as entertaining beasts prized for their fighting skills. Animal collecting reflected the culture that sanctified it.

In ancient India, religion serviced a more benign attitude towards the natural world. Vedic Indian culture prominent in the region from 3000 BC postulated the care of birds and deer inside ashramas (monasteries). Embracing Jainism, a non-violent spiritual doctrine that forbade the killing of all creatures, Hindu leaders during the Gupta period (467–320 BC) passed early conservation laws. Emperor Chandragupta and his son Asoka banned hunting for sport. Asoka also founded pinjarapoles (translated as 'cage protectors') – animal hospitals promising care for sick creatures and spiritual reward for committed workers.

Accounts from Rome and India reveal that ancient attitudes towards wildlife varied from the barbaric to the enlightened. However, despite their differences, many civilizations enshrined the collection and confinement of animals as a habit. Whether for conservation, entertainment, domestic purposes or aesthetic appeal, all kinds of mammals, birds and reptiles found themselves captured and killed by human stewards.[1]

THE EUROPEAN MENAGERIE

Animal collecting in medieval times remained the preserve of European dignitaries. Henry I kept a variety of exotic animals at Woodstock Park in the late eleventh century. After receiving the rare gift of an elephant from Louis IX, Henry III ordered appropriate animal housing to be constructed at the Tower of London to cater for his prized acquisition. Pope Leo X owned an elephant, while Pope Benedict XII boasted an enviable collection of ostriches. The practice of animal collecting proved piecemeal, unscientific and dependent on tribute. During the European Renaissance (1350–1600), fresh interest in science, philosophy, trade and conquest fuelled a significant rise in animal collecting, and led to the emergence of many new menageries. Exploration of Africa, Asia and the Americas revealed hitherto unheard-of species. Through networks of trade and diplomatic gifts, prominent European countries came to house an array of beasts not seen since the fall of the Roman Empire.

Personal menageries became fashionable among the wealthy. Enlightenment philosopher and scientist Francis Bacon declared the need for all rulers to have their own zoological parks. Bacon elaborated on an ideal area 'to be built about with Rooms, to stable in all rare Beasts, and to cage in all rare Birds; with two Lakes adjoining, the one of fresh Water, and the other of salt, for like variety of Fishes: And so you may have, in a small Compass, a Model of Universal Nature made private'. Bacon saw nature as something to analyse, to comprehend and, significantly, to control. His views encapsulated the humanist presentation of nature as eminently rational, understandable and reductive. Thanks to powers of intellect and the ability to reason, *Homo sapiens* assumed superiority over all other species. In the 1730s, Swedish botanist Carl von Linné forwarded his *Systema Naturae* of classification for the natural world, which radically shifted the rules of animal collecting. Prior to the Linnean model, classification systems had proved bewildering and abstract with animals rated according to human utility or simple aesthetics. Linné provided a scientific, rational and universal system based on genus and species – a categorization applicable to the entire animal kingdom.[2]

Ideas of scientific progress combined with the kudos attached to owning rare specimens. The evolving menagerie at the Tower of London, with its castle façade and defensive countenance, hardly fitted Bacon's zoological template, yet it housed an impressive array of species. The menagerie at Versailles (1663) proved more befitting of Bacon's gentrified ideal of organized faunal viewing. Cages surrounded a central pavilion, enabling guests to muse on successive animal characters by gazing from the plaza or by walking paths that skirted each enclosure. To reach the theatre of animals, the French elite rode gondolas along the Grand Canal. Violinists provided aural ambiance.

Wealthy aristocrats emulated royalty in establishing their own Baconian 'Model of Universal Nature'. Marrying traditional Christian teachings with new scientific rationalism, observers read the story of Noah as a biblical parable on the virtues of collection and classification. Animals none the less failed to wander on to boats and into storage crates in a docile and orderly fashion, two by two. Faunal acquisition proved treacherous for traders, and even more dangerous for their cargo. With little clue as to each creature's environmental, social or dietary needs, things often went disastrously wrong. *En route* to Venice in the early 1500s, trader Gonzalo Valdes fed a barrel filled with earth to an exotic iguana, who died soon after. The situation rarely improved on reaching European menageries, with keepers seldom prepared for caring for unusual and demanding creatures. Visions of healthy animal paradises expounded by Noah and Bacon eluded Renaissance collectors. With an ever increasing number of new species being discovered, and few means to secure them, many collectors favoured representative, or 'postage stamp', animal collections. Cabinets of stuffed animals proved easier to stock and exhibit than cages of live ones – the museum rather than the zoological garden thus gained precedence.

Along with scientific endeavour and social prestige, European menageries continued to service a human longing for blood-letting. Ivan the Terrible, who ruled Russia between 1530 and 1584, betrayed few stewardship principles in his Moscow bear pits. Viewed as representatives of Russian power and courage, bears became unconscious foot soldiers in class wars and religious altercations. Ivan entertained visiting elites with ursine versus peasant combat, while defiant monks met their maker courtesy of bruin claws. Staged animal fights in Hetzgarten (hunting gardens) in sixteenth-century Germany likewise paid homage to Roman gladiatorial bouts, all primal gore and barbarism. One battle almost led to the demise of sovereign Joachim II (1505–71), when an angry bear broke through barricades surrounding a fighting arena and headed towards the ruler. Hunters quickly intervened.

The presence of bear fights in Renaissance Europe indicated the limits of human sympathy for animals. Pertinently, the European menagerie took its name from the French word *ménage*, meaning to manage or control. Along with servants, monks and peasants, elephants and lions served as the subjects of royal masters. While the fad for animal confinement stoked scientific discovery, caged animals said more about elite owners, their vices and their grip on power. On reaching Tenochtitlán (now Mexico City) in 1519, Spanish explorer Hernando Cortés showed little respect for animals interned inside a huge zoological garden built by Aztec King Montezuma II. Treating it simply as an organic symbol of Montezuma's reign, Cortés destroyed the entire collection and slaughtered its 600 keepers.

NINETEENTH-CENTURY ANIMAL SHOWS AND ZOOS

As a prominent symbol of royal authority, the menagerie tied animal collecting to an antiquated social and political system. Industrialization, the rise of scientific societies, and a newly organized proletariat reshaped the cultural landscape of eighteenth- and nineteenth-century Europe. In turn, animal collecting evolved to cater for a mass audience. The private menagerie gave way to the public zoological garden, captive faunal assemblages shifting geographically from country palaces to city parkscapes in the process. On occasion, the transition between menagerie and zoo directly mirrored shifts in European political fortunes. During the French Revolution, an angry mob descended on the menagerie at Versailles, slaughtering the totem animals of King Louis XVI (Louis was himself famously guillotined in 1793). Six faunal survivors of the Revolution, including a rare quagga, were later rehoused at the Jardin des Plantes, a zoological garden open to all French citizenry and approved by none other than the National Revolutionary Convention.

Nascent scientific societies assisted the transition from menagerie to zoo. The newly formed National Museum of Natural History (Muséum d'Histoire Naturelle) oversaw the early operation of the Jardin des Plantes. London Zoo (1828) arose from the concerted efforts of the Zoological Society of London, an organization founded by Sir Stamford Raffles in 1826. In an early official prospectus, members expressed their 'deep regret to the cultivators of Natural History that we possess no great scientific establishments either for teaching or elucidating zoology'. The opening of London Zoological Gardens filled such a niche. On accession to the throne in 1830, William IV donated myriad animals formerly kept in the Tower of London to the fledgling zoo. Upon closure of the tower menagerie in 1832, keepers transferred the remaining stock.[3]

Boasting a newly opened animal garden, the Zoological Society of London quickly became an institution of worldwide repute. A combination of science and spectacle drew the urban gentry to the zoological landscape. The sheer range of species on view, coupled with the ability of keepers to arrange them by taxonomic classification, impressed educated guests. The zoo environment also encouraged scientific thought and debate. The first imported orang-utan attracted the interest of Charles Darwin, a new society member in 1831, who went on to write *The Origin of Species* (1859). Meanwhile, the growing store of creatures on public display inspired a fresh wave of private acquisitions. Education and study combined with an ardent collecting ethos. Affluent Englishmen willingly parted with their cash to acquire curious exhibits (both live and dead) from international animal dealers. The more unusual the species, the more cachet its owner achieved. Collections reeked of elitism. Consisting largely of wealthy and educated members, the Zoological Society initially resisted opening its gardens to the public. The accumulation of scientific knowledge failed to spell democratization automatically. Gates to the private playground were finally opened to the masses in 1847. London Zoo proved unrivalled for its scientific innovation in the decades that followed, boasting the world's first reptile house (1849), public aquarium (1853) and insect house (1881).

Sometimes the transition from menagerie to zoological park came not from revolution or scientific erudition, but from a gradual expansion in animal attractions. At Schönbrunn (derived from *schöner brunnen*, meaning 'beautiful fountain'), Austria's answer to Versailles, a zoological arrangement grew sporadically over several decades. Established in 1752, the menagerie at Schönbrunn Palace featured an impressive baroque architectural style and through its tenure housed elephants, wolves and even a giraffe. Its design template, which closely resembled the Versailles model, featured a circular pavilion with avenues flowing outwards towards geometrically arranged animal enclosures. Adored by royalty and public alike – Franz Josef (1830–1916) allegedly visited the collection every day, while Austrian citizens were free to enter as they pleased – Schönbrunn persisted as Vienna's premier animal attraction throughout the nineteenth century, with only minor changes. In the 1880s, curator Alois Klause finally transformed the menagerie into an official zoological park by adding bars, new enclosures and a wider range of species.

Aside from their fresh scientific dogmatism, the zoological parks of the 1700s and 1800s bore many similarities to their antecedents. Zoological ensembles drew heavily on past animal shows – the travelling circus merely replaced with a stationary and more sombre façade. Paying aesthetic homage to historic palaces and menageries, zoo landscapes favoured pompous and fantastical structures. Founded on a former royal hunting ground, Berlin Zoo opened in 1844. From the 1870s onwards, the institution attracted increasingly indulgent building projects. The venue gained fame for its outlandish palatial architecture, including a magnificent Egyptian temple for housing ostriches and a mosque accommodating monkeys. Early zoos also exhibited the same kind of animals that adorned older menageries. The presence of elephants and big cats – species favoured by visitors – conferred status on pioneer zoological establishments. Audiences expected to see large and fierce animals – charismatic mega-fauna with large teeth, tusks or trunks. Just as lion-filled menageries symbolized the stature of royalty in prior centuries, so well-stocked nineteenth-century zoological parks celebrated nationalism and conquest. London Zoo reflected the pride of the British Empire, caged animals testifying to imperial glories, exploration and land holdings. Trade, tribute and resource extraction allowed many European zoos to prosper. A colonial mind-set meanwhile melded the goal of imperial acquisition with scientific progress, empire with empiricism. The European zoological park emerged as an iconic landscape by presenting live trophies of the Age of Exploration to a public audience, while institutions such as the British Museum found acclaim by archiving the inanimate plunder of empire-builders. Traversing the zoological landscape reminded Europeans of their assumed superiority over exotic animals and other cultures. The zoological park, at heart, served as a popular symbol of power at home and abroad.[4]

In colonies themselves, zoos emerged as the pet projects of ambassadors or developed from holding areas initially designed for animal transportation to home countries. British diplomat Henry Southern helped establish the first zoo in Buenos Aires, Argentina (1840). In Vietnam, the French established Saigon Zoo in Ho Chi Minh City (1864) using the Jardin des Plantes as a blueprint. The premier status of London Zoo and the Jardin des Plantes fostered various attempts to mimic the colonial zoological enterprise. Widely regarded as the first Japanese zoo, Euno Zoo, Tokyo (1882), received funding from the national government, but was none the less inspired by the Jardin des Plantes. The first American zoological park opened in Philadelphia in 1874, thanks to ardent lobbying by the Zoological Society of Philadelphia. Members looked to British zoo keeping for guidance, with the chief engineer of the fledgling park travelling to London for insight. An imposing Victorian gatehouse welcomed Philadelphia's most dignified. Visiting the zoo in 1878, journalist M. Howland applauded the zoological society for attaining 'the air and general appearance of famous long-established like institutions in Europe'.[5]

Given the multicultural history of animal collecting, zoo building unsurprisingly derived from more than just the colonial mind-set. In Egypt, Giza Zoo (1891) emerged thanks to the combined, but uncoordinated efforts of native ecologist and Egyptian viceroy Ismail Pasha and British naturalist Stanley Smyth Flower. Pasha had been dedicated to the idea of a zoo since the opening of the Suez Canal in 1869, although the British claimed credit for the gardens that eventually sprang up. In India, early zoos similarly developed from the intersection of imperial and indigenous interests. Governor Richard Wellesley, responsible for Barrackpore Zoo, conceived of the zoo idea as a way to learn more about Indian natural history rather than as a simple vehicle of conquest. Rajah Rajendro Mullick Bahadar set up Marple Palace Zoo for similar educational purposes. Indian royalty financed Calcutta Zoo, whose first director, Ram Brahma Sanyal, wrote the world's first scientific management guide to zoos in 1892.

Animal trading in the 1800s became a profitable commercial enterprise. Motivated more by business interest than patriotic sentiment, dealers sold to circuses, private collectors and laboratories, as well as zoological societies. Renowned for their abilities to locate the strangest creatures, Texan Frank Buck and German Carl Hagenbeck led the animal trade in the late nineteenth century. A capable self-publicist, Buck drew on personal hunting trips to South America, South Asia and the West Indies for a series of 'Bring' Em Back Alive' adventure books. His trapping fame later engendered roles in several action-packed Hollywood jungle movies of the 1940s.

Fecund links between animal collecting and popular entertainment were much in evidence. Phineas T. Barnum convincingly merged entertainment with showmanship in advertising his touring menageries thus: '1,009 rare animals advantageously displayed in electric-lighted dens where they may be studied at close range in the mammoth travelling university of natural history'. Barnum also displayed fantastical corpses at his American Museum in New York, notably the 'Feejee Mermaid' (the withered body of a monkey joined to a fish tail and passed off as a real mermaid). Meanwhile, animal acts drew popular interest at Coney Island. Captain Jack Bonavita, a one-armed animal trainer (his other arm had been bitten off by a lion named Baltimore), ran a successful circus at Dreamland Park, until fire swept through Coney in 1911 and destroyed much of the menagerie. Elephants and parrots rubbed shoulders with all manner of human curiosities at the circus: all freaks alike to the enthralled masses.[6]

Zoo, circus and animal shows certainly competed for creatures, staff and punters. In 1882, Barnum procured Jumbo, an African bull elephant, from London Zoo for the substantial sum of $10,000. At one point, Jumbo had been the property of Jardin des Plantes, but Londoners welcomed him into their hearts when he arrived at the British zoo in 1865. Traders ultimately recognized little difference in the shopping lists provided by circuses, zoos and private collectors. The National Zoo in Washington, DC, thus received offers of four-winged roosters, albino racoons and other 'freak' creations from willing salesmen. Accustomed to the outlandish advertisements favoured by circus and sideshow exhibitors, visitors to the zoological park expected a lavish entertainment spectacle. Zoo directors duly pandered to public tastes by seeking out exotic creatures as well as inaugurating their own experiments in animal entertainment. In 1850, 300,000 visitors passed through the gates of London Zoo in order to stare in awe at Obaysch the hippopotamus. Early reptile houses provided similar thrills, especially during snake feeding sessions.[7]

Zoo directors none the less sought to differentiate their animal parks from competing animal shows and historic menageries. In the main, staff promoted education and knowledge over freakish titillation. Zoological parks bespoke social affluence, cultural and cerebral discourse, and civic modernity. By the end of the nineteenth century, conservation methods and scientific initiatives separated the zoological park from the travelling animal show. Changing designs and uses meanwhile signalled the end of the zoological park as a colonial property.

In Australia, the first zoological parks spawned from acclimatization pens used for imported animals. The Zoological Society of Victoria introduced exotic animals to the country in the 1860s, using the zoo platform as a means of rearing and domesticating game species and songbirds prior to their release. Adelaide Zoo (1883) opened thanks to the efforts of the South Australian Zoological and Acclimatization Society. Many creatures flourished courtesy of the project, though not all proved welcome additions to Australia's faunal complement. Introduced ungulates disrupted local habitat, while the Victoria Society was wrongfully blamed for bringing the rabbit to Australia.

In the United States, concerns over endangered species fuelled calls for zoological parks to serve as venues for conservation. The precarious state of the native bison population, brought on by sport and commercial hunting in the 1880s, led naturalist William Hornaday to campaign for zoological parks as refuges for the great American bovine. Hornaday saw the zoo as a sanctuary for animals threatened with extinction, a protected landscape where industry, hunting and agriculture could not impact on America's cherished fauna. He also recognized a need to extend city zoo enclosures in order to provide room to roam for large animals such as the bison. Hornaday joined forces with the New York Zoological Society – an institution comprised of members sympathetic to conservation measures, including, most notably, Theodore Roosevelt. Founded in 1895, the Society campaigned for 'a free zoological park' providing not only entertainment to the public, but education too. Such an institution would also aid 'in the preservation of the native animals of North America', the park collection tangible proof of 'the growing sentiment against their wanton destruction'. Zoos hence became a vehicle for highlighting the plight of endangered species, and began serving as breeding centres for the purposes of animal reintroduction. The New York Zoological Park (Bronx Zoo) opened in 1899, with Hornaday as its director. The enclave soon grew to include an ornate elephant house, a reptile house, a sea lion pond and a bison paddock. In 1907, authorities transported fifteen bison raised in

captivity to Wichita Mountain Preserve in Oklahoma. Along with conservationist measures instigated by Yellowstone National Park, the scheme at the
Bronx Zoo helped save the American buffalo.[8]

Zoos nevertheless proved imperfect sanctuaries for imperilled creatures.
The directors of Cincinnati Zoo, established in 1875, strove to sustain a
healthy population of passenger pigeons inside park confines, while extinction loomed outside. The collection featured twenty birds by 1881. In 1899,
the Zoo promised a $1,000 reward for any pair that could be hauled from
precarious freedom to captive safety inside the park landscape. 'Martha', the
last passenger pigeon in the world, died at Cincinnati Zoo in 1914. The
divergent fates of the American bison and the passenger pigeon ably indicated
the pros and cons of zoo conservation.

Park keepers exercised more care over their animal exhibits as the twentieth
century dawned. Authorities slowly recognized that the best way to care for
animals was to offer them facsimiles of their natural habitats, rather than place
them in simple cages arranged for aesthetics and easy viewing. At Giza Zoo in
Cairo, Egypt, moats rather than fences separated viewer from animal. A 1902
guidebook for Giza promoted a cogent conservation ethos in its aim to 'stimulate and foster in people a love for animals and plants and to promote the
science of biology'. Animal dealer Carl Hagenbeck revolutionized zoo planning by creating a Tierpark (a German zoo park) near Hamburg in 1907 famed
for situating animals in their natural settings (a technique now called 'natural
immersion'). Hagenbeck transformed 25 acres of potato fields into a series of
'panoramas' constructed from a range of artificial and natural materials. Arctic
and African enclosures gave the impression of neat slices of ecosystem transported to park quarters. Patrons gazed on picture-perfect montages of wilderness without iron bars. Crucially, by grouping animals according to their biotic
environment rather than by their scientific classification, Hagenbeck reunited
species on the same kindred turf. Initially, the inspirational Tierpark blueprint
proved too radical a break for some zoo directors by its focus on geographic
rather than taxonomic factors in zoo design. In latter years, the 'habitat zoo'
none the less emerged as the industry standard (see fig. 7).[9]

Unlike animal shows, which relied on gaudy advertisements and novelty
value for their popularity, the urban zoological park depended on a productive relationship with the city and the wider park movement for its survival in
the late nineteenth and early twentieth centuries. Although individual exhibits
became more environmentally ambitious, the zoo itself remained trapped
within city boundaries. Zoos sprang up within the confines of existing urban
playgrounds much to the horror of city park designers who favoured more
uncluttered forms of public recreation. From the 1860s, an impromptu
menagerie developed in Central Park thanks to gifts of unwanted pets and
cast-offs from circus shows (including Barnum's travelling menagerie).
Frederick Law Olmsted deplored the uncontrolled degeneration of his park
Eden and castigated London Zoo for taking up valuable greensward in
Regent's Park. Despite such protestations, the city zoo nevertheless built on

*Figure 7. Opening of Tierpark Hagenbeck, main entrance, 7 May 1907.
Reproduced courtesy of Archiv Hagenbeck. © Archiv Hagenbeck.*

established park ideals of recreation, entertainment, escapism and nature making. In 1891, a writer for the *Atlantic Monthly* duly proposed that 'the city park, if developed to its highest power, should give the necessary space for zoological gardens'.[10] Like the city park, the zoological park responded to the desires of urbanites for reminders of their rural past. Its naturalistic veneer offered temporary reprieve from industrial worlds. Somehow bringing monkeys to the urban jungle aided human acclimatization to the city. Zoos also bolstered civic pride and community identity.

Such attractions brought the city to the animal, as well as the animal to the city. In a sense, zoological parks themselves advanced the concept of fauna-inhabited cities. With animal districts, meandering paths and shopping areas, the zoo park certainly shared similarities with life beyond its confines. In Chicago, Lincoln Park Zoo was known simply as the 'animal town'. Meanwhile, urban society resolutely influenced life inside the enclave. Rowdy visitors often failed to treat faunal residents courteously. The Bronx Zoo struggled to enforce restrictions on alcohol use. Urban development ultimately restricted the size and development of zoological landscapes, keeping animals in cages rather than letting them loose in open spaces.

The advent of war underlined the difficult relationship between the city and the zoological park. Caught in the midst of military conflict, exotic animals suffered from geopolitical exigencies. World War I caused shortages and deprivation at many European zoos. A Hagenbeck-owned elephant named Jenny enrolled by the German army to clear trees and lift heavy loads miraculously survived the conflict. Others were not so fortunate. Two-thirds of the inmates of Schönbrunn Zoo (some 2,000 animals) died due to food shortages and illness. Due to their location in city centres, many zoological parks came under intense fire from bombing raids during World War II. Berlin Zoo lost most of its buildings, and only ninety-one animals survived the Allied attacks. The Japanese government ordered the destruction of larger zoo animals for the purposes of political propaganda (to blame the Allies for home sacrifices) and for safety reasons (in case accidentally released predators caused havoc). Elephants deliberately starved to death at Euno Zoo vividly demonstrated the horrors of war and belied the reputation of the zoological park as a faunal sanctum.

WILDLIFE PARKS

Most zoological parks survived the rigours of war. At Higashiyama Zoo in Nagoya, Japan, two elephants famously escaped death, while at Leningradsky Zoo in St Petersburg, Russia, 'Beauty' the hippo found her rations reduced from 56 kilograms of food to just 4–6 per day, yet still prevailed. Post-war rebuilding projects enabled parks to recover some of their lost animals, structures and revenues. With only its bear castle surviving wartime bombing, Frankfurt Zoo in Germany rebounded thanks to the efforts of zoo director Bernhard Grzimek, who embraced new conservation design philosophies in reconstructing the park. Dilapidated Japanese zoos, including Ueno, benefited from a range of animal donations from Hogle Zoo, Utah. A post-war boom in recreation further aided park recovery. Frankfurt employed poster advertisements and multi-species exhibits to lure new visitors, while the birth of Brumas, a polar bear, drew crowds to London Zoo in 1949.

In some cases, the post-war zoological park metamorphosed into a much larger and more spectacular version of itself: the safari or wildlife park. Paying homage to the African game park traversed by colonial forefathers, the sixth marquis of Bath converted the grounds of his Longleat estate into Britain's first safari park in the mid-1960s. A landscape designed by 'Capability' Brown in the 1750s found new life in the twentieth century as a zoological exhibit based on exotic locales and their animated residents. Attempting to simulate an African safari in the green groves of Wiltshire, Longleat's designers established several large enclosures, each one surrounded by fences and navigable by automobile. Imported beasts of the chase filled stretches of habitat that some centuries earlier had boasted native deer, wolves and wild pigs. Longleat's replication of the expansive savannah found in Kruger made England seem wild again. Despite the obvious (and insurmountable) ecological differences between the two countries, the claim of the safari park to offer 'Africa in the Heart of England' wooed those who possessed the requisite imagination to transplant the velt to rural Wiltshire. Longleat – emblematic of a new kind of animal park – allowed faunal charges to socialize and to exercise on a scale impossible in city zoos. The conservation aspect of the safari park featured highly in the promotional literature. Visitors were invited to Longleat to see 'Wild animals roam as Nature intended'. By the 1990s, the attraction had evolved into a chameleon-like entity influenced by all manner of amusement genres. Along with the traditional safari adventure, visitors could wander around a Doctor Who science fiction exhibit, a simulator amusement, pets' corner, a children's castle and a maze. Incorporating several park ideals, Longleat projected itself as an amusement park, a country park and an animal park, all in one.[11]

Common interests in conservation and science helped the safari park prosper. Zoological societies emerged as active lobbyists for wildlife parks. In British Columbia, Canada, Kamloops Zoological Society and the Kamloops Wildlife Park resulted from discussions at a public meeting and a starting budget of just $15. Thanks to significant donations from local businesses (including 122 acres of land), together with volunteer work, the Wildlife Park opened in 1965. San Diego Zoo designer Charles Faust aided in the project. A similar vision of like-minded individuals coming together for a mutual cause played out at Christchurch, New Zealand. In the early 1970s, the South Island Zoological Society proposed a new-style wildlife park in the region. In 1976, Orana Park – Maori for place of refuge or welcome – opened.

The safari park idea proved popular with designers who sought to extend traditional zoo landscapes. Safari-like additions to existing parks served to modernize the zoo concept and make it more amenable to conservation-minded critics. Expansive wildlife enclosures fostered successes in captive-breeding programmes and allowed directors to present their zoological parks as rightful homes for endangered fauna. The allure of the safari excursion also encouraged fresh visits to the zoo. First opened in 1959, India's Nehru Zoological Park generated new business by providing guided tours through lion, tiger, bear and gaur territories. In 1994, Singapore Zoological Gardens hosted the world's first Night Safari. Patrons travelled by tram through a rare tropical jungle under the cover of darkness, viewing up to 1,000 nocturnal species. Conservation had never been so exciting.

The popularity of the wildlife or safari park rested on its measured revision of the zoo park template. By its sheer size, the wildlife park magnified the conservationist message of zoology. The increase in space granted to exotic creatures equated to a concomitant rise in environmental respect. The next step on from Hagenbeck's 'natural immersion' Tierpark, the wildlife park pro-vided dedicated biotic zones based on animal rather than human preferences. By means of 'ecological theming', the wildlife park articulated a creditable rationale that animals only made sense if viewed in the context of their natural surroundings. Only then would visitors observe their true behaviour. What made a monkey a monkey was its habits and interaction with other monkeys, as well as its biological persona. To genuinely see such a creature mandated a trip to the rainforest, or, increasingly, a visit to the nearest wildlife park. Given that the history of animal entertainment revolved around choreography and performance, the success of the wildlife park depended on the willingness of audiences to revise their expectations of faunal behaviour. With this in mind, wildlife managers promoted realistic animal antics such as sleeping and eating as far more enthralling viewing than contrived simian picnics and lion-taming stunts. Drawing on the popularity of bird-watching as a pastime, the wildlife park asserted the mechanics of observational entertainment. The beauty of the safari park lay in its ability to create an interface between human and animal, to reconstruct the experience found in traditional zoos while adding ecological principles. By making cages larger, less noticeable and ecologically consistent, the safari park gave the illusion of a verdant wilderness crammed with exciting creatures. Drivers were warned to enter the parks at their own risk, especially when some species developed a penchant for disassembling car facia and wing mirrors. By manipulating our perceptions of space, animals no longer seemed trapped or caged, but rather, free and untamed. Far more successfully than London or Berlin zoos, safari parks fulfilled a human longing to enter a kingdom of animals, to get close to the lion in his den, to enter a domain where nature rules.

However, as simulations of wilderness, wildlife parks rarely achieved the total authenticity promised by the safari motif. Tourists wanted thrills and titillation, but scarcely desired an experience of the hardships associated with excursions to remote locations filled with the world's most formidable predators. Despite the sizeable acreage, managed landscapes failed to capture the spirit of the African savannah. Instead, the more contrived safari parks often resembled nature-based theme parks, fun-filled facsimiles of the great outdoors. In place of poorly paid staff dressed as giant mice and ducks in Disneyland stood real lions and tigers. Faunal performers populated the wildlife park, their designated role: to entertain. Prescribed routes, trash bins, gift shops, miniature trains and car lots undoubtedly detracted from the safari fantasy. Ironically, Disney, the organization responsible for introducing theme parks to the world, arguably offered the purest safari experience at its Animal Kingdom (1998), a satellite of the Magic Kingdom in Orlando, Florida. The Disney Corporation inevitably treated Animal Kingdom as one of its theme parks during design phases. Real creatures simply replaced audio-animatronic ones. Some 100,000 trees and 4 million shrubs replaced the usual plastic horticulture. Rather than employing ecological or taxonomic classification systems, Animal Kingdom provided separate 'worlds' based on *The Jungle Book*, *The Lion King* and other popular stories, an approach familiar to all Disney park devotees. Yet, despite its evident cartoon spin, Disney articulated a holism in its nature park that other venues rarely matched. Animal enclosures received the same attention to detail lavished on Sleeping Beauty's famous Castle. The Kilimanjaro Safari, covering some 120 acres of land, took guests close to rhino and giraffe courtesy of all-terrain vehicles. The wholesale disguising of zoo artefacts such as feeding troughs and cages alongside perfectly maintained African flora made Kilimanjaro one of the most authentic safari experiences outside Africa. Once again the Disney facsimile of real life wowed audiences. Some 6 million visited Animal Kingdom in its opening year.

Significantly, Disney's wildlife park was less predicated on species conservation than typical wildlife parks. Instead, Disney Imagineering brought together animals in order to entertain a human clientele. Disney spiel, cartoon stories and mass merchandising thereby simplified and cheapened the message of the Animal Kingdom. The Kilimanjaro Safari represented a theme park ride rather than a wilderness epiphany. Nature remained the plaything of Disney, the lion 'red in tooth and claw' invisibly but inextricably tethered to the synthetic mouse.

The same ambiguities of corporate-engineered conservation compromised Seaworld, California, a pioneering marine-based incarnation of the wildlife park. Opened in 1964, Seaworld modernized the nineteenth-century public aquarium by offering large displays, walk-through tunnels beneath giant tanks, whale and dolphin shows, and hands-on interaction with aquatic residents. Shamu, a captive orca became the star attraction amidst Seaworld's choreography of water entertainment. With its amenable blend of education, personal contact, conservation and amusement, the San Diego marine park proved immensely popular, attracting some 4 million visitors per season.

On the surface, Seaworld worked wonders, yet problems lurked below the waterline. As with Disney's Animal Kingdom, Seaworld encouraged visitors to satisfy their sense of environmental responsibility through consumption. By simply attending animal shows and buying mementos of their trip, guests convinced themselves that both park and attendee boasted a laudable ecological agenda. Rather than having time to individualize each marine experience, visitors were herded along conveyor-belt tours. Successive snapshots of interned marine animals afforded little opportunity for independent thought or detailed interpretive education. In addition, Seaworld arguably contradicted its publicly proclaimed conservation message by its private treatment of marine 'entertainers'. Orcas and dolphins resided in cramped environments, learning their 'rightful' behaviour from human trainers. The family-oriented film *Free Willy* (1993), along with publicity by dolphin and whale advocacy associations, highlighted the plight of marine mammals inside wildlife centres and amusement parks. Intelligent and sociable creatures had become simple circus entertainers, dressed in contrived conservation garb as a mechanism to assure public acceptability. On a scale of priorities, captive marine wildlife served entertainment first, profit second, and conservation third. Keiko the killer whale, star of *Free Willy*, resided in Reino Aventura amusement park, Mexico, suffering from skin lesions, until a conservation campaign financed his rehabilitation at the Oregon Coast Aquarium. In 2002, Keiko moved to free waters in the North Atlantic (though he has since died).

THE ZOOLOGICAL PARK QUESTIONED

On 4 January 1903, 1,500 spectators gathered to watch an elephant nicknamed Topsy give her last performance at Fred Thompson's Luna Park on Coney Island. Ever since her arrival in the United States in 1875, Topsy had entertained audiences across the country. Unfortunately, several keepers had been killed by Topsy, including an inebriated trainer who encouraged her to smoke cigarettes but met stern resistance. Recognizing the publicity and profit to be had from punishing the 'man-killer', Thompson advertised a public execution. Following a feeding of cyanide-laced carrots, Topsy received a lethal dose of electricity from none other than Thomas Edison. As the New York-based *Commercial Advertiser* described it, 'The big beast died without a trumpet or a groan.'[12]

Behind the death of Topsy lay a broader tale highlighting the poor treatment of animals in the late nineteenth century, an age when humans regarded exotic creatures as curiosities, commodities and freakish spectacles. Parks provided ideal public forums for displaying caged fauna and exhibiting human cruelty towards the natural world. By the end of the twentieth century, much had changed in the exhibition and treatment of animals. None the less, the offspring of Topsy continued to be used for entertainment purposes at a variety of parkscapes, from Disney's Animal Kingdom and Seaworld to thousands of zoological parks across the globe. Animals unceasingly served as animated attractions in amusement, theme and wildlife parks. In the 1970s, animal rights discourse engaged with the animal park in a critical fashion, highlighting the problems of faunal exploitation for the purposes of human gratification. Peter Singer's *Animal Liberation* (1975) became the makeshift bible of ardent animal rights campaigners. Investigative campaigns by animal welfare groups such as Zoocheck and Born Free also illuminated the hardships endured by park inhabitants. In 1990, the Royal Society for the Prevention of Cruelty to Animals (RSPCA) filed a report on animal captivity in China, including documentation on the horrors of Beijing Zoo, a place where chained elephants rested in their own faeces and visitors routinely tormented interned gorillas. A 2001 report on ten Indonesian zoos by the World Society for the Protection of Animals (WSPA) classified 99 per cent of animal enclosures as failing to meet even the most basic needs of faunal residents. Investigators documented the widespread beating of bears, orang-utans and elephants to make them perform in shows and before cameras. Some 50 per cent of inmates showed indications of the psychological condition 'zoochosis', trauma characterized by stereotypic behaviour such as continual pacing and swaying. The report received such publicity that several zoos agreed to significant overhauls.

For critics, the zoological park underlined, rather than challenged, a relationship of dominance between humans and the rest of the natural world. Zoos provided arenas where nature operated under the purview of sapient overlords, parks demonstrative of our power as well as our stewardship over the natural world. Traditionally constructed for human attendees rather than animal residents – the 'park' badge cementing the primacy of visitation – the zoo disguised the permanence of animals living out segregated and mediated lives. For animal rights activists, the zoo signified a faunal concentration camp, a prison where animals lost their identity, rather than a place where wilderness could be re-seeded. They believed that zoological parks in Europe, America and Asia were archaic remnants of a Victorian age, and needed to be closed down.

While many zoos declined in the late twentieth century, not all animal inmates languished in cages only to be harassed by tourists. In 1976, landscape architects came up with a plan to redesign Woodland Park Zoo in Seattle, based on the idea of landscape immersion, an approach harkening back to Hagenbeck's panoramas. Woodland Park expanded on the original Tierpark concept by encouraging its patrons to walk through settings, to be a part of the scene, and hopefully by their experience to recognize species interaction and ecological interdependence. By furnishing native forage and opportunities for movement, the project promoted an enriched life for animal patrons too. Founded by the local zoological society, San Diego's Zoo, Wild Animal Park and Center for Reproduction of Endangered Species (CRES) garnered acclaim for its conservation credentials. With a strong environmental message and high standards of veterinary science, San Diego Zoo in the 1990s bore little resemblance to its starting point in 1916 as a collection of caged creatures left over from an International Expo in Balboa City Park. Opened as a partner organization to the zoo in 1972, the San Diego Wild Animal Park demonstrated the importance of offering species natural habitats of decent size and quality. The 1,800 acre site fostered significant captive-breeding successes, most notably with Arabian oryx and cheetahs. Off limits to the public, CRES operated as the dedicated research wing of the zoological establishment. Meanwhile, in European cities, zoo managers finally recognized necessary limits to their geographic space. Bristol Zoo in England gradually shifted its attention from charismatic and exotic mega-fauna to displaying those creatures happiest in smaller environments, such as insects and reptiles. Through the latter decades of the twentieth century, standards of care improved substantially. With increasing restrictions on animal trafficking, zoo directors recognized that the future of their organizations and the fate of rare species remained interlinked. By saving endangered creatures, zoos could ensure their own validity and survival.

Though questioned about their conservation ethics, post-war zoos demonstrated a variety of uses to society outside the conventional arena of animal welfare. The zoological park continued to fulfil human longings for freedom, recreation and wilderness. According to Elizabeth Hanson, American zoos 'offered people an escape from the cement, stress and physical confinement of the city to a lush landscaped park'. Hanson rightly acknowledged how 'A trip to the zoo has long been presented as a journey into nature'. A fascination for the natural world drew people to the zoological park, despite the irony of animals assuming a captive existence in the concrete jungle precisely to satisfy such human predilections. Zoos provided a reminder of rural life, wild nature and undomesticated creatures. Caged lions thus served as symbols of raw wilderness.[13]

Comparison of the modern wildlife park to the medieval menagerie indicates how far we have come in our environmental sensibilities, and how the zoo format has evolved into a (some would say flawed) linchpin of animal conservation while shedding many of its barbaric roots. Zoological parks offer stories of scientific discovery, of learning about animal behaviour and habitat. In the nineteenth century, Barnum passed off natural curiosities as contrived as the 'Feejee mermaid' as biotic truth. Now we are that little bit wiser. Future zoological parks may well provide a valuable function as meeting points between humans and the rest of the natural world, albeit in mediated form. At the same time, the zoological park will remain compromised if it strives to do all the things we expect from both animals and parkscapes, if it continues to juggle thrills, entertainment, education, consumption, anthropomorphic petting *and* the saving of endangered species. As Hanson writes, 'Zoos occupy a middle ground between science and showmanship, high culture and low, remote forests and cityscape, and wild animals and urban people.' This middle ground may have served the zoo well in the past, but increasing criticism and falling attendance figures suggest caveats to the model. Inevitably, our own complex relationship with animals makes the zoological park an ambiguous entity. As David Hancocks argues, 'Around the world today, people adore, eat, fear, worship, and in laboratories, torture wild animals. The constancy is our inconstancy.' The animal park represents part of this maelstrom, part of our convoluted mind-set on nature. The priority of zoo managers should be to interpret animals on their own terms, to make the zoo a place for animals first, and humans second. Historically, the zoological park has been a place where we construct our animals rather than let them construct themselves. In the twenty-first century, the park idea needs to accommodate not just the wants of humans but the needs of animals.[14]

7 Expanding the Park Experience

By the latter half of the twentieth century, the park idea had generated thousands of protected zones across the globe. New and old national, state, city, zoological and theme parks entertained the masses. In the aftermath of World War II, increased leisure time, affluence and a surging interest in the outdoors strengthened the bond between people and parks. In the United States, national parks witnessed unrivalled tourist numbers. In its first 50 years of operation, Yellowstone National Park hosted fewer than a million visitors. In 1948 alone, Yellowstone received 1,013,531 guests, and in 1972 celebrated its 50,000,000th visitor. Elsewhere, tired amusement parks metamorphosed into polished theme parks. Families flocked to Disney's collection of wonderlands in California, Florida, Tokyo and Paris. The popularity of the park idea managed to wash over most, but not every, park structure. Falling attendance figures at London Zoo almost led to its closure in the late 1990s, while Coney Island, dilapidated and bereft of attractions, never recovered its turn-of-the-nineteenth-century glitz.

Other venues adopted the nomenclature of parkdom despite their failure to fit within conventional parameters of park design. Reflective of the broadening appeal of the park label, the post-war period saw the rise of trailer and caravan parks, industrial and research parks, heritage and culture parks, and electronic or virtual parks. Fresh appropriations of the park tag passed largely unnoticed in the public arena, with citizens rarely questioning the revolutionary variegation happening about them. However, attaching the park epithet to impromptu collections of mobile homes, industrial centres and resoundingly artificial technological landscapes went against the concept of the park most dominant in the nineteenth and early twentieth centuries – namely, a public, naturalized space promising escape from industrialized urbanity. In the short span of 50 years, the park umbrella expanded to encompass land forms and buildings far beyond its traditional remit. Arguably, the sheer variety of post-1945 parkscapes challenged the singular meaning of the park concept itself. Could one idea account for such unrivalled diversity, or join together such incongruent structures as Stanford Research Park, California, West Coast emerald of high-tech capitalism, and Stalin World, a Soviet sculpture park and monument to communism in Lithuania? Could the park idea survive its own multiplicity in the modern era, or was it rendered meaningless by the very process? This final chapter explores the broadening of the park idea in the post-1945 period, and ponders whether our reinventions of the park amount to paradise lost or paradise redefined.

CARAVAN AND TRAILER PARKS: MOVING THE PARK IDEA ON

In the 1920s and 1930s, camping trailers appeared for the first time on American roads. Basic and cramped affairs (historian Andrew Hurley dubs them 'inflated bread boxes on wheels'), trailers none the less allowed urban-ites to take to the country. Initially, auto campers simply parked on the road-side or in open fields, much to the annoyance of farm owners. Gradually, a system of campgrounds emerged to cater for 'tincan tourists'. Free municipal lots quickly gave way to fee-charging camps where landlords supplied light-ing, play areas and electricity. Towards the end of the Thirties, the best camps went by the name of trailer parks, the park emblem suggestive of a higher quality in recreational amenities as well as a salubrious natural setting. During the Great Depression, transient labourers also took advantage of urban-placed trailer lots, sparking fears of hobo camps in the city.[1]

The American dream of the post-war era promoted a sedentary life-style as the best route towards personal satisfaction. A white middle-class family residing in a detached suburban house complete with white picket fences and a neatly trimmed lawn proved the popular aspiration. With the advent of mass-produced assembly-line communities such as Levittown, Long Island, New York, built by William Levitt at the pace of 150 houses a week, a conformist, homogeneous ideal of suburbia rapidly gained ascendancy. However, not all Americans wanted or could afford such a life-style. Despite the best efforts of Levitt and his ilk, post-war housing shortages transformed the dream into a hazy mirage for many demobilized military personnel. Financial constraints and a wish for mobility also factored into the equation. At precisely the same time as suburbia became desirable, the trailer park entered its own heyday. The residential park found favour among those who, like suburbanites, craved their own home and consumer appliances but lacked the financial security or settled existence conducive to supporting a sizeable mortgage and a new house. For some, residency at a trailer park represented merely a stopgap measure. For others, it became a way of life. Life in the trailer park promised freedom, independence and affordability. It perfectly suited seasonal and migratory work patterns. Sporting larger sizes and fully fitted bathrooms, new trailer ranges in the Fifties favoured long-term use. As suburbia blossomed, so too did trailer parks. Some 12,000 of them existed across the United States.

Trailer life did have its share of problems. Park amenities often proved basic, while individual cabins lacked privacy and space. Few Americans considered the trailer park an ideal environment. By the 1970s, media articles and public misconceptions reduced the archetypal trailer park to a ramshackle shanty town, overcrowded and patronized by social misfits. Park residents found themselves stigmatized as losers and pejoratively dubbed 'trailer trash'. While parks provided havens for seniors in Florida, trailer life was mostly interpreted as a tawdry subculture of the poor and the backward. The park label failed to secure respectability for those living outside middle-class norms. Traditionally, parks represented landscapes to visit and to recreate in, not to reside in permanently. The worst examples of trailer parks, where litter, chaos and clutter predominated, bespoke the ruination of American family values and the degradation of hallowed park principles.

In the United Kingdom, the caravan phenomenon followed a similarly faddish course of mass popularity followed by dogged denigration. Caravan parks emerged in the post-1945 period thanks to the alliance of mass recreation, camping, affordable auto technology and the specifically English trait proclaiming 'My home is my castle'. Like the snail carrying its shell on its back, the true Brit of the 1960s and 1970s travelled the kingdom with miniature home in tow. Gleaming cars took to the roads pulling mobile homes that jangled with kitchen cutlery. Farmland and former campsites served as makeshift caravan parks, with the better organized locations offering public conveniences, gas hook-ups and easy access. Caravan culture promised blissful weekends away for those who romanticized the coupling of the great outdoors with the great indoors. The caravan park holiday incorporated travel, freedom, nature, sightseeing and the welcome sight of a good cup of tea in a plastic picnic cup.

In 1962, the British government published a caravan park handbook with the specific design intent of imposing order on new recreational spaces. Disdainful of cluttered rows of ramshackle trailers visible at most beaches and tourist attractions, officials proposed 'screening' caravan parks from passers-by. By careful choice of foliage, park owners could assimilate the caravan into the natural landscape, and thus hide the machine in the garden. Paying homage to the original park ideal of stewardship, order and aesthetics, government officials warned, 'A site can only properly become a caravan park if skilled attention is given to its location, layout and landscape.' Caravan park owners needed to take inspiration from 'Capability' Brown and plan their estates wisely. Yet the successful 'greening' of the caravan park failed to materialize. While Forest Park Caravan site in East Anglia, founded in 1967, situated its legion of static and tourer homes in 85 acres of woodland, other parks stayed true to a more utilitarian mentality of fitting as many units into one field as possible. As long as the public flocked to such places, park owners had nothing to fear. However, by the 1980s, many Englanders were lamenting the loss of rural cliffs and pastures to regimented assemblages of weather-beaten caravans. More luxurious vacations beckoned with the advent of affordable air fares. While some park owners modernized facilities and naturalized their settings, many sites returned to farming uses or were simply left fallow.[2]

RESEARCH AND INDUSTRIAL PARKS:
THE PARK AS WORKPLACE

Parks are typically places set apart from industry. Much of this attitude derives from the conscious separation of nature and machine during the nineteenth century. The Industrial Revolution spurred a mechanized life-style marked by mass migration away from rural life and daily proximity to nature, and towards urban toil and environmental dislocation. Deemed an enlightened response to the dirty, hard labour attached to the Industrial Revolution, the nineteenth-century city park promised temporary sanctuary from urban ills. The park emerged as a landscape deliberately set aside from industrialism, a natural island and reminder of old times.

However, the divide between nature and machine proved far from pre-ordained. At Pawtucket Falls, Lowell, Massachusetts, a social experiment was prosecuted in the 1820s that sought to ally the best of nature with the best of industrial society. Boston Associates on the Merrimack River believed that good business flowed from a salubrious working environment, and duly installed at Pawtucket a textile plant boasting fine architecture, green land-scaping and decent housing for its largely female workforce. Coming from a gardening family and sporting useful connections in the Massachusetts Horticultural Society, chief executive of Merrimack Manufacturing Company and the Proprieters of Locks and Canals, Kirk Boott drew on an illustrious green background. Boott oversaw the beautification of the nascent industrial scene of Lowell with elm-planting programmes and the establishment of Dutton Mall, a shaded promenade for peaceful Sunday strolls. A picture of Lowell by Benjamin Mather in 1825 captured a bucolic country estate rather than an industrial behemoth, with lush vegetation dominating the scene. The greening of Lowell continued with Shattuck Mall in the early 1840s, and Canal Walk, designed by horticulturist and hydraulics engineer James B. Francis, in 1847. For scholars Patrick Malone and Charles Parrott, such beautification amounted to an early example of 'green engineering'. At the same time, residents of Lowell's Anne Street gained licence to a sliver of land between their houses and the Merrimack Canal. 'Dedicated and set apart by the grantors for the purpose of beautifying and ventilating the City', in 1844, the greenway later became known as Anne Street Canal Park. Open to all, the park brought together residential, industrial, natural and democratic interests in the immediate area, and foreshadowed the US city park movement. Moreover, by their determined efforts, Boott, Francis and other enlightened officials at Lowell established America's first industrial park in all but name.[3]

Lowell undoubtedly served as a valuable model at a time when many doubted the possibility of pleasant living in an age marked by smog, mech-anization and widespread social upheaval. Its paternalistic remit of schooling working women in etiquette and religious instruction in particular drew admiration. The neatly organized textile mills at Pawtucket Falls provided a vision of benign industrialism. Meanwhile, the resultant beauty of the

Merrimack and Northern canals invited the popular epithet of 'Venice of America'. Pawtucket Falls earned a lofty reputation for its careful incorporation of rural nature in city landscaping. Yet, Lowell's designers never really solved the dilemma of how to marry industrial development with nature protection. Growing competition for space, together with the need for new railroad access, led to the curtailing of Lowell's green malls not long after their creation. Despite its organic façade and democratic zeal, Lowell was fundamentally a landscape of enterprise, with park strolls reserved for only one day out of seven. Similarly, in the realm of industrial reform, profit and competition eroded attempts by the Boston Associates to look after their female labour force. Neglected and exploited, some workers considered themselves 'wage slaves' repressed by cotton lords by the 1840s. Seemingly, Lowell's attempts at integrating class, gender, nature and industry together fell short of success.[4]

A century on, the industrial park re-materialized on the West Coast of the USA as a hybrid landscape incorporating university campus, suburbia, city park and business district. In the late 1940s, officials at Stanford University hoped to strengthen the reputation of their collegiate, as well as its financial position, by leasing a parcel of university-chartered land to outside interests. Professor of Radio Engineering Frederick Emmons Terman shrewdly recognized the potential to fuse university research in the field of electronics with corporate development. Terman envisaged a 'community of technical scholars' culled from both private and public sectors. Stanford Industrial Park emerged from 660 acres of cattle grazing land in 1951, its rural lineage transferred into a simple moniker: 'The Farm'. The pleasant setting combined with the prospect of tapping science graduates served to entice local companies. An early convert to the park idea, electronics firm Varian Associates employed respected German-American Erich Mendelsohn as chief architect for its first building, a single-storey modern workspace that set a trend for future park architecture. Kodak, General Electric and Hewlett Packard also located to the site. From its humble beginnings in a Palo Alto garage in 1939, Hewlett Packard became the unexpected flag-bearer of industrial park design. The corporation helped define the ethos of industrial parkdom, whereby recreation and greenery accompanied high technology and skilled labour. Imparting a modicum of Greco-Roman elegance, Packard's open, low-rise building complexes, constructed in the late Fifties, encircled ornate courtyards, home to volleyball courts and water fountains. Such naturalistic places intimated play, but also encouraged the stimulation of ideas, thus conjuring a productive entrepreneurial environment. Drawing on the age-old reputation of the park as a fertile plain of contemplation and intellectual creativity, the Packard courtyards allowed employees the freedom to muse on electronics in the great outdoors.

While Packard attracted new employees with its salubrious working conditions, the park itself gained international stature as an example of innovation in industrial geography. Post-war interest in futuristic science cities perfectly complemented the physical landscape taking form at Stanford.

Utopian technological realms, marked by sanitized automated living, tantalized and captivated visionary minds. Walt Disney conceptualized his own futuristic domicile (later constructed as EPCOT in Florida) during the 1950s. In 1958, Stanford featured in an exhibit at the Brussels World's Fair entitled Industrial Parks USA. The long tradition of World's Fairs assured a continual market for technical inventiveness and prototypes of living and working spaces. With its clean lines, symmetrical architecture and green aspect, the modernist landscape of Stanford duly impressed. The industrial park operated as a place of high expectations, of hidden technological wonders nestled in a semi-wild setting. Thanks to positive publicity, Stanford became the prototype for industrial parks worldwide.

In its own locality, Stanford Industrial Park attracted sizeable financial investment and public interest. The popularity of the park as an industrial hub spurred mass immigration. The nearest city, Palo Alto, more than doubled in population during the Fifties. By 1962, forty-two companies had located to Stanford. The wholesome reputation of the park readily interfaced with that of suburban, green and affluent Santa Clara County. Emphasis on serving military and aerospace markets in the 1960s gave way to computer innovation in the early 1970s, with the renamed Stanford Research Park (1974 onwards) fuelling the rise of Silicon Valley about it. The kudos of the park fortified around Enlightenment notions of a proud and peaceful scientific community, as well as classical references – Stanford staff configured as a neo-Athenian bunch of individuals gathered in courtyards pondering not the countenance of gods or the mechanisms of democracy but the subroutines of microprocessors. Belying the harsh realities of business competition, the park environment was typically cast as a nurturer of informal, friendly ties. While the rural setting remained largely intact, cattle dung had given way to computer chips on the Stanford 'farm' by the 1970s.[5]

Despite its innovative spirit, Stanford Industrial Park ultimately employed similar social and environmental mechanisms to those used at Lowell. While computer technology and textile production had few obvious commonalities, architects at both locations sought to harmonize nature with industry through the flexible format of the park. At Pawtucket and in Santa Clara country alike, trees and lawns served as agents of pastoralism, there to humanize and naturalize a machine-based economy. A park-like setting promised to negate the deleterious effect of mechanical dependency, servicing goals of betterment and cerebral stimulation in the process.

Unlike Lowell's magnates, stewards of Stanford University managed to keep their park relatively virtuous despite burgeoning economic growth. In the 1950s, overseers successfully suburbanized the park scene, encouraging developers to include grassy areas that, in the words of one Stanford representative, gave buildings their own 'suburban front lawns', just like residential estates in nearby Palo Alto. The green veneer common to definitions of suburbia and parkdom helped to meld the two concepts together, making them conspicuously similar. Recognizing the need to further regiment park development, Stanford imposed myriad building restrictions, including the screening of trash bins, parking lots, and loading bays, along with the hiding of utility lines and power generators. Responding to concerns from Palo Alto residents over the loss of Santa Clara county's bucolic salubrity, the university instigated rigorous building codes inside the park.[6]

Intriguingly, the controlled environment of Stanford came to resemble another Californian landscape also born in the 1950s: Disneyland. Both Disney and Stanford dealt in the aesthetic discourse of disguise, utilizing subtle natural inferences and meticulous landscaping to cover the business of enterprise. Disneyland operated as a fantasy realm dancing above a corporate profit motive, while Stanford served as a private theme park devoted to high technology. Stanford insisted on greening to conceal the industry within, to make sure the location resembled a park rather than a factory site. Disney hid its motive – tourism – behind cartoon figures and monuments. At neither location did people have a tangible relationship with the environment. Instead, nature served as a visual emblem of quality of life, a totem of easy living. Essentially, the clean futurist look common to both Disney and Stanford reflected the same ethos: scientific optimism, capitalism and 1950s social conservatism. Like Disneyland, Stanford Industrial Park invited a near uncontrollable belt of congestion and development around it (despite its environmental strictures). A dark side to the computer chip gradually emerged in the form of chemical pollution, land alienation and community segregation in Silicon Valley. By the early 1990s, the reputation of the park rested more on its knowledge bank than on any references to natural geography. As Manuel Castells and Peter Hall put it, 'Most of the famous orchards of the Silicon Valley mythology are gone.'[7]

Orchards or not, Stanford succeeded in establishing the conventions of industrial park design. The archetypal industrial (or research) park entailed single-storey buildings, green spaces, a campus-like ambiance, and geographical room for expansion. Its prime rationale lay in attracting investment and bolstering regional development. The park became an apologist for industry, a vehicle of urban and economic regeneration. Interest in the new park model encouraged other US universities and councils to re-envision their open spaces as hybrid landscapes offering industrial and research facilities in green settings. In North Carolina, the Research Triangle Park (RTP) emerged in 1959 as an answer to local unemployment and economic depression. A great swathe of woodland caught between three Raleigh–Durham universities, the RTP facilitated a new manufacturing buzz in the region. In 1965, IBM purchased land there. By 1990, more than 30,000 people employed by fifty organizations travelled daily to the research park. Other research centres blossomed along Massachusetts' Highway 128, with the Lowell region itself reindustrialized courtesy of Wang Laboratories and the computer boom. All told, by 1998, more than 200 industrial, science and research parks graced the US landscape.

The industrial park idea found favour in many other countries eager to kick-start their economies. In Cambridge, England, farmland that had belonged to Trinity College since 1546 served as the base for a new science park. A response to governmental pleas for universities to increase ties with industry, derelict land was duly cleared for use in 1970. By 1999, sixty-four companies had located there. In France, research parks assumed the mantle of 'technopoles'. Dubbed 'a technopolis for the 21st century', Sophia-Antipolis (1972) near Nice attracted a mixture of residential, recreational and techno-logical uses on a site governed by strict environmental regulations. Original plans dictated that two-thirds of the park had to remain green. Designer Pierre Laffitte hoped for a 'Latin Quarter in the countryside, a city afield devoted to creation, intelligence, and consequently to economic, cultural and social modernity'. Aided by government funding, Sophia-Antipolis played host to 400 companies and nearly 10,000 workers by 1989. The Chinese government meanwhile established TORCH in 1988, a programme designed to promote a national network of science parks through foreign investment. Pre-existing parks such as Shenzhen (1985), with its strong ties to Hong Kong business, fell under the purview of the programme. New Chinese industrial parks promised to rejuvenate ailing regions, and to replace poor agricultural eco-nomies with high-tech industry. In the ancient city of Xi'an, west-central China, four distinct industrial parks prospered in the government-funded Xi'an New Technology Industrial Development Zone. Home of countless palaces, the dynastic city of Xi'an successfully lured new corporate emperors including IBM and Coca-Cola to take power in the region. A former hub of military-industrial production in the Cold War, Xi'an, which translates as 'Western Palace', invited US and European corporate giants to reside along-side protected Terracotta Warriors and ancient temples.[8]

The first eco-industrial parks emerged in Denmark and the United States in the 1990s. Rather than camouflage industrial development with token greenery, developers recognized the potential for factories and research units within parks to pool resources in a manner favourable to the environment. At Kalundborg, near Copenhagen, 'industrial synergy' inclined several firms to exchange products. The local coal-fired power plant used unwanted gypsum from a wallboard plant, then diverted waste heat to local fish farms and Novo Nordisk Pharmaceutical Plant. The pharmaceutical manufacturer duly supplied sludge for agricultural use. The eco-industrial park lofted corporate communication and resource-sharing as core values. Such park-based inter-dependency served to reduce working costs and minimize environmental impacts.[9]

The advent of the eco-industrial park hinted at the possible resurgence of green philosophy inside business park boundaries. Working landscapes such as Kalundborg (or Cape Charles Sustainable Technology Park, Virginia) sug-gested that the park idea could be usefully broadened to take into account innovative environmental agendas. However, at the close of the twentieth century, ecological factors remained of secondary importance at most indus-trial, science and technology parks. The park label, adapted to suit the lexicon of business, remained orientated around fiscal rather than ecological growth.

In essence, industrial parks served as artificial seed-beds for industrial cross-fertilization, not as areas for endangered species or recycling centres. Parks were valued principally for their positive economic effects, promising a productive internal business culture alongside regional regeneration. The prolific rise in the number of industrial parks around the globe rarely translated into local distinctiveness. Courting the same international companies, and providing the same facilities, most industrial parks proved much like one another: formulaic landscapes based on the Stanford principle. In place of ecological or cultural references, the identity of each park rested on its corporate complement. Arguably, the salience of the park label itself was placed under threat from such industrial and government-induced anonymity.

At the same time, taking into account the long history of the park idea, industrial parks did share some similarities with earlier park landscapes. Where once the aristocracy resided in sumptuous estates, with ornate buildings operating as the geographical and symbolic hubs of their power, Hewlett Packard, IBM and Microsoft seized prime positions in new industrial enclaves. Following much genuflection by regional authorities, corporations forged business facilities in parks around the world as visual totems of their economic and political ascendancy. At Louis XIV's Versailles and Hewlett Packard's Stanford, lush greenery, the noble parkscape and modish architecture offered blatant indicators of wealth and prestige.

BRINGING THE PARK TO THE MALL

With mobile homes and industrial enterprises joining the ranks of wilderness wonderlands and urban playgrounds, the flexibility of the park concept appeared almost boundless in the post-1945 period. The granting of the park moniker to novel landscapes encouraged a base level of public acceptance. The phrase 'park' carried with it an array of celebratory connotations: recreation, nature, contemplation, quality of life and escapism. It was commonly understood as a utopian landscape, deemed capable of influencing society in an enlightened way by associations with civility, good manners, nature appreciation and pure enjoyment. Seeking to exploit the enduring appeal of parkdom, city planners in the post-war period subtly incorporated elements of green design into urban and commercial environments. The greening of shopping venues and downtowns from the 1950s onwards highlighted the pervasiveness of park philosophy among both government and corporate planners. While developers shied away from labelling their creations 'parks' as such, they none the less forged park-like spaces that sat comfortably alongside existing green landscapes.

Recreational pursuits spurred the first malls into existence. Played in London in the seventeenth century, paille-maille, a game similar to croquet, gained one thoroughfare the popular epithet of 'the Mall'. By the 1830s, malls denoted tree-lined promenades, such as those crafted at Lowell. Designed in 1922 by Jesse Clyde Nichols, the Country Club Plaza in Kansas City was the first suburban-style shopping centre, and served as the prototype for the modern mall. Nichols transformed Missouri swampland into a Spanish-themed shopping area replete with sculptures, courtyards and fountains, much akin to the architectural contrivances of a European park. The Country Club Plaza paved the way for the modernization of the mall concept around themes of mass consumption and entertainment.

It was in 1950s America that the shopping mall became ubiquitous, a populist icon demonstrative of peacetime aspirations for better living. The mall scheme responded to three significant cultural trends of the time: suburbaniza-tion, rising automobile use and middle-class affluence. Early malls subscribed to one basic design, the 'dumbbell', popularized by architect Victor Gruen, whereby two large ('magnet') stores marked the ends of a corridor housing a plethora of smaller boutiques. Diametrically opposed to the park idea of out-doors recreation, the self-contained air-conditioned shopping arena prevented adverse environmental conditions from intruding on mass consumption. The notable absence of windows furthered the sense of the mall as a 'placeless' structure, removed from traditional constructs of time and geography.

The park idea influenced this modern landscape of consumption taking form across the United States. At the centre of most malls lay a spectacular atrium with fountains shooting jets of water towards the roof and assemblages of verdant foliage. At Gruen's first covered mall, Southdale in Minneapolis, the three-storey Garden Court of Perpetual Spring, with its exotic palms and songbirds, highlighted the temperate nature of life inside the mall, especially on cold winter days in Minnesota. Gruen explained his intentions thus: 'By bringing the outdoors indoors, we are creating a new kind of environment – one of Eternal Spring – which provides a psychological and visual contrast and relief from indoor shops.' By breaking up the formulaic aesthetic struc-ture of store windows and sale posters, the addition of the organic promised a less bland, and less overwhelmingly sanitized, experience. Along with mall 'muzak', indoor plants and trees provided soothing reprieve from unbridled materialism. Park-style benches allowed contemplation and rest, while sign-posts laid out mall trails. The presence of the organic assisted in the natural-ization of mass consumption, aiding Americans in their adaptation to the new commercial environment. Park-like features transformed the shopping experience into something more tangible and meaningful, lifting the encounter beyond simple commerce. Such earnest attempts to bring both nature and the park to the shopping mall ultimately reflected discomfort over the social activity of shopping, a vestige carried over from Puritanism. Meanwhile, in order to mitigate any sense of narcissistic purchasing, mall designers drew on a variety of objects to conceal the real process of con-sumption. A veritable canon of 'disguises', including theatre, family events and indoor gardens, enabled, according to Jon Goss, 'a fantasised dissociation from the act of shopping'. Natural edifice helped offset the sheer materialism of it all. Park references also assisted in the creation of the mall as a civic space, a meeting ground for the local community. With all its altruistic associations, the hallowed park ideal had been co-opted for the purposes of retail therapy and consumer expenditure.[10]

Organic theming in the mall environment succeeded in cross-pollinating the natural with the artificial. Nature in the mall duly spread its roots to encompass rainforest cafés decorated with waterfalls and animals, and nature stores choked with affordable mementos of the great outdoors. The Nature Company, along with other stores based on celebrating exploration and wilderness adventure, borrowed a definition of 'nature' already advertised in the floral arrangements scattered across the mall. Read as colourful ornamentation, 'nature' proved eminently marketable. Dolphin key chains and rustic bird-feeders reminded shoppers of an exotic outside world brought inside to the safety of the mall. In a sense, nature stores served as the consumer-based zoo parks for the late twentieth century, with all manner of creature simulacra available to look at, touch *and* take home.

As chapter 5 elaborated, shopping malls shared much in common with modern theme parks. As products of 1950s America, Gruen malls and Disney parks championed a strong work ethic and social conservatism. As attractions designed in large part for the white middle-class fraternity fleeing Cold War anxieties, neither the mall nor the park actively welcomed minorities or nonconformists. Park and mall authorities exerted significant control over the carnivalesque atmosphere in terms of audience and form. Part of the didacticism of the mall, jolly architectural features along with vibrant poster displays, cemented notions of satisfaction gleaned through purchase. Likewise, at Disney, seeing Mickey Mouse brought joy to all, with families brought together through a mutual interest in consumption.

The park and the mall gradually moved closer together, to the extent that by the 1990s Margaret Crawford commented on how 'the two forms converge – malls routinely entertain, while theme parks function as disguised marketplaces'. Such commonality meant that by the end of the century, theme parks literally took pride of place in larger shopping venues, while miniature malls could be found in Disney promenades. The Mall of America, in Bloomington, Minnesota, the largest mall in the United States at 4,200,000 square feet, opened in 1992 featuring four themed retail areas. The Mall of America's 'North Garden' depicted 'Main Street USA', yet its sheer historical inauthenticity reminded one more of Disneyland's own Main Street rather than any abject reality. The Mall of America also featured Knott's Camp Snoopy, a theme park that by 2004 included over thirty attractions. The park promised to enrich the shopping experience for local families and international tourists.[11]

Moving north of the 49th parallel, West Edmonton Mall, in Canada, dwarfed the average town and lured a global clientele. Built in the early 1980s, WEM gained its estimable reputation by virtue of its size (weighing in at 5,200,000 square feet) and recreational credentials. The Albertan giant featured not only stores but a theme park, a water park, a golf course, a theme park-styled hotel, a chapel and several nightclubs. WEM amounted to a self-enclosed fantasy world rivalled only by Disney's creations. It offered a tour of the park diaspora under one roof. Meanwhile, the seamlessness by which citizens passed from park ride to store checkout to sport activity attested to the collapse of conventional boundaries between recreation, consumption and entertainment. The different themes, period styles and geographical allusions, the fusion of plastic and real plants, all gathered together in one space, further tested the ability of individuals to differentiate the real from the unreal. In the case of Old Chicago (1974), an indoor amusement park and mall 35 miles south-west of the windy city, time and geography appeared to collapse entirely. Old Chicago resurrected the legendary 1893 Chicago exposition in modern garb for the latest generation of tourists and consumers.

Extant parks meanwhile had to compete with the mall for public attention. Mainstream society voted with its feet, many people preferring the reliability, predictability and temperate climate of mall shopping. In time, citizens learned to use the mall as a surrogate park. Exercise could be had in the safe, clean, and windproof environment – leading to the phenomenon of early morning 'mall-walkers' and even joggers. The 'great indoors' offered perfect safety. By comparison, city and national parks seemed dangerously open and unmonitored. Larger malls deliberately undercut parks as tourist attractions, with one advertisement for West Edmonton Mall highlighting the succession: 'Tourists will no longer have to travel to Disneyland, Miami Beach, the Epcot Park . . . California Sea World, the San Diego Zoo, the Grand Canyon . . . It's all here at the WEM.' With a need to attract visitors, the reverse seemed inevitable. Parks had to sell themselves as malls and adopt commodity culture. Originally envisioned as places removed from rampant commercialism, parks invited fresh retail ventures. Not far from WEM, the main street of Banff National Park by the 1990s featured its own shopping alleys, cinema and even a small mall.[12]

Meanwhile, the presence of organic mementos inside the mall fostered the expectation that nature could be bought at virtually any locale. Packaged wilderness, 'Nature' with a capital N, was expected to be for sale at both nature store *and* national park. Parks thus became caught up in the universality of the 'mall experience' – with a wide range of entertainment and souvenirs a prerequisite at all public attractions. While in the past, parks (in myriad guises) facilitated elements of consumption through the hunting of animals and the provision of aesthetic rewards, the post-1945 years led to a reframing of the park idea that reflected the increasing dominance of consumerism. Managers adapted to the desires of their clientele by focusing on 'selling' their parks as attractive entertainment landscapes. However, by such a process, stewards unwittingly blurred the boundaries that set the park aside from the rest of society, sacrificing the original park idea in the forging of a new consumer paradise. On visiting Yellowstone, those accustomed to the mall environment naturally focused their attention on familiar icons such as souvenir stores and eateries, with wilderness reduced to an exercise in purchasing. Arguably, a balance needed to be reached between the preservation of the original park ideal and its adaptation to new social precedents. Otherwise, some parks looked set to join the generic consumer landscapes – the everyday malls – building up on their periphery.

Cross-fertilization also occurred within the park diaspora. Back in the 1800s, the city park had sought to mitigate some of the problems associated with urbanization and industrialization. A century on, city planners again experimented with park ideas, but this time drawing on the Disney canon. Thanks to its intricate interfacing of work, leisure, community and commerce, the Disneyland blueprint found favour among planners looking to reinvigorate urban spaces. The success of theme parks in controlling antisocial behaviour (particularly criminality) while promoting local commerce and organizing spatial dynamics encouraged some city authorities to apply similar design principles to their own downtown facilities. In Seattle, officials employed the Disney Development Company to help restore the Seattle Center, originally constructed for the 1962 World's Fair, and by the 1980s in urgent need of repair. Just like Olmstedian city parks designed to offset urban decay, Disneyfication offered a proactive response to the paralysed state of modern spaces. The themed regeneration of downtowns and an overarching focus on family entertainment both flowed from Disney ideology. Friendly theme park-style designs were expected to encourage better urban behaviour and prove attractive to guests. While few towns compared to the wanton theming of Las Vegas – to academic Mark Gottdiener, the 'theme park capital of the United States' – subtle re-engineering of urban spaces around the tenets of tourism and greenery indicated enduring park principles at work. In 1996, Disney engineered the perfect park-town of Celebration in Florida. A 'real' place with 'real' houses, Celebration amounted to an intricately organized Disney-themed township for the white middle classes, a cartoon Levittown for the twenty-first century. For those addicted to weekend trips to Disney World, Celebration offered a permanent escape. The saccharine allure of Celebration tempted many. However, park theming, when applied to cityscapes, brought with it fresh problems. Behind the amiable veneer, Disneyfied landscapes traded in privatization, localization and social control. E. Soja saw in Los Angeles 'a giant agglomeration of theme parks, a life space comprised of Disney worlds', a decrepit environment marked by its territorial divisions, capital accumulation and bewildering postmodern tendencies. Even at Celebration, criticisms mounted over the poor quality of workmanship, the organization of the local school, and the absence of ethnic minorities. Life was blandly utopic. In Seattle, Disney's plans for the Seattle Center were eventually dismissed, primarily due to the lack of involvement by community residents along with alleged corporate ignorance of local history. Evidently there were limits as to how far the theme park idea could be applied outside park confines.[13]

NEW CULTURAL PARKS

The potential for park landscapes to impart cultural and political metaphors continued unabated in the post-1945 period. Parks offered refuges filled with historical artefacts as well as signposts pointing to future prospects. Designated in 1952 as a place of commemoration, Hiroshima Peace Memorial Park, Japan, included within its boundaries an array of poignant reminders of 6 August 1945, the day that the *Enola Gay* dropped an atomic bomb on the city. Physical records of the catastrophe, such as a domed building that partially survived the devastation, sat alongside figurative memorative pieces such as the Tower of a Thousand Cranes, in honour of child leukaemia victim Sadako Sasaki, who, while sick, folded 1,000 origami cranes, each a symbol of fortune and long life. Hiroshima Park served as a sanctuary of memory, a frozen ground zero in time. By traversing the landscape, visitors not only relived (or imagined) the horrors of war, but also encountered historical interpretation (found in the Peace Memorial Museum) and pleas for pacifism. Next to a cenotaph dedicated to the victims of the bomb (with some 180,000 names) stood 'The Flame of Peace' (1964), said to burn until the vanquishment of nuclear weapons from the Earth. The quiet, green, sombre outlook of the park affirmed sensations of what world peace might translate into. Hiroshima Peace Memorial Park offered itself as a pivotal temporal landscape, a place where citizens could look back on a destructive past, but also glance positively forward. The landscape intentionally operated as a moral guide, a subtle didactic instrument. The message of peace overwhelmed the stories of war inside the park.

As well as pondering the meaning of loss, parks borne from World War II also celebrated triumph. The concept of Victory Park (Park Pobedy) in Moscow first emerged in 1947 as a way to commemorate the overthrow of Nazi Germany. However, convoluted political machinations kept the park idea in limbo. In 1958, more than 150 projects submitted in an open design competition for Victory Park were casually dismissed by a Soviet committee. The President of the Art Academy remarked that 'no project sufficiently expressed the triumphant victory, the idea of the feat that had been accomplished by the Soviet people and its army'. More tellingly, the decision allowed less democratic planning methods to assume primacy. However, bureaucratic inertia, ideological disputes over content, concerns over how to fit monuments within the Russian landscape, and even untimely deaths forestalled the park project. A sudden spurt of progress in the late 1970s was halted by budgetary restraints in consequence of financing the upcoming Moscow Olympics. Interpretative discussions fiercened with the advent of *Glasnost* in the 1980s, with protracted arguments over the building of a Russian Orthodox church on-site. Victory Park finally opened in 1993, 50 years after liberation. For five decades, the imagined park landscape served as a virtual battleground for competing views of Soviet history, memory and political ideology. Plans were continually reframed to suit the power brokers of the time, with government procrastination imperilling each vision in turn. The park proved so contentious because, on one level, such a landscape was viewed as permanent and staunchly symbolic. What the park had to say about the past mattered immensely.[14]

Opened on April Fool's Day, 2001, Soviet Sculpture Park in Lithuania took just 2 years to emerge despite its own embroilment in public controversy. The work of canned mushroom magnate Viliumas Malinauskas, Soviet Sculpture Park gathered together discarded and defamed sculptures of the Soviet era inside a 30 acre forest reserve. Statues otherwise targeted for destruction due to their intimate associations with the Cold War and communism found refuge in a protected park landscape. Most Lithuanians, harbouring few fond memories of Soviet occupation, questioned the idea of celebrating such blatant symbols of autocracy. However, notable sculptors recognized the growing collection of statues for their artistic rather than political qualities. 'It's not the ideology that matters, it's the art,' cried legendary Lithuanian sculptor Konstantinas Bogdanas, maker of 'many, many' Lenin statuettes. Malinauskas meanwhile regarded the ensemble of marble and metal statues in terms of tourist revenue.

When Soviet Sculpture Park opened, visitors found themselves greeted by Lenin and Stalin impersonators, akin to Mickey Mouse and Pluto welcoming children at the gates of Disneyland. Hidden among the foliage resided a multitude of stoic Communist leaders in the form of giant figurines. While undoubtedly some tourists managed to focus on the aesthetic worth of Soviet Sculpture Park, the art, steeped in politics, only served to remind others of Soviet abominations. One critic described it as 'a bizarre trip through the iconography of Soviet repression'. Unrepentant, Malinauskas boasted to journalists: 'It combines the charms of a Disneyland with the worst of the Soviet Gulag prison camp.' Although the $2 entrance fee undercut most theme parks by some margin, 'Stalin World' (as the sculpture park became known) shared with Disney World an inability to deal sensibly with historical context. A lack of sensitivity towards those Lithuanians who had suffered under Soviet rule could be seen in the 'ironic' placement of Soviet mortars in the children's play area and the theming of the park around a concentration camp, replete with barbed wire and gun towers. Plans were also unveiled for a railroad from the city of Vilnius to Stalin World, with visitors climbing aboard cattle wagons after the fashion of Soviet era deportees, the simulated horror of a trip to the Gulag ghoulishly married to the innocence of a Disney World train journey. Stalin World, like any other theme park, rendered history as vacuous and facile, jolly and innocent. However, 'history' remained living reality for many of the park's visitors and neighbours. For all its artistic and historical significance, Stalin World exuded a dubious morality by its projections of a Holocaust-style theme park.[15]

Elsewhere, a spate of religiously framed park building invited controversy. The Holy Land Experience theme park in Orlando, Florida, opened in February 2001 to much criticism. To its opponents, the Holy Land, a walk-through re-creation of biblical scenes, reduced the Bible to a mere entertainment spectacle, cashing in on Christians like a three-dimensional extension of a TV-evangelist show. Its financing by Zion Hope, a Christian ministry for Jews, also created offence. The website <RoadsideAmerica.com> commented on the features of the new park, noting that, 'Holy Land Experience has no thrill rides to compete with local heavyweights like Disney World and Universal Studios, but is the only one of the three to have a six-story, half-scale replica of the front of Herod's temple'. The Holy Land hoped to attract those looking for both novelty and salvation in the Sunshine State.[16]

Just one year later, the Free Church of Satan announced plans for a rival attraction on the West Coast, the 'Perdition' theme park, California, complete with Journey to Hell rollercoaster and rock 'n' roll stage. According to the *Sunday Times*, Satanists wanted their own theme park as a 'riposte' to the Holy Land Experience. Meanwhile, local Christians in Sighisoara, Romania, protested plans for 'Dracula Land' theme park. Announced by the Transylvanian government in 2001 as a scheme to boost tourism, the Dracula theme park was to be built at the birthplace of Count Vlad Tepes (Vlad the Impaler), the inspiration behind Bram Stoker's original novelization. Fearing an onslaught of Satanists to the area, Lutheran pastor Hans Bruno Frohlich conceded, 'You can build a theme park, but not one that attacks Christian values.' The park landscape had suddenly become a venue for a holy war of the twenty-first century framed around the unlikely constructs of consumer culture and rollercoaster rides.[17]

Seemingly incapable of presenting sober issues with requisite sensitivity, the theme park idea appeared best suited to popular entertainment. Dollywood, Tennessee, which opened in 1986 as a shrine to country singer Dolly Parton, captured the Disney feel perfectly with its schmaltzy family feel and indulgent focus on celebrity. By 1993, annual receipts reached $9,000,000. Dollywood succeeded because it never took itself too seriously. The park focused on simple fun as its remit. Yet, outside the extravagances of theming, parks were able to reflect on substantive issues, as Hiroshima Peace Memorial Park ably demonstrated. The park format offered much potential in the realm of healing and commemoration – hence the prominence of greenery and parkscapes in schematics put forward to fill the void left at the site of the New York World Trade Center after the terrorist attacks of 11 September 2001.

SECOND NATURE PARKS

The post-1945 period witnessed a broadening of the park concept and a blossoming of unconventional parks with newfangled purposes. In the United States, parkscapes emerged at unexpected places, none more so than at former nuclear and military bases, environments once used for atomic testing and troop manoeuvres but set aside in the twenty-first century as protected wildernesses.

In 1979, the US conservationist magazine *Cry California* carried a series of cartoons entitled 'Revisiting the Nukes: Impressions of the Future'. One cartoon suggested that atomic reactors – unholy and contaminated landmarks of militarism – would outlast the Pyramids. Another sketch situated a nuclear plant as a tourist attraction, with passengers on a nearby freeway lured by billboards advertising 'See the historic radioactive ruins' and souvenir 'contaminated soil' for sale. In interpreting the nuclear age, few foresaw the establishment of parks on former atomic or military territories. Those who did, volunteered the park label as an ironic statement. Photographer Richard Misrach documented the twisted landscape of Bravo 20 bombing range north of Fallon, Nevada, as a case in point. Misrach saw Bravo 20 as a physical document of 'the war the Navy waged on Nevada', its giant craters and exploded vehicle remnants testimony to the overt militarization of the American West. Legally defined as public territory where visitors could rightfully picnic, Bravo 20 had been stolen from the American people for Cold War expediencies and had been bombed successively for three decades. Misrach offered Bravo as ideal parkland. Situating the military site within a discourse of greater inclusion in the US park fraternity, of official dictates valuing ecological and historic monuments as much as aesthetic vistas, Misrach announced 'America's first environmental memorial: Bravo 20 National Park'. Mapping out the contours of his own park idea, Misrach foresaw a 'devastation drive' and a 'boardwalk of the bombs' as two highlights of the new tourist-friendly landscape. Bravo 20 National Park would serve as an instructive journey across ground zero and beyond, a palpable warning of military-engineered destructiveness. Witnessing the beauty and the horror of the unworldly terrain would also, Misrach hoped, teach visitors to embrace wilderness and humanity rather than weapons testing and global conflict.[18]

In order to make headway, Bravo 20 National Park required a significant bomb disposal programme as well as an agreement by the US Navy to relinquish its land claim. When Misrach wrote the piece in 1990, his park idea seemed nothing more than a protester's pipe dream. Yet, in the years that followed, a number of parks sprang up at nuclear and military 'sacrifice zones' across the United States. In June 2000, President Bill Clinton signed into existence Hanford Reach National Monument in Washington State. In the 1940s, Hanford Engineering Works had proved pivotal to the Manhattan Project, America's clandestine government ordinance to build the world's first atomic bomb. B Reactor at Hanford produced the first weapons-grade plutonium for use in the nuclear arms race. Production continued until 1988. Despite decades of military use, radioactive contamination applied to only 5 per cent of the Hanford reservation, leaving the rest of the enclave preserved as valuable shrub-steppe wilderness. The park designation honoured the quality of local ecology. Meanwhile, a solitary park information board, situated on a highway pull-out overlooking B Reactor, testified to the region's distinguished nuclear history. The reactor itself garnered status as a National Historic Monument.

Hanford was not alone in attracting national park stewardship. The Park Service also assumed responsibility for former nuclear missile silos near Badlands National Park, South Dakota, and McDonald Ranch, where the first nuclear weapon was prepared, at the Trinity Test Site in New Mexico. Military lands not entered in the official national park compendium also achieved some form of protected status. In May 1999, US Energy Secretary Bill Richardson established Rock Creek Reserve at the Rocky Flats Environmental Technology Site, Colorado. The region carried the dubious moniker of 'Rocky Flats Horror Picture Show' among some environmentalists, who drew attention to on-site toxic hotspots as the true result of years of plutonium processing. Nevertheless, the US Fish and Wildlife Service joined forces with the Department of Energy to co-manage an 800-acre nature reserve on the site. A Natural Resources Management Plan published in April 2001 included plans for extending the park to include 1,700 acres and proposed the reintroduction of 'sensitive' native fauna.[19]

By the 1990s, the US Department of Energy (DOE) had designated several of its chief land assets as National Environmental Research Parks. Such parks operated as 'outdoor laboratories' for environmental studies of climatology, geology and biodiversity. The park tag also involved research into the restoration of native habitat and endangered species. In April 1992, Nevada Test Site (NTS), host for an astounding 928 nuclear tests, achieved park designation. At 1,375 square miles of protected terrain, the Nevada park competed with Yosemite in terms of acreage. The DOE drew attention to a plethora of biotic communities flourishing 'in a relatively natural balance' at the nuclear park, in spite of its chequered history and continued use for military projects (see fig. 8). Proof of its new environmental credo, the federal agency published pictures of wild horses roaming the NTS. The park also extended protection to cultural resources, including a camping area used successively by Native Americans, horse hunters and, in the 1850s, the US mail service. Such artefacts sat somewhat uncomfortably alongside army-constructed ghost towns nullified during atomic blasts.[20]

In the guise of Hanford Reach and Nevada Test Site, the park label advanced the powerful image of nature blossoming at ground zero. Eagles, coyotes and lizards prospered where bombs had once rained, free to roam without fear of industrial or suburban encroachment. Off limits to the wider populace for several decades, nuclear sites arguably benefited in ecological terms from their enforced separation from civilization. Issues of toxic and radioactive contamination aside, nature preservation emerged as an accidental by-product of military secrecy. For some commentators, such sites even compared favourably with more orthodox park landscapes. Author Rebecca Solnit witnessed true beauty in the people and the wildness of Nevada Test Site, traditionally thought of as an 'Armageddon' landscape, while the natural virtues of Yosemite seemed somehow tarnished through its bustling tourism. Arguably, a radical new Eden had emerged out of destruction, a nature park from national sacrifice.[21]

The notion of a post-nuclear wilderness challenged traditional interpretations of the nuclear age as artificial and deadly. That nature had survived the worst ravages of nuclear testing suggested a welcome and unexpected potential for biotic regeneration. Still, nuclear parks carried a technological, militaristic imprint that rendered them lesser landscapes in the popular mind

Figure 8. Bristlecone Pine Rainier Mesa and Stockade Wash, Nevada Test Site. US Department of Energy photograph. Reproduced courtesy of US Department of Energy. © US Department of Energy.

when compared to well-tended city parks or bucolic national parks. In the late twentieth century, the public ultimately preferred parks that testified to loftier principles, and managed to look the part. Westerners wanted their parks to conjure up visions of unsullied nature and altruistic intentions – mangled machines and bomb shells suggested something different.

Finding true paradise none the less proved a challenging prospect, given that every landscape was touched in some form by pollution, pesticides or radioactive particles. In the quest for a pure parkscape, a group of English entrepreneurs and financiers in the late 1990s envisaged their own Eden inside a series of biodomes in Cornwall. Perfectly insulated from the rigours of airborne contaminants, the Eden Project opened to the public in 2001, offering a wilderness garden in an artificial nutshell. Bringing the great out-doors indoors, the Eden Project showed one possible future for the park idea inside protected glass and plastic canopies. Visitors passed through distinctive re-creations of African tropics and Mediterranean gardens. Unsullied by human industry, or overcast skies, Eden tantalized its spectators with exotic biota and an environmentalist message. Project devotee Tim Smit explained Cornwall's Eden as an elaborate celebration of science and nature, with its multiple ecological zones a far cry from the consumer dorms of Disney. 'If this place becomes no more than an upmarket theme park it will have been the most gigantic waste of money,' he surmised.[22]

The Eden Project impressed by its celebration of floral variegation and human ingenuity. The work of a legion of horticulturists, Eden amounted to a 'living theatre of plants and people', as the tourist brochure enthused. The perfection of the image was overwhelmingly utopic, and, by definition, religiously optimistic. Nobody dared quip that the domes amounted to a Jurassic Park without dinosaurs, a mediated nature experience in its own way as fake as Disney. For many, the Eden Project instead represented an engineering, agricultural marvel. The scheme attested to human predilections for moulding nature and wandering through garden creations at leisure. What better take on the park idea(l) at the dawn of the new millennium than a day trip to Eden.[23]

In fact, the Cornish enclave conveyed a dual message well hidden behind the verdant foliage. The horticultural project testified to human salvation through conservationist ethics, but also ruminated on the global spread of ecological devastation. The domes at Eden lauded pure nature by keeping out impurities. Such a situation hardly seemed enviable. Wilderness remained captured inside a curious 'ship in a bottle' display. Eden thus did not seem that natural. It hardly amounted to the open freedom or primeval grandness of Yosemite or Yellowstone. Some might argue that Cornwall's Eden shared more with Nevada Test Site as a dual landscape pregnant with unworldly qualities, an extraterrestrial domain hardly in harmony with the rural contours of the English south-west. Project staff themselves described the aesthetics as 'from outer space, like the dazzling spaceship of *Close Encounters*'. In actuality, the Eden Project had far more in common with another 1970s science fiction film, *Silent Running*, in which humans left an irradiated earth in spaceships hauling wilderness biodomes in tow, transporting the park idea across the final frontier.[24]

TECHNOLOGY, ROBOTS AND THE DAWNING OF THE VIRTUAL PARK

The Eden Project still projected the park as an essentially organic experience. Designers aspired to keep the intrusion of technology to a minimum, engineering skills serving as a conduit towards naturalism in the fashion of Olmsted's Central Park. Yet, while hardly embracing post-industrial values, Eden, like other parkscapes forged in the post-1945 period, relied on technology for salvation. The futuristic domes of Eden performed the cardinal role of ecological facilitators, giant post-Victorian greenhouses that enabled the circumvention of weather systems and the propagation of exotic species. The domes highlighted the vital role of technology in the twenty-first-century park. Eden joined forces with industrial, science and theme parks in advertising technology as at the very hub of park design.

Ultimately, the welcoming of technology inside the park reflected the dominance of technology outside. In the post-1945 period, high technology took root within the park stable as a way to immerse clientele in fantasy. Animatronic characters (including a robotic Abraham Lincoln) populated Disney parks. With their movements dictated by signs, queues and Mickey Mouse guides, guests behaved like their robotic brethren. Observing this passive but regimented fantasy world, Umberto Eco pointed out how 'its visitors must agree to behave like its robots'. By the late twentieth century, technology-driven parks had seemingly reduced people to automatons, and robots to park guides.[25]

Such a portent was not lost on Michael Crichton, writer and director of the science fiction film *Westworld* (1973). Projecting the Disney ethos into the future, *Westworld* related the joys and horrors of an entirely automated theme park, Delos, where visitors offered 'the vacation of the future today' chose to stay in android-populated re-creations of Rome, medieval Europe, or the American frontier. In 'Westworld', travellers entered a perfect simulation of the Wild West. However, rather than the timid voyeurism of Disneyland, the space park offered its guests active roles in the entertainment. Visitors freely challenged android gun-fighters to duels and welcomed 'fully functioning' prostitutes to their beds. *Westworld* took the historic purposes of the park – play and movement – to an extreme. In the process, attendees swiftly lost the ability to differentiate fiction from reality, or robotics from flesh. The park became a world unto itself, a completely independent, autonomous society. However, in Crichton's take, the perfect simulation was flawed by android self-consciousness and faulty circuitry. An unexpected robot-led revolt highlighted the dangers of realizing such a fantastical world. Forced to engage in real and deadly conflict with an android gunslinger played by Yul Brynner, sapient park visitors proved strangely impotent. *Westworld* imparted the pleasures and perils of automating parks beyond human control – a theme of 'science run amok' that Crichton later reprised in *Jurassic Park*.

Like Delos, technologically driven parks regularly looked backwards for inspiration. In their architectural homage to ancient Greece and Rome, park designers had always sought to offer their guests simulations of idealized pasts. At Disney, Frontierland and Main Street USA drew on popular infatuations with the Wild West and turn-of-the-century small town America. Such locales never existed in the precise forms reanimated by Mickey Mouse. Yet technology allowed designers to create a Disneyfied history that people felt comfortable with. Technology, in the form of robotics and landscape engineering, enabled three-dimensional simulations so immersive that visitors found themselves rereading the past through park media. At high-tech theme worlds such as Disneyland, replication extended beyond the boundaries of simple architectural homage or cultural referencing. As Umberto Eco relates, 'The theme of hyper realistic reproduction involves not only Art and History, but also Nature.' Technological parks included in their simulations the remaking of nature in a mechanical cast, a prime example being the Disney tree.

But why replace nature with an organic-looking machine? 'At Disney, nature is appearance, machine is reality,' explained Michael Sorkin. Arguably, the preference for fake flora inside technological parks suggested a resonant human need for reconstruction, for improving on organic and social designs. In wider society, imitation and simulation proved pervasive. With plastic trees and rubberized animals, parks served as experiments in the perfection of replication and the perfect manifestation of human ingenuity.[26]

With many of today's parks installed as havens for simulated nature, the necessity of preserving material nature might be called into question. Preferences for simulation and replication have reached their zenith in the dawning of the virtual park – a landscape wholly designed, built and given 'life' in a computer-engineered environment. At DreamlandPark.com, opened in 2002 by Twilyte VR Entertainment, netizens can enter an on-line park featuring all manner of attractions (or 'worlds') to visit, from 'Paradise' to the gambling haven 'Bingo'. Punters at Dreamland Park are positively encouraged to add their own three-dimensional constructions to the virtual ensemble – to offer their own vision of the park idea. Meanwhile, virtual versions of Central Park, Yosemite and Fenway Park have all been generated on the Internet with varying degrees of authenticity.[27]

The social construction of nature reaches its apogee in such artificial climes, with the park no longer a physical or tangible space, instead a technological and imaginary configuration. Virtual parks indicate a shift away from the concrete and towards the binary. The electronic park thereby promises the triumph of the artificial (and purely cultural) over the organic (and non-human) in the park ideal. In the future, parks may not endure as places to visit physically, but rather exist only as dislocated, non-corporeal web domains. Why travel to a real park for a fantasy fix, when a perfect facsimile beckons with a click of the mouse? Such ideas may seem radical and unlikely, but one lesson of the post-1945 park adventure is that simulation can outperform reality – as the superior attendance figures at Disneyland compared to Yosemite suggest.

For all their manufactured demeanour, virtual parks do, however, indicate a level of interest in the great outdoors. To simulate signifies, after all, an excursion in flattery. Arguably, the most artificial creations of humanity are also the most pure reflections of our idealizations; to turn the park into a virtual domain perhaps attests to an enduring love of the idea itself. For Sorkin, 'the abiding theme of every park is nature's transformation from civilisation's antithesis to its playground.' If so, then virtual parks complete an age-old process. Finally, nature has been civilized, made human. Such electronic reserves may, in turn, herald the total democratization of the park idea, where once the park invited only the highest echelons of society.[28]

Radically, in the future, parks may no longer require geographical territory. The park idea may make its transition into cyberspace, a realm far removed from the park's earthly origins. However, just as likely is the maintenance of old and historic parks for succeeding generations. While *Westworld* provides one vision of the park of the future, Gene Roddenberry's *Star Trek* serves up another prospect. At the beginning of *Star Trek V: The Final Frontier* (1989), Captain James T. Kirk mountaineers on Mount Capitan at Yosemite. He then participates in a traditional campfire sing-along with his veteran crew. As these Hollywood visions intimate, the post-1945 period highlights a desire to make 'our Edens' in many different forms. The park concept is moulded to fit memorial, scientific, religious and historic purposes. Such a multiplicity of sentiments indicates that the park has some life in it yet.

Conclusion: The Park Ideal from Paradise to Utopia

In one of the many memorable scenes in the action movie *Jurassic Park* (1993), park director John Hammond (played by Richard Attenborough) seeks to reassure his guests as to the safety of his new 'prehistoric' theme park. When things start to go pear-shaped at the remote island off Costa Rica, Hammond relates to chaos theorist Ian Malcolm (Jeff Goldblum) how every theme park experiences teething problems, even the original Disneyland. Malcolm responds by pointing out that not every theme park features live dinosaurs – when the Pirates of the Caribbean ride, for example, breaks down, tourists are left disappointed but not running for their lives.

Jurassic Park grossed over $50,000,000 in its opening weekend in the United States, and went on to become an international blockbuster. Film critics saw in *Jurassic Park* a warning sign about technology run amok, a moral commentary on the scientific revolution (and the future possibilities) of DNA splicing. It was equally an exercise in kids' entertainment, all digital monsters and adrenalin action sequences. Significantly, *Jurassic Park* was rarely related to ideas about the park.

Jurassic Park combined two park concepts normally kept separate: the park as an amusement centre (akin to Coney Island) and the park as a natural museum (as in Kruger or the Galapagos). Visiting Hammond's 'Jurassic Park' promised the ultimate thrill ride, an adventure through a lost valley of dinosaurs. Compared to nondescript theme park rides based loosely on the prehistoric age, with plastic dinosaurs strategically placed to intimidate, 'Jurassic Park' offered a more tangible experience with ancient fauna. Restoring lost species to the present, owner John Hammond brought to life a whole wing of the British Natural History Museum. Previously viewed as skeleton exhibits held together by pins and plaster of Paris, dinosaurs took on form and flesh as live creatures in an island gallery. By restoring extinct species (including *Tyrannosaurus Rex*), writer Michael Crichton went one further than ranger-led plans in national parks to bring back extirpated fauna such as the grey wolf and the alpine ibex. Jurassic Park reinvented life, and reanimated it in a bestial enclosure. As biological specimens, island residents found themselves caged like animals in a nineteenth-century zoo, dangerous and rare beasts corralled for the public to scrutinize. Meanwhile, that the park went wrong – with dinosaurs challenging their human benefactors – replayed a common fear of circus and zoo staff – of the tiger biting its keeper.

Just like Frederick Law Olmsted, 'Capability' Brown and Walt Disney, John Hammond had a grand vision of the park ideal. 'Jurassic Park' promised much by its medley of scientific and natural wonder, novelty and entertainment, grand scenes and spectacle. It was a park like no other. At the same time, Hammond's tropical enclave built on established tropes in the park concept. While far less tumultuous than the rollercoaster rides on offer through 'Jurassic Park', the same themes and values have resonated during our own journey through the park diaspora.

FROM EDEN TO DISNEY

From Eden to Disney, the design of parks has shifted dramatically. Beginning as a divinely crafted enclave marked by few tools or implements, the modern park, in several of its incarnations, boasts sophisticated engineering and machine-oriented idolatry. Technologically saturated landscapes such as the science park, the research park and the theme park push the park ideal towards the frontiers of knowledge and exploration. The park has become a place of technical experiment and mastery, a conclusion best exemplified by the vast recesses of Nevada National Environmental Research Park, a place entirely given over to military research and testing. Potentially, as in the case of *Westworld*, we have opened ourselves to lands controlled by machine messiahs. Compared to the divinely ordained Garden of Eden, Disney World is made by elaborate machines, and kept running by computers. City parks in the nineteenth century, by their natural veneer, sought to ameliorate the isolation and alienation brought on by exposure to the Industrial Revolution. Things have changed. The park in the twentieth century openly embraced technology. The machine has been welcomed into the park (where before it was hidden), to the extent that mechanized entertainment, rather than natural thrills, has become the prime symbol of leisure in several parkscapes. The steel rollercoaster, rather than the wilderness sojourn, is what many children look for on the modern park horizon.

The image of parks has equally moved on. Spectacle has always been an important aspect of design, with favoured landscapes (such as Versailles or the Grand Canyon) promising unparalleled aesthetic delights. Perfecting the scenery has led to all manner of subtle landscape reconfiguring, from the addition of boardwalks to the removal of unwanted 'pests' and unsightly trees. However, the quest for the perfect image has gradually led to a new trend in park schematics, one that circumvents ecological parameters and ignores the earthy canvas. Increasingly, the notion of spectacle has become associated with illusion and simulation in the modern park canon. While organic features complemented the lavish fetes at Versailles, nature seems increasingly peripheral in modern parkscapes. Instead, virtual parks and theme parks celebrate the triumph of the artificial, the rule of the image over geographical reality.

Parks have become places of fakery and replication. The creed of naturalism verges on becoming a computer-rendered effect rather than an organic reference point. Such artificial, image-orientated landscapes exert control over visitors in an intricate fashion. Whereas the gentry touring Stourhead found themselves following a meandering trail, free to idle and muse, Disney guides and signs inform vacationers as to how to behave, where to walk, and how to respond to the park itself in a more regimented way. Aesthetic directionism has grown with the rise of the artificial park. As landscapes become more man-made, more control is exercised over touring denizens.

In the Garden of Eden, just two people wandered in its realms. Today, millions of people gather in parks around the globe. The popularity of parkscapes is momentous. As a key entertainment and leisure venue, the park is here to stay. Such success brings with it an associated cost, however. From tortuous queues for rollercoaster rides at Alton Towers to auto convoys through Yosemite, the park ideal has become a victim of its own popularity – people are 'loving the parks to death'. Far from blind to the unfolding circus of visitors, park stewards have responded with measures to co-ordinate services better and even to restrict use in peak times. Theme parks have instigated single-rider tickets to fill seating gaps. Caps on automobile access in some national parks have forced people to abandon their vehicles, taking buses and walking trails instead. The drive-through park may yet join the drive-through movie theatre as an anachronistic entertainment landscape.

The rising popularity of parks relates, in large part, to their role as public landscapes. The elitism of the English landscape park, privy to the rich and the royal, has been replaced by modern city parks open to all and sundry. Yet, the potential for the park to return to its more exclusive roots remains. According to Mike Davis, the sprawling, segregated city of Los Angeles indicates the decline of 'urban liberalism, and with it the end of what might be called the Olmstedian vision of public space' at the end of the twentieth century. Davis foresees and fears in equal measure the loss of public mixing and social reformism that underscored Olmsted's urban park creations. In Los Angeles, public space is increasingly marginalized, city parks closed down and left 'derelict', 'pedestrian democracy' undercut, while exclusive greened gateway communities rise up on city perimeters. The municipal park, at least in its urban form, may yet become a victim of a broader war between public and private use, class and moneyed interests.[1]

Popular esteem is also linked to the broadening of the park ideal. In the post-1945 period, the park ideal evolved to cater for new landscape possibilities and fresh social dictates. Parks have become consumer paradises (in the guise of Disney), residential blocks (in the form of trailer parks) and places of work (as in industrial parks), each tailoring their space to attract a particular clientele. Where once the park symbolized only a landscape for recreation, it now presents a far greater compendium of human activity. It is a 'catch-all' landscape used to connote salubriousness. This broad reinvention of the park ideal has yet to reveal fully its effects on both nature and society.

Whether the park ideal remains cogent depends, in part, on the preservation of a few core ideas. The park ideal needs to be understandable and comprehensible in order to survive. Fortunately, even on the frontiers of park design, at Disneyland and Stanford Industrial Park, traditional staples of the park concept, of recreation, greenery, inspiration and social uplift, all endure. Parks similarly remain landscapes of power. The park as a kingly prize, epitomized by Louis XIV's resplendent Versailles, has metamorphosed into the corporate giant's headquarters. Luxuriant greenery continues to signify superficial opulence and stately riches. Below the surface, park landscapes bespeak an age-old negotiation between culture and nature. The park concept entails the synthesis of both social and organic artefacts, a coming together of dual forces. Contemporary parks include Kruger, where wildebeest roam and nature figures largely, and Disney, where Mickey Mouse frolics and technology makes it all possible. Ultimately, parks represent dialectical landscapes, places where we quite literally work out our relations with the natural world.

The myth of the park as a perfect island also persists. Since the Garden of Eden, the park has been depicted as a special place set aside from civilization, a bordered and distinct zone. Millions of vacationers have prized the park for this very concept of separation – valuing the landscape as a mythic escape from reality and everyday burdens. Entering the park, moving through its gates, yields a psychological effect akin to entering paradise itself. Yet, the park (except perhaps in its virtual guise) sports a continuing connection to real landscapes, politics and people. Controversies over resource access, environmental despoliation, land rights and sovereignty have dominated planning discussions over the years. Parks always interact with their surrounding environments. At Disneyland and Yellowstone alike, post-1945 success spawned a legion of hotels, freeways and stores on their boundaries. Conservationists at least have come to recognize the relational aspects of parks to surrounding environments – and have set about protecting wildlife corridors that incorporate both parklands and exterior spaces. Seeing the park as part of a much broader landscape remains crucial to understanding the park itself.

Finally, the park ideal offers a narrative of hope. It is a geographical space reflecting all manner of social, political and environmental impulses. Park landscapes serve as the phoenixes of human betterment. This sense of hope originally derived from a crude sense of nature didacticism that inferred that being in natural surroundings automatically led to improvement. It has now expanded to include other paradigms. As vernacular landscapes, parks commonly offer stories people want to hear. From Eden to Disney, good triumphs over evil within the park fraternity. Parks have become salvific experiences. As Karal Ann Marling declares, 'A trip to Disney is like going to heaven.' Within this trajectory of the park ideal, two visions come to the fore, one of the park landscape as a paradise lost, the other as a utopia glimpsed.[2]

PARKS AS PARADISE LOST

Parks have always serviced human fascination with paradise. The Persian word *pardes*, which translates as garden, orchard, pleasure ground or park, forms the literal foundation for the word 'paradise'. Paradise has accordingly always been green. Persian royal hunting grounds proved to be early examples of the melding of parkdom with themes of unbounded pleasure, recreation and reward. Biblical text referred to the Garden of Eden as the original paradise, a peaceable, bucolic kingdom of humans and animals. This definition of paradise – as a heavenly, godly and naturalistic realm – has dominated Western European thought ever since. For the early Christian parish, a heavenly paradise signified just rewards for toils in the real world. Made by God on this Earth, the Garden of Eden was also seen to have tantalizing real world origins. John Milton, in *Paradise Lost* (1674), wrote: 'to reward His faithful, and receive them into bliss, Whether in heav'n or earth; for then the earth Shall all be paradise'. Meanwhile, European explorers searched for the true Garden of Eden, conquering new worlds and peoples in the process. As we have seen, paradise (and the park idea) gradually earned associations with constructions of primitivism, the noble savage, wilderness and innocence. In the United States, George Catlin proposed 'a nation's park' to enclose extant Indians and bison – losing paradise tantamount to the collapse of America's heritage. Later, conservationists moved to restore parcels of wild nature as living museums with similar thoughts in mind. For nature-lover John Muir, the mountains of Yosemite, where he conjoined his Christian faith with a more biocentric philosophy, signified a paradise enclave. Yosemite became one of the world's earliest national parks and, for America, a national treasure. More recently, Crichton's *Jurassic Park* related one man's search for paradise, while the formation of the Eden Project in Cornwall embodied a further reanimation of pure and untainted nature.[3]

Many good things have resulted from the popular and enduring conception of parks as paradises. Such a sensibility has fuelled human responsibility towards the natural world. Vital ecological fragments have come under governmental protection. Many parks across the globe provide valuable refuges for endangered species of plant and animal life. Nature parks, as rare vignettes where ecology truly matters, highlight the role of the non-human in a world increasingly dictated by sapient exigencies. In the twenty-first century of pesticide contaminants and global warming, parks offer spaces as close to the 'other' world of nature as we can get. Their relatively unspoiled countenance makes them special, earning them credence as otherworldly paradises. As cultural Edens too, parks have performed an estimable function. Paradise is viewed as a realm where rivalries and conflicts disappear, where contemplation and bliss take root.

However, distinct flaws exist in this construction of the park as paradise. Such notions have projected a comprehension of the natural world as a spectacle to visit. Nature has been rendered as a weekend escape, and, in consequence, something separate from everyday living. In Genesis, Adam and Eve were cast out of the Garden after succumbing to temptation – paradise no longer a place where they worked or lived. This denouement had repercussions for human–nature relations and for the park idea. Nature has become a museum object, a cultural artefact and a place only for visiting. It is paradise lost and found, a Jurassic park, and a locale of separation. The absence of park visions in Aboriginal spirituality is instructive here. When mythology situated humans as part of nature, the park had no meaning. Only when civilizations separated themselves from the natural, did the purpose of the park become obvious.

PARKS AS UTOPIA

Whereas notions of the park as paradise make sense, the idea of the park as utopia initially confounds. Utopia, after all, is typically imagined as a city on the hill, in the mould of Thomas More's Amaurot (*Utopia*, 1516) or Campanella's *City of the Sun* (1602). A product of Renaissance Europe, Utopia, as a civic, urban and scientific mode of living just beyond the reach of man, hardly matches with the preternatural images of wilderness that predominate in park design. Utopia bespeaks the perfection of civilization, a perfect state of governance and politics, rather than a world removed from society, be it in the guise of Yosemite or Disneyland. It is first and foremost a place of people, not nature. More himself railed against the landscape parks of England and their aristocratic owners, writing in *Utopia*: 'As if forests and parks had swallowed up too little of the land, those worthy countrymen turn the best inhabited places in solitudes; for when an insatiable wretch, who is plague to his country, resolves to enclose many thousand acres of ground, the owners, as well as tenants, are turned out of their possessions, by tricks, or by main force.' The urbanized civic state of Utopia was located far from country estates and regent parklands.[4]

Yet, popular visions of utopia have included the park within city gates. Like paradise (seen by scholars Frank and Fritzie Manuel to have shaped many versions of utopia by a common language of religious inference), the park remains caught up in utopian dreams. Notions of both 'park' and 'utopia' are commonly viewed as products of Western culture. Writers and visionaries crafted their utopias as a way to mirror, and thus highlight, problems of contemporary society. Lewis Mumford discovered how in 'Almost every utopia is an implicit criticism of the civilization that served as its background'. Utopia, at the same time, emerges from the rubble as a beacon of light, a projected optimistic path for a downtrodden society to take. As venerable social experiments, parks equally serve as geographically inclined responses to social ills and vices, making an imprint on the land where utopias can be found on the written page. Park schematics thus proved far from accidental. Initially evident as stark symbols of authority and power, the park canon has grown to include sophisticated social criticism and cultural idealism. Successive designs reacted to new political directions – notably, the emergence of the city park movement in synthesis with mass democracy. Parks have provided material escape from industrial and social ailments in a similar mode to how intellectual imaginings of utopia have given solace. The park landscape has commonly functioned as a paradigm of reaction against contemporary social problems, promising a green tonic, a natural remedy, to civic alienation. Where once Gilgamesh journeyed to Humbaba's hunting park looking for the plant of immortality, enlightened park creators in later years ably recognized the potential of park landscapes themselves to serve as social elixirs. Frederick Law Olmsted cast nature as social uplift, his designs promising the renewal of core human values: dignity, peace and personal esteem. The park as a place of natural balance represented a refuge in a sea of urban chaos. Utopian aspirations were clearly in evidence. Central Park was a masterpiece of human as well as landscape engineering. Sir Ebenezer Howard's Garden City movement of the early 1900s drew on similar impulses, marrying greenery, civility and public order. As idealized spaces of leisure, contemplation and hope, parks presented utopian landscapes in the making.[5]

While utopian philosophy has drifted through the park ideal, literary imaginings of utopia have likewise included their share of green references. A man-made island, with a capital city of Amaurot at its centre, Thomas More's 'Utopia' responded to the specific political and social deficiencies of medieval England. His lavish garden city of Amaurot boasted a fresh water supply and three-storey townhouses, each sporting large enclosed gardens. In More's description, the population of Utopia 'cultivate their gardens with great care, so that they have both vines, fruits, herbs, and flowers in them; and all is so well ordered, and so finely kept, that I never saw gardens anywhere that were so fruitful and so beautiful as theirs'. More's civic fantasy exerted an influence on urban planning and public amenity provision later on, yet his Utopia failed to include a park framework.[6]

Enlightenment philosopher Francis Bacon mapped out his utopia, the 'New Atlantis', in 1627. Bacon presented a world full of machine-engineered abundance, from furnaces to sweet-smelling perfume-houses. This amounted to a utopia very different from the one sketched by Thomas More. Along with hyperreal orchards and gardens, the product of significant tinkering with the 'taste, smell, colour, and figure' of each plant, Bacon included parks and animal enclosures in his Atlantis. Designed 'not only for view or rareness, but likewise for dissections and trials', parks served as experimental landscapes, more animal testing centres than wilderness enclaves. Just like Atlantis's 'mathematic house' given over to instruments of geometry, parks were party to the ethos governing Bacon's utopia: the art and impulse of a rational, mechanized and scientific mind-set. According to Bacon's ideal, nature and the park were both dissected down to their bare bones – and conceived in terms of their utility to service the advancement of knowledge and power.[7]

This enduring link between green spaces and utopia receives scrutiny from Gibson Burrell and Karen Dale in their contribution to *Utopia and Organization*. The authors classify a number of foundational principles of utopia: the establishment of boundaries (between the best inside and the beastly outside), the protection afforded to utopians, harmonious control over such denizens, the prominence of planning, and the endurance of formality. For Burrell and Dale, these organizing tenets are striking for their resemblance to typical garden design. The formation of park landscapes subscribes to similar precepts. A critical point here is how utopias and parks are both places that people like to visit, be it in their minds or with their bodies. Ultimately, parks seem closer to utopia than many of us are prepared to admit.[8]

If one park stands out as a conscious attempt at utopia 'made', it is Disneyland. The magical kingdom of Disney represents a manufactured fantasy realm for kids, adults, international tourists and US citizens alike. The cartoon world stands for the perfection of childhood, for the sanctity of naive recreation. Compared to nearby Los Angeles, a dystopic landscape lambasted by a legion of critics, most recently, and famously, Mike Davis, Disney is fantastical. For French philosopher Jean Baudrillard, Disney is American utopia achieved, a leisure landscape framed in terms of an interactive, immersive cartoon movie reel with visitors playing supporting roles. The spool keeps running without interruption. Nothing is allowed to go wrong – everything is perfect and perfected, as in our visions of utopia. Just like utopia, Disney centres on day-dreaming the ideal life. As Lewis Mumford wrote in his *Story of Utopias*, 'utopia stands in common usage for the ultimate in human folly or human hope – vain dreams of perfection in a Never-Never Land or rational efforts to remake man's environment and his institutions.' The presence of 'Peter Pan's Flight' at the original Disneyland only cements this sense of Disney's parks as classic 'Never-Never Lands'. The Disney experience itself sprang from one man's dream-world – Walt Disney's imagined place – now rendered in plastic and concrete in California, Florida, Tokyo and Paris, and facilitated by a rational, detailed masterpiece of architectural and social design. An important question none the less remains: can utopia ever really be achieved, even with meticulous planning? By definition, utopia merges the Greek for 'good place' (*eu topos*) with the semblance of 'no place' (*ou topos*), resulting in an unattainable, but mesmerizing fantasy land. As More surmised in the original *Utopia*, such a place is unreachable. As a concept and a landscape goal, utopia remains restricted by its imaginary underpinnings. Disney embodies one attempt to capture the image of utopia and make it real. For many, this encapsulates its wonder, the reason why they visit. Yet, as Baudrillard affirms, the Disney (and for him American) utopia is all about hyperreality, simulation and perception. It is thoroughly unreal.[9]

Ultimately, the park ideal has, as yet, proved incapable of furnishing the human race with paradise or utopia. Forcing landscapes to conform to spiritually influenced visions of paradise has historically proved a troubled exercise based on species manipulation and the forced removal of indigenous peoples. The difficult creation of locales such as Yosemite and Kruger has rendered them imperfect paradises. The park ideal, while compatible with utopianism in its preference for social ordering and optimism, also differs on matters of elemental function. Parks hardly represent total models on which to base entire societies. Most remain oriented towards the specifics of recreation and leisure, and exclude matters of work and residency. Over time, science parks and business parks may change this aspect. However, as Disney's flawed attempt to fashion its theme park template into the town of Celebration proved, the park ideal is not automatically transferable to life outside its boundaries, to utopia writ large. As journalists Douglas Frantz and Catherine Collins point out, many believed in 'the myth that living in Celebration would be the closest thing to living at Disney World'; however, the park fantasy failed to deliver the perfect residential experience. While the theoretical rewards of making life outside the park more park-like seem significant, results have proved less than spectacular in practice. True to its original remit, the park remains an enclosure – utopia and paradise human imaginings perhaps impossible to craft.[10]

That said, fecund ties between utopia, paradise and parkscape remain. According to the Bible, the human story begins in paradise, and ends in Jerusalem, a biblical utopia, in the book of Revelation. The park ideal meanwhile has shifted from the Garden of Eden to the twenty-first century 'Holy City' of Disneyland (and with it, Celebration). The Manuels, writing in the 1970s, commented on the enduring appeal among humans for returning to paradise while looking forward to an ideal future: 'To bathe in the waters of paradise or utopia for a precious while has made existence bearable for man under the most ghastly conditions.' Through history, parks have followed in this distinguished tradition. Part of an endless fascination with perfect nature and cultural idealism, the park concept has been, and will continue to be, reinvented to suit our intellectual whims.[11]

Notes

INTRODUCTION: DEFINING THE PARK

1   Raymond Williams, *Keywords: A Vocabulary of Culture and Society* (London: Fontana, 1976), 219.
2   Alfred Runte, *Yosemite: The Embattled Wilderness* (Lincoln: University of Nebraska Press, 1990); Jane Carruthers, *The Kruger National Park: A Social and Political History* (Pietermaritzburg: University of Natal Press, 1995); Janet Wasko, *Understanding Disney: The Manufacture of Fantasy* (Cambridge: Polity, 2001); Elizabeth Barlow, *Landscape Design: A Cultural and Architectural History* (New York: Harry Abrams, 2001); John Dixon Hunt, *Gardens and the Picturesque* (Cambridge, MA: MIT Press, 1992); Roy Rosenzweig and Elizabeth Blackmar, *The Park and the People: A History of Central Park* (Ithaca, NY: Cornell University Press, 1992); Stephen J. Pyne, *How the Canyon Became Grand: A Short History* (New York: Penguin, 1998). The contribution of Carl Hagenbeck to zoo design is discussed by Nigel Rothfels, *Savages and Beasts: The Birth of the Modern Zoo* (Baltimore: Johns Hopkins University Press, 2002). For further details on recommended titles, see 'A Guide to Further Reading'.
3   Charles E. Beveridge and Carolyn Hoffman, eds, *The Papers of Frederick Law Olmsted*, Supplementary Series, Vol.1: *Writings on Public Parks, Parkways and Park Systems* (Baltimore: Johns Hopkins University Press, 1997), 309, 216.
4   Ibid. 328, 211, 216.
5   Anthony Burgess and Robert E. Park, *The City* (Chicago: University of Chicago Press, 1967 [1925]); Mike Davis refers to the map of Chicago as 'The most famous diagram in social science', in *Ecology of Fear: Los Angeles and the Imagination of Disaster* (London: Picador, 2000 [1998]), 364.

CHAPTER 1. FROM ANCIENT GROVES TO VERSAILLES

1   Marie Luise Gothein, *History of Garden Art: From the Earliest Times to the Present Day*, 2 Vols., ed. Walter Wright (London: J. W. Dent, 1928), i. 30.
2   Ibid. 40.
3   Xenophon, *Cyropaedia*, quoted in J. K. Anderson, *Hunting in the Ancient World* (Berkeley: University of California Press, 1985), 58.
4   Evan Eisenberg, *Ecology of Eden* (New York: Picador, n.d.), 151.
5   E. V. Rieu, *The Odyssey* (Harmondsworth: Penguin, 1946), 115.
6   Pliny the Younger, *Natural History*, quoted in J. Donald Hughes, *Pan's Travail: Environmental Problems of the Greeks and Romans* (Baltimore: Johns Hopkins University Press, 1994), 170.
7   Seneca, *Epistles*, quoted in ibid.

8 See J. Donald Hughes, 'Artemis: Goddess of Conservation', *Forest and Conservation History*, 34 (Oct. 1990), 193.

9 J. Donald Hughes, 'Early Greek and Roman Environmentalists', in *Historical Ecology: Essays on Environmental and Social Change*, ed. L. Bilsky (New York: Kennikat Press, 1980), 48–9.

10 Julia S. Berrall, *The Garden: An Illustrated History from Ancient Egypt to the Present Day* (London: Thames & Hudson, 1966), 39.

11 Ibid. 42.

12 John Michael Hunter, *Land into Landscape* (London: George Goodwin, 1985), 25.

13 Quoted in Anderson, *Hunting in the Ancient World*, 86.

14 Ibid. 101.

15 Pliny the Elder, *Naturalis Historia*, 12.111. Also see Kathryn L. Gleason, '*Porticus Pompeiana*: A New Perspective on the First Public Park of Ancient Rome', *Journal of Garden History*, 14 (1994), 19.

16 Gothein, *History of Garden Art*, i. 46.

17 The account, by Archbishop Romuald of Salerno, is cited in John Julius Norwich, *The Kingdom of the Sun, 1130–1194* (London: Faber & Faber, 1976), 156–7.

18 *De Profectione Ludovici VII in Orientem*, quoted in Henry Maguire, 'Gardens and Parks in Constantinople', *Dumbarton Oaks Papers*, 54 (2000), 252. Available online at <http://www.doaks.org/etexts.html>.

19 See Oliver Rackham, *The History of the Countryside: The Full Fascinating Story of Britain's Landscape* (London: J. M. Dent, 1986), 123–4.

20 William Greswell, *The Forests and Deer Parks of Somerset* (Taunton: Barnicott & Pearce, Athenaeum Press, 1905), 242.

21 Hunter, *Land into Landscape*, 77.

22 Ibid.

23 Ibid. 53.

24 Stewart Harding and David Lambert, eds, *Parks and Gardens of Avon* (Bristol: Avon Gardens Trust, 1994), 16.

25 Greswell, *Forests and Deer Parks*, 242.

26 Harding and Lambert, eds, *Parks and Gardens of Avon*, 15.

27 Charles Chenevix Trench, *The Poacher and the Squire: A History of Poaching and Game Preservation in England* (London: Longmans, Green & Co., 1967), 71.

28 Hunter, *Land into Landscape*, 87.

29 Thomas, quoted in Susan Lasdun, *The English Park: Royal, Private and Public* (London: André Deutsch, 1991), 60.

30 See Louis XIV, *The Way to Present the Gardens of Versailles* (Paris: Réunion des Musées, 1982).

31 Robert W. Berger, *In the Garden of the Sun King* (Washington, DC: Dumbarton Oaks Research Library and Collection, 1985), 21.

32 Berrall, *The Garden*, 211.

33 Gothein, *History of Garden Art*, i. 75–6.

34 Hugh Prince, *Parks in England* (Isle of Wight: Pinhorns, 1967), 5.

CHAPTER 2. THE ENGLISH LANDSCAPE PARK

1 Joseph Addison, *The Spectator*, no. 414 (25 June 1712). See also John Dixon Hunt and Peter Willis, eds, *The Genius of the Place: The English Landscape Garden 1620–1820* (London: Paul Elek, 1975), 51.

2 Alexander Pope, 'An Epistle to Lord Burlington' (1731), in Hunt and Willis, eds, *The Genius of the Place,* 212.

3 John Dixon Hunt, *Gardens and the Picturesque* (Cambridge, MA: MIT Press, 1992), 128.

4 Brown, quoted in Dorothy Stroud, 'Our Landscape's Debt to the 18th Century', *Geographical Magazine* (May 1952), 20.

5 William Gilpin, 'Remarks on Forest Scenery' (1791), in Hunt and Willis, eds, *The Genius of the Place,* 339.

6 Tom Williamson, *Polite Landscapes: Gardens and Society in Eighteenth-Century England* (Baltimore: Johns Hopkins University Press, 1995), 107.

7 Similar parks could be found at Rousham, Oxfordshire, and Painshill, Surrey.

8 Julia S. Berrall, *The Garden: An Illustrated History from Ancient Egypt to the Present Day* (London: Thames & Hudson, 1966), 266.

9 Williamson, *Polite Landscapes,* 73.

10 Kenneth Woodbridge, *The Stourhead Landscape* (London: National Trust, 2002), 17.

11 Interview with Matthew Ward, Head Gardener, Prior Park, Bath, 20 Dec. 2002.

12 Repr. in Bryan Little, *Prior Park: Its History* (Bath: Prior Park College, 1975), 18.

13 The National Trust, 'Prior Park Landscape Garden Conservation Plan 2002', 15. Held at Prior Park Landscape Garden Estates Office, Prior Park, Bath.

14 Rosemary Feesey, *A History of Wivenhoe Park: The House and Grounds* (Colchester: Benham & Co., 1963), 7.

15 Williamson, *Polite Landscapes,* 140.

16 Quoted in Hugh Prince, *Parks in England* (Isle of Wight: Pinhorns, 1967), vii.

17 Pierre Bourdieu uses the concept of 'cultural capital' to define the skills, objects and attitudes used by an individual to navigate certain social fields or networks. The park might be seen as such a resource. See Pierre Bourdieu, 'Social Space and the Genesis of Groups', *Theory and Society,* 14/6 (1985), 723–44.

18 Stroud, 'Our Landscape's Debt', 17.

19 Woodbridge, *Stourhead Landscape,* 17.

20 Berrall, *The Garden,* 311.

21 See Jennifer Price, *Flight Maps: Adventures with Nature in Modern America* (New York: Basic Books, 1999), 114–24.

22 Isaac Jefferson, *Life of Isaac Jefferson of Petersburg, Virginia, Blacksmith* (1847), ed. Charles W. Campbell. Cited at <http://www.lib.virginia.edu/speccol/exhibits/nature/jefferson.html>.

23 Peter Coates, *Nature: Western Attitudes since Ancient Times* (Cambridge: Polity; Berkeley: University of California Press, 1998), 123; Thomas Jefferson, 'Memorandums made on a Tour to Some of the Gardens of England', repr. in Hunt and Willis, eds, *The Genius of the Place,* 333.

24 For the history of the National Trust, see Jennifer Jackson and Patrick James, *From Acorn to Oak: The Growth of the National Trust, 1895–1994* (London: Macmillan, 1994); Peter Mandler, *The Fall and Rise of the Stately Home* (London: Yale University Press, 1997); Howard Newby, ed., *The National Trust: The Next Hundred Years* (London: National Trust, 1995); Paula Weideger, *Gilding the Acorn: Behind the Façade of the National Trust* (London: Simon & Schuster, 1994).

25 Newby, ed., *National Trust,* 24.

26 Benedict Anderson, *Imagined Communities: Reflections on the Origin and Spread of Nationalism* (London: Verso, 1991 [1983]), 5–7. Additional texts on heritage, monuments and collective memory are listed in the Bibliography.

27 Hewison read this renewed interest in parks as indicative of 'a country obsessed with its past, and unable to face its future'. See Robert Hewison, *The Heritage Industry: Britain in a Climate of Decline* (London: Methuen, 1987), 9.

28 Anthea Taigel and Tom Williamson, *Parks and Gardens* (London: B. H. Batsford, 1993), 144.

CHAPTER 3. THE CITY PARK: BRINGING THE COUNTRY TO THE METROPOLIS

1 Julia S. Berrall, *The Garden: An Illustrated History from Ancient Egypt to the Present Day* (London: Thames & Hudson, 1966), 28.

2 Susan Lasdun, *The English Park: Royal, Private & Public* (London: André Deutsch, 1991), 74–5.

3 John Dryden, *Marriage à la Mode*, ed. Mark S. Auburn (London: Edward Arnold, 1981), 91.

4 See E. P. Thompson, *Customs in Common* (London: Merlin Press, 1991), 113.

5 Neville Braybrooke, *London Green: The Story of Kensington Gardens, Hyde Park, Green Park, & St James' Park* (London: Victor Gollancz, 1959), 27.

6 Roy Rosenzweig and Elizabeth Blackmar, *The Park and The People: A History of Central Park* (Ithaca, NY: Cornell University Press, 1992), 5.

7 Thomas More, *Utopia* (London: Penguin, 1965 [1516]), 73.

8 Paul Zucker, *Town and Square: From the Agora to the Village Green* (New York: Columbia University Press, 1959), 2.

9 Wood, quoted in Stewart Harding and David Lambert, *Parks and Gardens of Avon* (Bristol: Avon Gardens Trust, 1994), 53.

10 Tobias Smollett, *The Expedition of Humphry Clinker* (London: Hutchinson & Co., 1771), 116.

11 Anthea Taigel and Tom Williamson, *Parks and Gardens* (London: B. T. Batsford, 1993), 130.

12 John W. Reps, *The Making of Urban America: A History of City Planning in the United States* (Princeton: Princeton University Press, 1965), 330.

13 Lasdun, *English Park*, 137.

14 Galen Cranz, *The Politics of Park Design: A History of Urban Parks in America* (Cambridge, MA: MIT Press, 1982), 5.

15 Ibid. 157.

16 Thomas Bender, *Toward an Urban Vision: Ideas and Institutions in Nineteenth Century America* (Baltimore: Johns Hopkins University Press, 1975), 13.

17 Speech quoted in J. C. Loudon, 'A Catalogue of Trees and Shrubs' (1840), Derby Local Studies Library.

18 Leo Marx, *The Machine in the Garden: Technology and the Pastoral Ideal in America* (New York: Oxford University Press, 1964).

19 See Lasdun, *English Park*, 142, 140, 130, 128.

20 Cited by Frederick Law Olmsted, 'The People's Park at Birkenhead, near Liverpool. By W., Staten Island, New-York' (1851), in *Papers of Frederick Law Olmsted*, Supplementary Series, vol. 1: *Writings on Public Parks, Parkways, and Park Systems*, ed. Charles E. Beveridge and Carolyn Hoffman (Baltimore: Johns Hopkins University Press, 1997), 72–3.

21 Russel Nye identified Fairmont Park, Philadelphia, landscaped in 1812, as an important precedent, but other scholars emphasize the lack of dedicated park spaces in US cities

prior to the 1850s. See Russel Nye, 'Eight Ways of Looking at an Amusement Park', *Journal of Popular Culture,* 15/1 (Summer 1981), 63; Reps, *Making of Urban America,* 331; Dorceta E. Taylor, 'Central Park as a Model for Social Control: Urban Parks, Social Class & Leisure Behavior in Nineteenth-Century America', *Journal of Leisure Research,* 31/4 (1999), 429.

22 Reps, *Making of Urban America,* 330.

23 Ibid. 331.

24 Frederick Law Olmsted, 'People's Park at Birkenhead', 70–3.

25 Taylor, 'Central Park as a Model for Social Control', 430.

26 Frederick Law Olmsted, 'Public Parks and the Enlargement of Towns' (1870), in *Papers of Frederick Law Olmsted,* ed. Beveridge and Hoffman, i. 196.

27 Ibid. 189.

28 *New York Evening Post,* 31 May 1856.

29 Rosenzweig and Blackmar, *Park and the People,* 64.

30 *New York Herald,* 29 Dec. 1859.

31 Rosenzweig and Blackmar, *Park and the People,* 136.

32 Bender, *Toward an Urban Vision,* 159.

33 Reps, *Making of Urban America,* 344.

34 *San Diego Union,* 4 Nov. 1869.

35 *Butte Miner,* 25 May 1889.

36 *New York Herald,* 27 Dec. 1858.

37 S. B. Sutton, ed., *Civilizing American Cities: A Selection of Frederick Law Olmsted's Writings on City Landscapes* (Cambridge, MA: MIT Press, 1971), 202.

38 Stephen Germic, *American Green: Class, Crisis and the Deployment of Nature in Central Park, Yosemite and Yellowstone* (Lanham, MD: Lexingten Books, 2001), 2.

39 Quoted in Rosenzweig and Blackmar, *Park and the People,* 10.

40 Cranz, *Politics of Park Design,* 28.

41 Ibid., 196.

42 Quoted in Galen Cranz, 'Women in Urban Parks', *Signs: Journal of Women in Culture and Society,* 5/3 (1980), s80.

43 Rosenzweig and Blackmar, *Park and the People,* 323.

44 Taylor, 'Central Park as a Model for Social Control,' 462.

45 John Montgomery Ward, 'Our National Game', *Cosmopolitan* (Oct. 1888), 448; Lawrence Ritter, *Lost Ballparks: A Celebration of Baseball's Legendary Fields* (New York: Penguin, 1992), 10.

46 Ritter, *Lost Ballparks,* xi; Philip Lowry, *Green Cathedrals* (Manhattan, KS: AG Press, 1986), 19; For Ebbet's Field, see Ron Smith, *The Ballpark Book,* rev. edn (St Louis, MO: Sporting News Books, 2003), 222–9.

47 Giamatti quoted at <http://baseball-almanac.com/quotes/fenway_park_quotes.shtml>. Also see Ritter, *Lost Ballparks,* 50–61; Karl B. Raitz, ed., *The Theater of Sport* (Baltimore: Johns Hopkins University Press, 1995) for the changing relationship between sports and their venues.

48 Alan Tate, *Great City Parks* (London: Spon Press, 2001), 108.

49 Ibid. 71.

50 Cranz, *Politics of Park Design,* 101.

51 Tate, *Great City Parks,* 11.

52 Ibid. 45.

53 See William H. Whyte, *The Social Life of Small Urban Spaces* (Washington, DC: The Conservation Foundation, 1980).

54 Jane Jacobs, *The Death and Life of Great American Cities* (London: Jonathan Cape, 1961), 89–90.

55 Quoted in ibid. 76.

56 Tate, *Great City Parks*, 23.

57 David Higgs, ed., *Queer Sites: Gay Urban Histories since 1600* (London: Routledge, 1999), 15.

58 Topos: European Landscape Magazine, eds, *Parks: Great Spaces in European Cities* (Munich: Callwey, 2002), 5.

CHAPTER 4. NATURE AND RECREATION IN
THE NATIONAL PARK

1 Angus Waycott, *National Parks of Western Europe* (Southampton: Inklon, 1983), 7–8.

2 Wallace Stegner, 'The Best Idea We Ever Had', in *Marking the Sparrow's Fall: The Making of the American West*, ed. Page Stegner (New York: Henry Holt, 1998), 137; Donald Worster, *Nature's Economy: A History of Ecological Ideas* (New York: Cambridge University Press, 1994), 261; Roderick Nash, quoted in John Hendee, *Wilderness Management* (Washington, DC: Department of Agriculture, 1978), 43.

3 George Catlin, *North American Indians*, ed. Peter Matthiesen (New York: Penguin, 1989 [1841]), 263.

4 Henry David Thoreau, *Three Complete Books: The Maine Woods, Walden, Cape Cod* (New York: Gramercy, 1993), 98.

5 Quoted in Rebecca Solnit, *Savage Dreams: A Journey into the Landscape Wars of the American West* (New York: Vintage Books, 1994), 239.

6 See Michael Milstein, *Yellowstone: 125 Years of America's Best Idea* (Billings, MT: Billings Gazette, 1996), 8.

7 *Helena Herald*, 28 Feb. 1872; Nathaniel Langford, 'Annual Report of the Superintendent of the Yellowstone National Park for the year 1872' (Washington, DC: Government Printing Office, 1872), Bancroft Library, University of California, Berkeley.

8 See Osborne Russell, *Journal of a Trapper*, ed. Aubrey Haines (Lincoln: University of Nebraska Press, 1965), 46; Aubrey Haines, *The Yellowstone Story: A History of Our First National Park*, 2 vols (Yellowstone National Park, WY: Yellowstone Association, 1996), 90; W. Turrentine Jackson, 'The Creation of Yellowstone National Park', *Mississippi Valley Historical Review*, 29/2 (1942), 188, 189–90.

9 John Muir, *Our National Parks* (Madison: University of Wisconsin Press, 1981 [1901]), 1.

10 'The Corner Stone was Laid', *Wonderland*, 30 Apr. 1903.

11 John Muir, *The Yosemite* (New York: Doubleday, 1962 [1912]), 97.

12 See Alfred Runte, *National Parks: The American Experience* (Lincoln: University of Nebraska Press, 1979), 7; Richard White, 'The Nationalization of Nature', *Journal of American History*, 86/3 (1999), 976–86.

13 Runte, *National Parks*, 7.

14 Henry David Thoreau, 'Walking', in Ralph Waldo Emerson/Henry David Thoreau, *Nature/Walking* (Boston: Beacon Press, 1991), 95.

15 Muir, *Yosemite*, 3.

16 Frederick Law Olmsted, 'Yosemite and the Mariposa Grove: A Preliminary Report, 1865' (Yosemite, CA: Yosemite Association, 1995).

17 See Charles E. Beveridge and Carolyn Hoffman, eds, *The Papers of Frederick Law Olmsted: Supplementary Series vol. 1: Writings on Public Parks, Parkways and Park Systems* (Baltimore: Johns Hopkins University Press, 1997).

18 Quoted in Alston Chase, *Playing God in Yellowstone: The Destruction of America's First National Park* (San Diego: Harcourt Brace, 1987), 105.

19 Tobias Smollett, *The Expedition of Humphry Clinker* (London: Hutchinson & Co., 1771), 110.

20 Olmsted, 'Yosemite and the Mariposa Grove'.

21 Joseph Grinnell and Tracy Storer, 'Animal Life as an Asset of National Parks', *Science*, n.s. 44, 1133 (15 Sept. 1916), 375–80.

22 See Karen Jones, *Wolf Mountains: A History of Wolves Along the Great Divide* (Calgary: University of Calgary Press, 2002), for predator policy in US and Canadian parks.

23 The irony was that the open vistas so appealing to Euro-American tastes largely reflected Indian fire-burning regimes.

24 Muir, *Yosemite*, 197.

25 Robert Sterling Yard, *The National Parks Portfolio* (Washington, DC: Government Printing Office, 1917), 5, 3. For issues of parks and transport, see Alfred Runte, *Trains of Discovery: Western Railroads and the National Parks* (Flagstaff, AZ: Northland Press, 1984); Marguerite Shaffer, *See America First: Tourism and National Identity, 1880–1940* (Washington, DC: Smithsonian, 2001); Paul Sutter, *Driven Wild: How the Fight Against Automobiles Launched the Modern Wilderness Movement* (Seattle: University of Washington Press, 2002).

26 Milstein, *Yellowstone*, 64.

27 Thomas Dunlap, *Nature and the English Diaspora: Environment and History in the United States, Canada, Australia and New Zealand* (Cambridge: Cambridge University Press, 1999), 119.

28 John Shultis, 'The Creation of National Parks and Equivalent Reserves in Ontario and the Antipodes: A Comparative History and its Contemporary Expression', in *Changing Parks: The History, Future and Cultural Context of Parks and Heritage Landscapes*, ed. John S. Marsh and Bruce W. Hodgins (Toronto: Natural Heritage/Natural History, 1998), 193.

29 *Lithgow Mercury*, 9 June 1899.

30 Shultis, 'Creation of National Parks', 197.

31 Quoted in William Lothian, *A Brief History of Canada's National Parks*, vol. 1 (Ottawa: Parks Canada, 1976), 23.

32 See Janet Foster, *Working for Wildlife: The Beginning of Preservation in Canada* (Toronto: University of Toronto Press, 1998), 22; Robert Craig Brown, 'The Doctrine of Usefulness: Natural Resource and National Park Policy in Canada, 1887–1914', in *Parks and Protected Areas in Canada*, ed. P. Dearden and R. Rollins (Toronto: Oxford University Press, 1993), 20.

33 Lothian, *A Brief History*, 23.

34 For discussion of the repentant hunter, game conservation and colonialism, see Richard Fitter and Peter Scott, *The Penitent Butchers: Seventy-five years of Wildlife Conservation* (London: Collins, 1978); John MacKenzie, *The Empire of Nature: Hunting, Conservation and British Imperialism* (Manchester: Manchester University Press, 1988), 262–94.

35 Roderick Nash, *Wilderness and the American Mind*, 3rd edn (New Haven: Yale University Press, 1982), 355–7.

36 For colonial images of an African Eden and the relationship between conservation, science and empire, see Melissa Leach and James Fairhead, *Misreading the African Landscape: Society and Ecology in a Forest–Savanna Mosaic* (Cambridge: Cambridge University Press, 1996); Richard Grove, *Green Imperialism: Colonial Expansion, Tropical Island Edens and the Origins of Environmentalism, 1600–1860* (Cambridge: Cambridge

University Press, 1995); MacKenzie, *Empire of Nature*; Jonathan Adams and Thomas McShane, *The Myth of Wild Africa* (Berkeley: University of California Press, 1992).

37 Quoted in Jane Carruthers, 'Creating a National Park, 1910 to 1926', *Journal of Southern African Studies*, 15/2 (1989), 204.

38 James Stevenson-Hamilton, *South African Eden: From Sabi Game Reserve to Kruger National Park* (London: Cassell & Co., 1952 [1937]), 106–7.

39 Jane Carruthers, *The Kruger National Park: A Social and Political History* (Pietermaritzburg: University of Natal Press, 1995), 56.

40 See Carruthers, 'Creating a National Park', 209; Stevenson-Hamilton, *South African Eden*, 207.

41 The preserve in the foothills of the Himalayas was named for the renowned hunter of man-eating lions turned conservationist, photographer and best-selling writer of *The Maneaters of Kumaon* (1944).

42 George M. Wright, Joseph S. Dixon and Ben H. Thompson, *Fauna of the National Parks of the United States: A Preliminary Survey of Faunal Relations in National Parks*, Contributions of Wildlife Survey, Fauna Series no. 1 (Washington, DC: Government Printing Office, 1933).

43 Stevenson-Hamilton, *South African Eden*, 260–1.

44 Ibid.

45 Memo from James Harkin to Mr Cory, 20 May 1925, RG84, vol. 137, file U.300, pt. 3, Public Archives Canada, Ottawa.

46 Quoted in Runte, *National Parks*, 169.

47 Lary Dilsaver, ed., *America's Park System: The Critical Documents* (Lanham, MD: Rowman and Littlefield, 1997), 51.

48 *Daily Oklahoman*, 28 Apr. 1940.

49 Nash, *Wilderness and the American Mind*, 358.

50 'The Convention Relative to the Preservation of Flora and Fauna in their Natural State', 8 Nov. 1933. Available online at <http://www.univie.ac.at/RI/KONTERM/ intlaw/konterm/vrkon_en/html/doku/fauna33.htm#1.0>.

51 Richard West Sellars, *Preserving Nature in the National Parks: A History* (New Haven: Yale University Press, 1997), 152.

52 *Calgary Herald* article reprinted in the *Ottawa Morning Journal*, 30 June 1945.

53 Nash, *Wilderness and the American Mind*, 360.

54 William Wordsworth, *A Guide through the District of the Lakes* (Bloomington: Indiana University Press, 1952 [1810]), 127.

55 See Charles Stewart, 'A National Park for Scotland', *Nineteenth Century and After*, 55/327 (May 1904), 822–6.

56 John Sheail, 'The Concept of National Parks in Britain, 1900–1950', *Transactions of the Institute of British Geographers*, 66 (Nov. 1975), 42.

57 Ibid. 48.

58 See Michael Cohen, *The History of the Sierra Club, 1892–1970* (San Francisco: Sierra Club Books, 1988), 260.

59 David Brower, *Work in Progress* (Salt Lake City: Peregrine Smith Books, 1991), 97–110.

60 Cohen, *History of the Sierra Club*, 443.

61 Runte, *National Parks*, 171.

62 Ibid. 175.

63 Nash, *Wilderness and the American Mind*, 333.

64 *Billings Gazette*, 14 Nov. 2003.

65 Erik Eckholm, *Down to Earth* (New York: W. W. Norton, 1982), 8.

66   Hanekom later retracted his comment. See Jane Carruthers, 'Dissecting the Myth: Paul Kruger and the Kruger National Park', *Journal of Southern African Studies*, 20/2 (1994), 264.

67   Edward Abbey, *Desert Solitaire: A Season in the Wilderness* (New York: Ballantine Books, 1968), 277–8.

68   Michael Frome, 'National Parks or Theme Parks?', Fiftieth Annual Banquet of Olympic Park Associates, Seattle, Washington, 7 Nov. 1998.

69   Aaron G. Bruner, Raymond E. Gullison, Richard E. Rice and Gustavo A. B. da Fonseca, 'Effectiveness of Parks in Protecting Tropical Biodiversity', *Science*, 291 (5 Jan. 2001), 125–8.

70   Quoted in Jim Birckhead, Terry De Lacy and Laura Jane Smith, eds, *Aboriginal Involvement in Parks and Protected Areas* (Canberra: Aboriginal Studies Press, 1992), 46.

CHAPTER 5. AMUSEMENT PARKS AND THEME PARKS

1   'See You in Tivoli' park brochure, 2003, courtesy of Tivoli Gardens.

2   A. H. Saxon, *P.T. Barnum: The Legend and the Man* (New York: Columbia University Press, 1989), 132. See also P. T. Barnum, *The Life of P.T. Barnum Written by Himself* (Urbana, IL: University of Illinois Press, 2000 [1855]).

3   Congress: Edo McCullough, *Good Old Coney Island: A Sentimental Journey into the Past* (New York: Fordham University Press, 2000 [1957]), 267–70; Thompson, cited in Russel B. Nye, 'Eight Ways of Looking at an Amusement Park', *Journal of Popular Culture*, 15/1 (Summer 1981), 65. For freak shows, see Robert Bogdan, *Freak Show: Presenting Human Oddities for Amusement and Profit* (Chicago: University of Chicago Press, 1988).

4   Ingalls, cited in Karal Ann Marling, ed., *Designing Disney's Theme Parks: The Architecture of Reassurance* (Paris: Flammarion, 1997), 21; Nye, 'Eight Ways', 65.

5   See Michael Immerso, *Coney Island: The People's Playground* (New Brunswick, NJ: Rutgers University Press, 2002), 39.

6   See Judith A. Adams, *The American Amusement Park Industry* (Boston: Twayne, 1991), 49, on Luna's clientele. For the importance of Fred Thompson, see Woody Register, *The Kid of Coney Island: Fred Thompson and the Rise of American Amusements* (New York: Oxford University Press, 2001). Thompson recognized the value of new rides and relentlessly providing everyday spectacles. For Thompson, Luna was about 'movement, movement, movement everywhere', 86.

7   Immerso, *Coney Island*, 39. Freud saw Coney as 'magnified Prater', ibid. 81.

8   Quotations taken from Peter Bennett, *Blackpool Pleasure Beach: A Century of Fun* (Blackpool: Blackpool Pleasure Beach, 1996), 144, 32, 19.

9   *The Experience! Blackpool Pleasure Beach* (1997 videocassette).

10   Nye, 'Eight Ways', 65.

11   For Coney and class issues, see Kathy Peiss, *Cheap Amusements: Working Women and Leisure in Turn-of-the-Century New York* (Philadelphia: Temple University Press, 1986), 115–38. On Kennywood, see Adams, *American Amusement Park Industry*, 75.

12   The influence of Disney extends far beyond that of park design, or the remit of this study. See Janet Wasko, *Understanding Disney: The Manufacture of Fantasy* (Cambridge: Polity, 2001), and Alan Bryman, *Disney and his Worlds* (London: Routledge, 1999), for worthwhile introductions. For films and Disney, see Eleanor Byrne and Martin McQuillan, *Deconstructing Disney* (London: Pluto Press, 1999).

13   Disney, quoted in Margaret J. King, 'Disneyland and Walt Disney World: Traditional Values in Futuristic Form', *Journal of Popular Culture*, 15/1 (Summer 1981), 120.

14 Aviad E. Raz, *Riding the Black Ship: Japan and Tokyo Disneyland* (Cambridge, MA: Harvard University Press, 1999), 187.

15 Marling, ed., *Designing Disney's Theme Parks*, 74.

16 For further exploration of Frontierland, see Michael Steiner, 'Frontierland as Tomorrowland: Walt Disney and the Architectural Packaging of the Mythic West', *Montana: The Magazine of Western History*, 48/1 (Spring 1998), 2–17.

17 Finch, cited in King, 'Disneyland and Walt Disney World', 116; Marling, ed., *Designing Disney's Theme Parks*, 85.

18 Hench, cited in Adams, *American Amusement Park Industry*, 97.

19 Stephen M. Fjellman, *Vinyl Leaves: Walt Disney World and America* (Boulder, CO: Westview Press, 1992), 10.

20 Henry A. Giroux, *The Mouse that Roared: Disney and the End of Innocence* (Lanham, MD: Rowman and Littlefield, 1999), 35–6.

21 James M. Cameron and Ronald Bordessa, *Wonderland Through the Looking Glass: Politics, Culture and Planning in International Recreation* (Maple, Ontario: Belsten, 1981), 109–13; George Ritzer, *The McDonaldization of Society* (Thousand Oaks, CA: Pine Forge, 1993), 1.

22 Alan Bryman, 'The Disneyization of Society', in *McDonaldization: The Reader*, ed. George Ritzer (Thousand Oaks, CA: Pine Forge, 2002), 52. For the original work, see Alan Bryman, 'The Disneyization of Society', *Sociological Review*, 25/5 (Feb. 1999), 25–47.

23 Giroux, *Mouse that Roared*, 55; The Project on Disney, *Inside the Mouse: Work and Play at Disney World* (Durham, NC: Duke University Press, 1995), 106.

24 Raz, *Riding the Black Ship*, 197.

25 Jean Baudrillard, 'Disneyworld Company', *Liberation*, 4 Mar. 1996. Baudrillard defines hyperreality as 'models of a real without origin or reality: a hyperreal', in *Simulations* (New York: Semiotext, 1983), 2. See also Baudrillard, *America* (London: Verso, 1988 [1986]), 55–7.

26 Glucksmann, quoted in Andrew Lainsbury, *Once Upon an American Dream: The Story of Euro Disneyland* (Lawrence: University Press of Kansas, 2000), 42.

27 Cameron and Bordessa, *Wonderland*, 113; Umberto Eco, *Travels in Hyperreality* (London: Pan Books, 1987 [1986]), 41, 43; Raz, *Riding the Black Ship*, 88 (TDL orientation quiz for 'cast members').

28 For the dangers of Disney, see Project on Disney, *Inside the Mouse*, 115–17, and Anthony Lovett and Matt Maranian, *LA Bizzaro!: The Insider's Guide to the Obscure, the Absurd, and the Perverse in Los Angeles* (New York: St Martin's Press, 1997), 98–101. Also worth consulting is Wayne Ellwood, ed., 'The Mousetrap: Inside Disney's Dream Machine', *New Internationalist*, 308 (Dec. 1998), special issue.

29 'Roller Coaster Lovers Get a New High', *USA Today*, 2 May 2003.

30 Alexander Wilson, *The Culture of Nature: North American Landscape from Disney to the Exxon Valdez* (Cambridge, MA: Blackwell, 1992), 181.

31 Eco, *Travels in Hyperreality*, 44.

32 Willis, quoted in Project on Disney, *Inside the Mouse*, 185.

33 Knott's Berry Farm in California started out as a fruit stall in the Depression. The evolution of entertainment landscapes such as Seaworld, which take nature as their theme, are discussed in the next chapter.

34 Official park website, <www.europapark.de>; Europa Park tour brochure (2003), courtesy of Europa Park.

35 Cameron and Bordessa, *Wonderland*, 114.

36 Raz, *Riding the Black Ship*, 3.

37 Lainsbury, *Once Upon an American Dream*, 34, 33.

38 'Coca-colonization': Frederick Ferney, 'L'Amér Look des Anti-Américains', *Le Nouvel Observateur*, 3–9 Jan. 1986, 26; John Tabliabue, 'A Comic-Strip Gaul Battles Disney', *New York Times*, 9 Aug. 1995, 3; <www.parisdigest.com/withchildren/parcaste.html>.

39 Project on Disney, *Inside the Mouse*, 85.

40 Fjellman, *Vinyl Leaves*, 60; 'Mickey Mouse History': Mike Wallace, cited in Giroux, *Mouse that Roared*, 41.

41 Marling, ed., *Designing Disney's Theme Parks*, 29.

CHAPTER 6. TRAPPING NATURE IN THE ANIMAL PARK

1 See Sally Walker, 'Zoological Gardens of India', in *Zoo and Aquarium History: Ancient Animal Collections to Zoological Gardens*, ed. Vernon N. Kisling, Jr (Boca Raton, FL: CRC Press, 2001), 252–4.

2 Bacon, cited in Vernon Kisling, 'Ancient Collections and Menageries', in *Zoo and Aquarium History*, 30.

3 Society prospectus, cited in David Hancocks, *A Different Nature: The Paradoxical World of Zoos and their Uncertain Future* (Berkeley: University of California Press, 2001), 42–3.

4 For the zoo as a colonial enterprise, see Harriet Ritvo, 'The Order of Nature: Constructing the Collections of Victorian Zoos', in *New Worlds, New Animals: From Menagerie to Zoological Park in the Nineteenth Century*, ed. R. J. Hoage and William A. Deiss (Baltimore: Johns Hopkins University Press, 1996), 43–50, and idem, *The Animal Estate: The English and Other Creatures in the Victorian Age* (Cambridge, MA: Harvard University Press, 1987).

5 M. Howland, 'The Philadelphia Zoo', *Harper's Magazine*, 58 (1878), 703.

6 Advertisement noted in Hancocks, *A Different Nature*, 87.

7 The sale of Jumbo 17 years later was blamed on his unpredictable behaviour, but the loss of Britain's premier faunal celebrity still caused national consternation. Despite stubborn resistance on boarding his shipping crate, Jumbo sailed to America, where he attracted record crowds. A freak train accident killed him in 1885.

8 Society aims detailed in Kisling, 'Zoological Gardens', 162.

9 *Plan and Guide to the Zoological Gardens Giza Near Cairo, Egypt* (1902), found in Wilhelmus Labuschagne and Sally Walker, 'Zoological Gardens of Africa', in Kisling, ed., *Zoo and Aquarium History*, 335.

10 See Alpheus Hyatt, 'The Next Stage in the Development of Public Parks', *Atlantic Monthly*, 67 (1891), 215–24.

11 'Longleat: So Much That's New to See and Do', tourist brochure (*c.* 1995).

12 *Commercial Advertiser*, 5 Jan. 1903.

13 Elizabeth Hanson, *Animal Attractions: Nature on Display in American Zoos* (Princeton: Princeton University Press, 2002), 2.

14 Ibid. 7; Hancocks, *A Different Nature*, 5.

CHAPTER 7. EXPANDING THE PARK EXPERIENCE

1 See Andrew Hurley, *Diners, Bowling Alleys and Trailer Parks: Chasing the American Dream in Post War Consumer Culture* (New York: Basic Books, 2001), 199.

2 Ministry of Housing and Local Government, *Caravan Parks: Location, Layout, Landscape* (London: HMSO, 1962), 41.

3 Patrick M. Malone and Charles A. Parrott, 'Greenways in the Industrial City: Parks and Promenades along the Lowell Canals', *Industrial Archaeology*, 24/1 (1998), 19, 28.

4 The historic significance of Lowell led to the area being set aside as a National Historical Park in the late twentieth century.

5 Dianne Sussman, 'The 1950s: So Long, Sleepy Town', *Palo Alto Weekly*, 13 Apr. 1994.

6 John M. Findlay, *Magic Lands: Western Cityscapes and American Culture after 1940* (Berkeley: University of California Press, 1992), 131.

7 Manuel Castells and Peter Hall, *Technopoles of the World: The Making of 21st Century Industrial Complexes* (London: Routledge, 1994), 26.

8 See <http://www.sophia-antipolis.org> for details of the French effort and comments by Pierre Laffitte. Technopoles are also discussed by Castells and Hall, *Technopoles of the World*, 85. For further details of Xi'an and other Chinese parks, see Susan M. Walcott, *Chinese Science and Technology Industrial Parks* (Aldershot: Ashgate, 2003).

9 See the Center for Economic Conversion, Mountain View, California, web site: <www.conversion.org/cec/>.

10 Victor Gruen, quoted in 'The Garden Court', press release, 7 Oct. 1956, Southdale Center, now posted at <www.southdale.com>; Jon Goss, 'The "Magic of the Mall": An Analysis of Form, Function, and Meaning in the Contemporary Retail Built Environment', *Annals of the Association of American Geographers*, 83/1 (Mar. 1993), 19.

11 Margaret Crawford, 'The World in a Shopping Mall', *Variations on a Theme Park: The New American City and the End of Public Space*, ed. Michael Sorkin (New York: Hill & Wang, 1992), 16. For comments on North Garden, see Mark Gottdiener, *The Theming of America: Dreams, Visions, and Commercial Spaces* (Boulder Co: Westview Press, 1997), 89–90.

12 WEM advertisement: Goss, 'The Magic of the Mall', 28.

13 Gottdiener, *Theming of America*, 3; Edward Soja, *Postmodern Geographies: The Reassertion of Space in Critical Social Theory* (London: Verso, 1989), 246; see also see Michael J. Dear, *The Postmodern Urban Condition* (Oxford: Blackwell, 2000), and Douglas Frantz and Catherine Collins, *Celebration, USA: Living in Disney's Brave New Town* (New York: Henry Holt, 1999).

14 Nurit Schleifman, 'Moscow's Victory Park: A Monumental Change', *History and Memory*, 13/2 (Fall/Winter 2001), 6.

15 Adam B. Ellick, 'From Zappa to Lenin: Lithuanian Sculptors Chronicle the Times through the Soviet Era to Today', *City Paper (The Baltic States)*, Hyperlink <www.baltic-sww.com/lenin_to_zappa.htm>; 'Stalin World', *City Paper (The Baltic States)* HYPER-LINK <www.balticsww.com/stalin_world.htm>; Van Smith, 'Welcome to Stalin World: Vivat! Terror, Tourism, and Soviet Art', *Baltimore City Paper*, 5–11 Mar. 2003; 'Lithuanian opens Soviet Theme Park', *CNN* <www.edition.cnn.com/2001/world.europe/04/03/grutas.theme/>.

16 RoadsideAmerica.com, 'Protests Means Publicity and Profits For Holy Land Experience' 11 Mar., 2001, available at <www.roadsideamerica.com/tnews/QueryNews. php3?Tip_Description=Holy+Land+Experience#news5736>; also <www.roadside america. com/attract/ FLORLholyland.html>.

17 'Devil Theme Park is a Hot Property,' *Sunday Times*, 27 Oct. 2002; Lucian Kim, 'Can "Dracula Land" put Transylvania in the Black?', *Christian Science Monitor*, 31 Oct. 2001.

18 Steven M. Johnson, 'Revisiting the Nukes', *Cry California* (Summer 1979), 20–1; Richard Misrach, *Bravo 20: The Bombing of the American West* (Baltimore: Johns Hopkins University Press, 1990), xv; 95, 95–8.

19 John Wills, ' "Welcome to the Atomic Park": American Nuclear Landscapes and the "Unnaturally Natural" ', *Environment and History*, 7 (2001), 463.

20 <www.nv.doe.gov/nts/researchpark.htm>; see 'The Great DOE Land Rush?', *Science*, 282 (23 Oct. 1998), 616–17; Virginia H. Dale and Patricia D. Parr, 'Preserving DOE's Research Parks,' *Issues in Science and Technology*, 14/2 (1998), 73–7.

21 US Department of Energy, 'Finding of No Significant Impact: Integrated Natural Resources Management Plan and Environmental Assessment for Rock Creek Reserve', Apr. 2001, for the purposes of compliance with the National Environmental Policy Act, 1969. Copy distributed by the US Department of Energy, Rocky Flats Field Office, Golden, Colorado. Rebecca Solnit , *Savage Dreams: A Journey into the Landscape Wars of the American West* (New York: Vintage, 1994), 228–9, 367–8.

22 In Mike Petty, ed., *Eden: The Guide*, (London: Eden Books, 2001), 1.

23 Ibid. 3.

24 Ibid. 46.

25 Umberto Eco, *Travels in Hyperreality: Essays* (London: Pan Books in association with Secker & Warburg, 1987 [1986]), 48.

26 Ibid. 49; Sorkin, ed., *Variations on a Theme Park*, 223.

27 Visit HYPERLINK <www.dreamland park.com/>. See also John Wills, 'Digital Dinosaurs and Artificial Life: Exploring the Culture of Nature in Computer and Video Games', *Cultural Values*, 6/4 (2002), 395–417.

28 Sorkin, ed., *Variations on a Theme Park*, 210.

CONCLUSION: THE PARK IDEAL FROM PARADISE TO UTOPIA

1 Mike Davis, 'Fortress Los Angeles: The Militarization of Urban Space', in *Variations on a Theme Park*, ed. Michael Sorkin (New York: Hill & Wang, 1992), 156, 158.

2 Karal Ann Marling, ed., *Designing Disney's Theme Parks: The Architecture of Reassurance* (Paris: Flammarion, 1997), 168.

3 John Milton, *Paradise Lost* (London: S. Simmons, 1674), book XII, 461–4.

4 Italian Tomasso Campanella described his utopia as a city constructed on a 'high hill', marked by seven circular walls, with a temple at its centre. See Campanella, 'City of the Sun', in *Famous Utopias*, ed. Charles Andrews (New York: Tudor, 1901), 275; Sir Thomas More, 'Utopia', also in *Famous Utopias*, 139.

5 Frank Manuel and Fritzie Manuel, *Utopian Thought in the Western World* (Cambridge, MA: Belknap Press, 1979), 33; Lewis Mumford, *The Story of Utopias* (New York: Viking, 1962 [1922]), 2.

6 More, 'Utopia', in *Famous Utopias*, ed. Andrews, 166.

7 Francis Bacon, 'The New Atlantis', in *Famous Utopias*, ed. Andrews, 265.

8 Gibson Burrell and Karen Dale, 'Utopiary: Utopias, Gardens and Organization', in *Utopia and Organization*, ed. Martin Parker (Oxford: Blackwell, 2002), 108–9.

9 Mumford, *Story of Utopias*, 1; see Mike Davis, *City of Quartz: Excavating the Future in Los Angeles* (London: Verso, 1990), and —, *Ecology of Fear: Los Angeles and the Imagination of Disaster* (London: Picador, 2000 [1998]); Jean Baudrillard, *America* (London: Verso, 1988 [1986]), 77; see also Krishan Kumar, *Utopianism* (Milton Keynes: Open University Press, 1991), 82–4.

10 Douglas Frantz and Catherine Collins, *Celebration USA: Living in Disney's Brave New Town* (New York: Henry Volt, 1999), 314.

11 Manuel and Manuel, *Utopian Thought*, 62.

A Guide to Further Reading

What follows amounts to a brief survey of literature on the park idea. Relevant material can be gleaned from a whole range of disciplines, including landscape architecture, garden history, cultural studies, geography, environmental history, biology, art and political science. The aspiring park expert should be prepared to become a generalist predator, or take a leaf out of 'Capability' Brown's book, and navigate the landscape with natural science, philosophy, poetry and aesthetics all in mind.

For overviews of the interaction between humans and the landscape from antiquity to the present day, Jellicoe and Jellicoe (1975) and Pregill and Volkman (1993) present good starting points and are replete with stunning illustrations. More antiquarian in nature, yet still useful, are chronicles of famous gardens by Berrall (1966) and Gothein (1928). Hunter (1985) and especially Barlow (2001) serve up a mixture of landscape study and cultural history. Broader studies tracing human attitudes to nature are worth consulting. See Coates (1998), Glacken (1967) and Thomas (1984) for analysis of shifting environmental mentalities. The American experience is particularly well covered by Huth (1957), Nash (1982) and Marx (1964), while Dunlap (1999) provides an admirable comparative study of settler societies and nature in the USA, Canada, Australia and New Zealand.

In terms of the park idea itself, no dedicated work exists that maps its evolution and global dissemination – an oversight that stoked our enthusiasm for writing this book. However, there are a variety of texts dealing with specific parks and geographical regions. Taigel and Williamson (1993) and Lasdun (1991) offer historical surveys of the park concept as it unfolded on British shores. For park making in the ancient world, scholarship by J. Donald Hughes (1980; 1990; 1994) is stimulating reading, notably for its consideration of the relationship between conservation and spirituality. For related discussions regarding Christianity, nature and environmental ethics, see L. White (1971), Gottlieb (1995) and Gray (1981). Ideas about Eden, paradise imagery and the colonial collecting ethos are reflected on by Foster (1998), Prest (1981) and Grove (1995). J. K. Anderson (1985) and Trench (1967) ponder historic associations between parks, hunting and class, while Gleason (1994) focuses on the artistry behind Roman experiments in civic space.

Certain park geographies have garnered special attention from scholars due to their famous owners, renowned landscape designers or resonant cultural allure. Versailles represents a particularly well-tended case, on which works by Berger (1985) and Lablaude (1995) impress most. Also worth a look is Louis XIV's guide (1982), an illuminating text setting out the Sun King's impression of the gardens laid out in his honour. Across the English Channel, a sizeable literature exists on the landscape park. Taking Alexander Pope's famous dictum for its title, Hunt and Willis's *Genius of the Place* (1975) provides a well-apportioned anthology delineating British ideas on landscape, philosophy and design through the voices of contemporary essayists, philosophers and aestheticians. Meanwhile, the shifting fads of garden design and the careers of notable architects (especially 'Capability' Brown) remain the focus of attention for Stroud (1975) and Hyams (1971). Woodbridge (2002, 1970), A. Mitchell (1996) and Clarke (1987) study the English park in microcosm via engaging studies of landscape change at Stourhead and Prior Park. Recent scholarship, meanwhile, has shifted from conceiving the park as simply a work of art to emphasizing its embedded cultural values. Williamson (1995) deconstructs the organic canvas to discover a space marshalled by all kinds of issues from class politics and elite recreational desires to local subsistence economics. The relationship between British parks and national identity is ably tackled by several authors. Daniels (1993) and Olwig (2002) provide stimulating commentary on the powerful symbolism of such terms as 'country' and 'landscape' in Britain and the USA, while Weltman-Aron (2001) plots the influence of the English mode in France. Issues of elitism and tradition resonate in contemporary debates surrounding the landscape park and heritage tourism, for which see Hewison (1987), Mandler (1997) and Hunter (1996).

Turning to the urban sphere, the park has provoked interest from town planners and sociologists for its design aspects, its aspirations of social engineering, and its spatial dynamics. Cranz (1980, 1982) offers an exemplary survey of the cultural and gender assumptions behind US park blueprints, while Jacobs (1961) and Whyte (1980) navigate the topic from the standpoint of urban renewal. For Jacobs, the dereliction of many city parks serves notice on the failure of civic improvement programmes, thereby calling into question the efficacy of the park concept itself. Whyte offers an entirely different appraisal, canonizing the park as an indicator of city health, with well-used green spaces a sure sign of civic vigour. The park remains open to interpretation, signalling different meanings to different scholars.

Within the historical fraternity, academic attention has congregated around the urban landmark of Central Park and the prolific career of Frederick Law Olmsted. For those seeking information on New York's esteemed 'green lungs', Rosenzweig and Blackmar's exhaustive *The Park and the People* (1992) remains the best account, while Barlow (1972) and Roper (1983) offer sturdy ovations to its illustrious designer. Given his contribution to the park ideal in city and national guises, not to mention extensive wanderings across the parklands of Europe, readers are well advised to browse the works of Frederick

Law Olmsted directly. Beveridge and Hoffman (1997) serve up a particularly instructive edited collection. Urban parks outside the Olmstedian frame have been relatively overlooked, although compendiums by Topos (2002) and Tate (2001) embody fine attempts at broadening the discourse by discussing the origins and evolution of distinct urban spaces across North America and Europe.

National park literature is voluminous, but tends to focus on the American example (and to a lesser extent the African). Runte's *National Parks: The American Experience* (1979) probably remains the best historical account of park making in the US tradition. America's 'crown jewel' preserves are graced by a number of quality tomes. Runte (1990) and Pyne (1998) provide lively histories of Yosemite and Grand Canyon. Yellowstone has received detailed review. Park Service historian Aubrey Haines imparts his capacious knowledge in the two-volume celebration of *The Yellowstone Story* (1996). The more populist, and lavishly illustrated, *Yellowstone: 125 Years of America's Best Idea* (Milstein 1996) captures the spirit of the preserve and the popular romanticism surrounding its governing idea. More critical appraisals emanate from Bartlett (1985) and Chase (1987), who single out tourism and 'natural regulation' policies as critical problems. Science and wildlife policy are examined in the US preserves by Sellars (1997) and developments either side of the 49th parallel by Jones (2002) and Lowry (1994). Carruthers (1989, 1994, 1995) remains the expert on Kruger, while MacKenzie (1988) and Fitter and Scott (1978) inform on relations between parks, conservation and hunting in an imperial frame. For coverage of Canada and Britain, see Marsh and Hodgins (1998), Dearden and Rollins (1993), MacEwen and MacEwen (1987) and Sheail (1975). For the distinctive Scottish experience, see Lambert (2001) and Smout (2000). Information on preserves in the Antipodes is relatively sparse, although Australia's Kakadu National Park receives a praiseworthy social and environmental history from Lawrence (2000). Controversies between indigenous peoples and park conservation initiatives have been well covered of late, and scholarship has tended to favour a critical perspective. For the US scenario, see Spence (1999), Keller and Turek (1998) and Burnham (2000). Drawing on extensive Aboriginal testimony, Birckhead, De Lacy and Smith (1992) have edited a provocative tome on the Australian scene. An estimable comparative analysis of policy in the USA, Canada and Australia can be found in Gardner and Nelson (1981), although developments have moved on since publication. A useful update considering events in the USA and Tanzania can be found in Igoe (2003).

If Yellowstone is the national park most subject to academic analysis, then the same is true for Disney in the field of amusement parks. Perhaps due to its cultural saturation, distinctive imagery and savvy commercial practices, Disney receives extensive consideration. A fine introduction to the world of Mickey Mouse can be found in Wasko (2001). Fjellman (1992) and Marling (1997) provide useful takes on park infrastructure, ideology and landscape design. Raz (1999) documents the Disney experience abroad in a stimulating tone dealing with work patterns and cultural cross-fertilization in Japan. The Project on Disney (1995) ventures a sharply critical appraisal of the Magic Kingdom and the authoritarian employment regime operating behind its wholesome veneer. Notable precursors Coney Island and Blackpool are given deserved treatment by McCullough (2000 [1957]), Immerso (2002) and Bennett (1996). A large body of material from critical theorists and sociologists is also worth consulting in regard to theme parks and (post)modernity. Baudrillard (1983, 1988 [1986]), Eco (1987 [1986]), Ritzer (1993, 2002) and Bryman (1995, 1999) are particularly useful in this regard, especially for theories on consumption and simulation.

The world of the animal park is comparatively bereft of literature. Scholars have lavished attention on Disney's plastic trees and animatronic fauna, but their real-life caged cousins remain somewhat neglected. There are, however, a few instructive texts well worth perusing. Hoage and Deiss (1996), Kisling (2001), and Baratay and Hardouin-Fugier (2002) offer broad surveys of zoos and the history of animal collection over time, while Hanson (2002) concentrates on the USA. Autobiographical accounts from the likes of filmmaker Armand Denis (1963) and Gerald Durrell (1984), the inspiration behind Jersey Zoo, provide light-hearted glimpses into the mentality of the collector-conservationist. Interested readers might also want to sound out broader surveys delineating the conflicted environmental and moral relations between humans and other animals. Ritvo (1987), Manning and Serpell (1994), and Mighetto (1991) offer reliable starting points.

Those intrigued by the fortunes of the park ideal since 1945 face a particularly esoteric literary collection. Few specific works exist on the park idea's more recent – and more bizarre – incarnations. Hurley (2001) provides a vivacious study of trailer parks among other working-class American icons, the diner and the bowling alley. Stanford industrial park is considered by Findlay (1992) in his exploration of California's fantasy landscapes, while Castells and Hall (1994) consider the global spread of the 'technopole', a fusion of corporatism, technological utopia and park schematics. Malone and Parrott (1998) provide some historical context to the business park phenomenon through their survey of the 'greening' of Lowell's industrial mills in the 1800s. Meanwhile, the wider scholarship on urban planning, the Disney influence in contemporary society, and the social function and dissemination of 'theming' are tapped in a number of provocative studies. Davis (2000 [1998]) and Frantz and Collins (1999) offer alternative visions in their studies of the dystopic landscape of Los Angeles and the urban paradise of Disney's Celebration town. The unlikely prospect of parks emanating from bomb holes is only just receiving academic scrutiny – Misrach (1990) and Wills (2001) provide insightful commentaries on this developing, and controversial, notion. Finally, with contemporary pundits postulating the rise of a virtual world and the technological possibilities of artificial life, treatises by Crang et al. (1999) and Soja (1989) are of relevance to the park diaspora, as is critical theorizing on the end of nature and the social construction of wilderness by the likes of McKibben (1990), Cronon (1995), Price (1999), Soulé and Lease (1995), and Wilson (1992).

Given the range and quality of relevant texts, the park enthusiast could spend many hours in the local bookstore and the library. A word of caution thus seems appropriate. In *The Ends of the Earth* (1989: 289) environmental historian Donald Worster offers excellent counsel: 'We must now and then get out of parliamentary chambers, out of birthing rooms and factories . . . get out of doors altogether, and ramble into fields, woods, and the open air. It is time we bought a good set of walking shoes, and we cannot avoid getting some mud on them.' With so many parks out there, we should know when to put down our books and investigate.

Bibliography

Abbey, Edward (1968), *Desert Solitaire: A Season in the Wilderness* (New York: Ballantine Books).

Adams, Jonathan and McShane, Thomas (1992), *The Myth of Wild Africa* (Berkeley: University of California Press).

Adams, Judith A. (1991), *The American Amusement Park Industry* (Boston: Twayne).

Anderson, Benedict (1991 [1983]), *Imagined Communities: Reflections on the Origin and Spread of Nationalism* (London: Verso).

Anderson, D. and Grove, R., eds (1987), *Conservation in Africa: People, Policies and Practice* (Cambridge: Cambridge University Press).

Anderson, J. K. (1985), *Hunting in the Ancient World* (Berkeley: University of California Press).

Bal, Mieke, Crewe, Jonathan and Spitzer, Leo (1998), *Acts of Memory: Cultural Recall in the Present* (Hanover, NH: Dartmouth College, University Press of New England).

Baratay, Eric and Hardouin-Fugier, Elisabeth (2002), *Zoo: A History of Zoological Gardens in the West* (London: Reaktion).

Barlow, Elizabeth (1972), *Frederick Law Olmsted's New York* (New York: Praeger).

Barlow, Elizabeth (2001), *Landscape Design: A Cultural and Architectural History* (New York: Harry Abrams).

Barnum, P. T. (2000 [1855]), *The Life of P.T. Barnum Written by Himself* (Urbana, IL: University of Illinois Press).

Bartlett, Richard (1985), *Yellowstone: A Wilderness Besieged* (Tucson: University of Arizona Press).

Baudrillard, Jean (1983), *Simulations* (New York: Semiotext).

Baudrillard, Jean (1988 [1986]), *America* (London: Verso).

Baudrillard, Jean (1996), 'Disneyworld Company', *Liberation*, 4 March.

Beinart, William and Coates, Peter (1995), 'Nature Reserves and National Parks', in *Environment and History: The Taming of Nature in the USA and South Africa* (London: Routledge), 72–92.

Bender, Thomas (1975), *Toward an Urban Vision: Ideas and Institutions in Nineteenth Century America* (Baltimore: Johns Hopkins University Press).

Bennett, Peter (1996), *Blackpool Pleasure Beach: A Century of Fun* (Blackpool: Blackpool Pleasure Beach).

Berger, Robert B. (1985), *In the Garden of the Sun King* (Washington, DC: Dumbarton Oaks Research Library and Collection).

Berrall, Julia S. (1966), *The Garden: An Illustrated History from Ancient Egypt to the Present Day* (London: Thames & Hudson).

Beveridge, Charles E. and Hoffman, Carolyn, eds (1997), *The Papers of Frederick Law Olmsted*, Supplementary Series vol. 1: *Writings on Public Parks, Parkways and Park Systems* (Baltimore: Johns Hopkins University Press).

Birckhead, Jim, De Lacy, Terry and Smith, Laura Jane, eds (1992), *Aboriginal Involvement in Parks and Protected Areas* (Canberra: Aboriginal Studies Press).

Birnbaum, Charles and Karson, Robin, eds (2000), *Pioneers of American Landscape Design* (New York: McGraw-Hill).

Bogdan, Robert (1988), *Freak Show: Presenting Human Oddities for Amusement and Profit* (Chicago: University of Chicago Press).

Bostock, Stephen (1993), *Zoos and Animal Rights: The Ethics of Keeping Animals* (London: Routledge).

Bourdieu, Pierre (1984 [1979]), *Distinction: A Social Critique and the Judgement of Taste* (Cambridge, MA: Harvard University Press).

Bourdieu, Pierre (1985), 'Social Space and the Genesis of Groups', *Theory and Society*, 14/6, 723–44.

Braybrooke, Neville (1959), *London Green: The Story of Kensington Gardens, Hyde Park, Green Park, and St James' Park* (London: Victor Gollancz).

Brooks, J. and Boal, I. (1995), *Resisting the Virtual Life* (San Francisco: City Light Books).

Brower, David (1991), *Work in Progress* (Salt Lake City: Peregrine Smith Books).

Bruner, Aaron G., Gullison, Raymond E., Rice, Richard E. and Da Fonseca, Gustavo A. B. (2001), 'Effectiveness of Parks in Protecting Tropical Biodiversity', *Science*, 291, 125–8.

Bryman, Alan (1995), *Disney and his Worlds* (London: Routledge).

Bryman, Alan (1999), 'The Disneyization of Society', *Sociological Review*, 25/5, 25–47.

Burgess, Anthony and Park, Robert E. (1967 [1925]), *The City* (Chicago: University of Chicago Press).

Burnham, Philip (2000), *Indian Country, God's Country: Native Americans and the National Parks* (Washington, DC: Island Press).

Burrell, Gibson and Dale, Karen (2002), 'Utopiary: Utopias, Gardens and Organization', in *Utopia and Organization*, ed. Martin Parker (Oxford: Blackwell), 106–27.

Byrne, Eleanor and McQuillan, Martin (1999), *Deconstructing Disney* (London: Pluto Press).

Cameron, James M. and Bordessa, Ronald (1981), *Wonderland Through the Looking Glass: Politics, Culture and Planning in International Recreation* (Maple, Ontario: Belsten).

Campanella, Tomasso (1901), 'City of the Sun', in *Famous Utopias*, ed. Charles Andrews (New York: Tudor), 273–317.

Carruthers, Jane (1989), 'Creating a National Park, 1910 to 1926', *Journal of Southern African Studies*, 15/2, 188–216.

Carruthers, Jane (1994), 'Dissecting the Myth: Paul Kruger and the Kruger National Park', *Journal of Southern African Studies*, 20/2, 263–83.

Carruthers, Jane (1995), *The Kruger National Park: A Social and Political History* (Pietermaritzburg: University of Natal Press).

Cartwright, John (1991), 'Is There Hope for Conservation in Africa?', *Journal of Modern African Studies*, 29/3, 355–71.

Castells, Manuel and Hall, Peter (1994), *Technopoles of the World: The Making of 21st Century Industrial Complexes* (London: Routledge).

Catlin, George (1989 [1841]), *North American Indians*, ed. Peter Matthiesen (New York: Penguin).

Chase, Alston (1987), *Playing God in Yellowstone: The Destruction of America's First National Park* (San Diego: Harcourt Brace).

Clarke, Gillian (1987), *Prior Park: A Compleat Landscape* (Bath: Millstream Books).

Clarkson, Jonathan and Cox, Neil, eds (2000), *Constable and Wivenhoe Park: Reality and Vision* (Wivenhoe Park: University of Essex).

Coates, Peter (1998), *Nature: Western Attitudes since Ancient Times* (Cambridge: Polity; Berkeley: University of California Press).

Cohen, Michael (1988), *The History of the Sierra Club, 1892–1970* (San Francisco: Sierra Club Books).

Cosgrove, Denis and Daniels, Stephen, eds (1989), *The Iconography of Landscape: Essays on the Symbolic Representation, Design and Use of Past Environments* (Cambridge: Cambridge University Press).

Crabtree, J. R. (1991), 'National Park Designation in Scotland', *Land Use Policy*, 8/3, 241–52.

Crandell, Gina (1993), *Nature Pictorialized: 'The View' in Landscape History* (Baltimore: Johns Hopkins University Press).

Crang, Mike, Crang, Phil and May, Jon eds (1999), *Virtual Geographies: Bodies, Space and Relations* (London: Routledge).

Cranz, Galen (1980), 'Women in Urban Parks', *Signs: Journal of Women in Culture and Society*, 5/3, s79–s95.

Cranz, Galen (1982), *The Politics of Park Design: A History of Urban Parks in America* (Cambridge, MA: MIT Press).

Cronon, William (1995), *Uncommon Ground: Toward Reinventing Nature* (New York: W. W. Norton).

Dale, Virginia H. and Parr, Patricia D. (1998), 'Preserving DOE's Research Parks', *Issues in Science and Technology*, 14/2, 73–7.

Daniels, Stephen (1993), *Fields of Vision: Landscape Imagery and National Identity in England and the United States* (Cambridge: Polity).

Davis, Mike (1990), *City of Quartz: Excavating the Future in Los Angeles* (London: Verso).

Davis, Mike (2000 [1998]), *Ecology of Fear: Los Angeles and the Imagination of Disaster* (London: Picador).

Dear, Michael J. (2000), *The Postmodern Urban Condition* (Oxford: Blackwell).

Dearden, P. and Rollins, R., eds (1993), *Parks and Protected Areas in Canada* (Toronto: Oxford University Press).

Denis, Armand (1963), *On Safari* (London: Collins).

Dilsaver, Lary, ed. (1997), *America's Park System: The Critical Documents* (Lanham, MD: Rowman and Littlefield).

Dryden, John (1981), *Marriage à la mode*, ed. Mark S. Auburn (London: Edward Arnold).

Dunlap, Thomas (1999), *Nature and the English Diaspora: Environment and History in the United States, Canada, Australia and New Zealand* (Cambridge: Cambridge University Press).

Durrell, Gerald (1984), *The Stationary Ark: A Warm, Wise, and Funny Account of his Struggles to Create the Perfect Zoo* (New York: Simon and Schuster).

Eckholm, Erik (1982), *Down to Earth*, (New York: W. W. Norton).

Eco, Umberto (1987 [1986]), *Travels in Hyperreality: Essays* (London: Pan Books in association with Secker & Warburg).

Eisenberg, Evan (n.d.), *Ecology of Eden* (New York: Picador).

Ellis, Stephen (1994), 'Of Elephants and Men: Politics and Nature Conservation in South Africa', *Journal of Southern African Studies*, 20/1, 53–69.

Ellwood, Wayne, ed. (1998), 'The Mousetrap: Inside Disney's Dream Machine', *New Internationalist*, 308, special issue.

Evans, David (1997), *A History of Nature Conservation in Britain* (London: Routledge).

Feesey, Rosemary (1963), *A History of Wivenhoe Park: The House and Grounds* (Colchester: Benham Co.).

Fein, Albert, ed. (1967), *Landscape into Cityscape: Frederick Law Olmsted's Plans for a Greater New York City* (Ithaca, NY: Cornell University Press).

Ferney, Frederick (1986), 'L'Amér Look des Anti-Américains', *Le Nouvel Observateur*, 3–9 January.

Findlay, John (1992), *Magic Lands: Western Cityscapes and American Culture after 1940* (Berkeley: University of California Press).

Fitter, Richard and Scott, Peter (1978), *The Penitent Butchers: Seventy-Five Years of Wildlife Conservation* (London: Collins).

Fjellman, Stephen M. (1992), *Vinyl Leaves: Walt Disney World and America* (Boulder, CO: Westview Press).

Foster, Janet (1998), *Working for Wildlife: The Beginning of Preservation in Canada* (Toronto: University of Toronto Press).

Foster, Karen Polinger (1998), 'Gardens of Eden: Exotic Flora and Fauna in the Ancient Near East', *Bulletin Series, Yale School of Forestry and Environmental Studies*, 103, 320–9.

Francaviglia, Richard (1999), 'Walt Disney's Frontierland as an Allegorical Map of the American West', *Western Historical Quarterly*, 30/2, 155–82.

Frantz, Douglas and Collins, Catherine (1999), *Celebration, USA: Living in Disney's Brave New Town* (New York: Henry Holt).

Freemuth, John (1991), *Islands under Siege: National Parks and the Politics of External Threats* (Lawrence: University Press of Kansas).

Frome, Michael (1992), *Regreening the National Parks* (Tucson: University of Arizona Press).

Gardner, J. and Nelson, J. G. (1981), 'National Parks and Native Peoples in Northern Canada, Alaska and Northern Australia', *Environmental Conservation*, 8/3, 207–15.

Germic, Stephen (2001), *American Green: Class, Crisis and the Deployment of Nature in Central Park, Yosemite and Yellowstone* (Lanham, MD: Lexington Books).

Giroux, Henry A. (1999), *The Mouse that Roared: Disney and the End of Innocence* (Lanham, MD: Rowman and Littlefield).

Glacken, Clarence (1967), *Traces on the Rhodian Shore: Nature and Culture in Western Thought from Ancient Times to the End of the Eighteenth Century* (Berkeley: University of California Press).

Gleason, Kathryn L. (1994), '*Porticus Pompeiana*: A New Perspective on the First Public Park of Ancient Rome', *Journal of Garden History*, 14, 13–27.

Goss, Jon (1993), 'The "Magic of the Mall": An Analysis of Form, Function, and Meaning in the Contemporary Retail Built Environment', *Annals of the Association of American Geographers*, 83/1, 18–47.

Gothein, Marie Luise (1928), *History of Garden Art: From the Earliest Times to the Present Day*, 2 vols., ed. Walter Wright (London: J. M. Dent).

Gottdiener, Mark (1997), *The Theming of America: Dreams, Visions, and Commercial Spaces* (Boulder, CO: Westview Press).

Gottlieb, Roger, ed. (1995), *This Sacred Earth: Religion, Nature and Environment* (New York: Routledge).

Gray, Elizabeth Dodson (1981), *Green Paradise Lost: Remything Genesis* (Wellesley, MA: Roundtable Press).

Greswell, William (1905), *The Forests and Deer Parks of Somerset* (Taunton: Barnicott & Pearce, Athenaeum Press).

Griffiths, Tom and Robin, Libby, eds (1997), *Ecology and Empire: Environmental History of Settler Societies* (Edinburgh: Keele University Press).

Grinnell, Joseph and Storer, Tracy (1916), 'Animal Life as an Asset of National Parks', *Science*, n.s. 44/1133 (15 Sept.) 375–80.

Grove, Richard (1995), *Green Imperialism: Colonial Expansion, Tropical Island Edens and the Origins of Environmentalism, 1600–1860* (Cambridge: Cambridge University Press).

Haines, Aubrey (1996), *The Yellowstone Story: A History of our First National Park*, 2 vols. (Yellowstone National Park, WY: Yellowstone Association).

Hancocks, David (2001), *A Different Nature: The Paradoxical World of Zoos and their Uncertain Future* (Berkeley: University of California Press).

Hanson, Elizabeth (2002), *Animal Attractions: Nature on Display in American Zoos* (Princeton: Princeton University Press).

Harding, Stewart and Lambert, David, eds (1994), *Parks and Gardens of Avon* (Bristol: Avon Gardens Trust).

Hendee, John (1978), *Wilderness Management* (Washington, DC: Department of Agriculture).

Hewison, Robert (1987), *The Heritage Industry: Britain in a Climate of Decline* (London: Methuen).

Higgs, David, ed. (1999), *Queer Sites: Gay Urban Histories since 1600* (London: Routledge).

Hoage, R. J. (1989), *Perceptions of Animals in American Culture* (Washington, DC: Smithsonian).

Hoage, R. J. and Deiss, William A. (1996), *New Worlds, New Animals: From Menagerie to Zoological Park in the Nineteenth Century* (Baltimore: Johns Hopkins University Press).

Howland, M. (1878), 'The Philadelphia Zoo', *Harper's Magazine*, 58.

Hughes, J. Donald (1980), 'Early Greek and Roman Environmentalists', in *Historical Ecology: Essays on Environmental and Social Change*, ed. Lester Bilsky (New York: Kennikat Press), 45–59.

Hughes, J. Donald (1990), 'Artemis: Goddess of Conservation', *Forest and Conservation History*, 34, 191–7.

Hughes, J. Donald (1994), *Pan's Travail: Environmental Problems of the Greeks and Romans* (Baltimore: Johns Hopkins University Press).

Hunt, John Dixon (1992), *Gardens and the Picturesque* (Cambridge, MA: MIT Press).

Hunt, John Dixon and Willis, Peter, eds (1975), *The Genius of the Place: The English Landscape Garden 1620–1820* (London: Paul Elek).

Hunter, John Michael (1985), *Land into Landscape* (London: George Goodwin).

Hunter, Michael (1996), *Preserving the Past: The Rise of Heritage in Modern Britain* (Stroud, Gloucestershire: Alan Sutton).

Hurley, Andrew (2001), *Diners, Bowling Alleys and Trailer Parks: Chasing the American Dream in Postwar Consumer Culture* (New York: Basic Books).

Huth, Hans (1957), *Nature and the American: Three Centuries of Changing Attitudes* (Berkeley: University of California Press).

Hyams, Edward (1971), *Capability Brown and Humphrey Repton* (London: J. M. Dent).

Hyatt, Alpheus (1891), 'The Next Stage in the Development of Public Parks', *Atlantic Monthly*, 67, 215–24.

Igoe, Jim (2003), *Conservation and Globalization: A Study of National Parks and Indigenous Communities from East Africa to South Dakota* (London: Wadsworth).

Immerso, Michael (2002), *Coney Island: The People's Playground* (New Brunswick, NJ: Rutgers University Press).

Jackson, Jennifer and James, Patrick (1994), *From Acorn to Oak: The Growth of the National Trust, 1895–1994* (London: Macmillan).

Jackson, W. Turrentine (1942), 'The Creation of Yellowstone National Park', *Mississippi Valley Historical Review*, 29/2, 188–90.

Jacobs, Jane (1961), *The Death and Life of Great American Cities* (London: Jonathan Cape).

Jefferson, Isaac (1847), *Life of Isaac Jefferson of Petersburg, Virginia*, Blacksmith, ed. Charles W. Campbell (n.p.).

Jellicoe, Geoffrey and Jellicoe, Susan (1975), *The Landscape of Man: Shaping the Environment from Prehistory to the Present Day* (London: Thames & Hudson).

Jennison, George (1937), *Animals for Show and Pleasure in Ancient Rome* (Manchester: Manchester University Press).

Jones, Karen (2002), *Wolf Mountains: A History of Wolves along the Great Divide* (Calgary: University of Calgary Press).

Karp, Ivan and Lavine, Steven (1991), *Exhibiting Cultures: The Poetics and Politics of Museum Display* (Washington, DC: Smithsonian).

Keller, Robert and Turek, Michael (1998), *American Indians and National Parks* (Tucson: University of Arizona Press).

Kim, Lucian (2001), 'Can "Dracula Land" put Transylvania in the Black?', *Christian Science Monitor*, 31 Oct.

King, Margaret J. (1981), 'Disneyland and Walt Disney World: Traditional Values in Futuristic Form', *Journal of Popular Culture*, 15/1, 116–40.

Kirsch, Scott (1997), 'Watching the Bombs Go Off: Photography, Nuclear Landscapes, and Spectacular Democracy', *Antipode*, 29/3, 227–55.

Kisling, Vernon N. Jr (2001), *Zoo and Aquarium History: Ancient Animal Collections to Zoological Gardens* (Boca Raton, FL: CRC Press).

Koshar, Rudy (2000), *From Monument to Traces: Artifacts of German Memory, 1870–1990* (Berkeley: University of California Press).

Kuletz, Valerie (1998), *The Tainted Desert: Environmental and Social Ruin in the American West* (New York: Routledge).

Lablaude, Pierre-André (1995), *The Gardens of Versailles* (London: Zwemmer).

Lainsbury, Andrew (2000), *Once Upon an American Dream: The Story of Euro Disneyland* (Lawrence: University Press of Kansas).

Lambert, Robert A. (2001), *Contested Mountains: Nature, Development and Environment in the Cairngorms Region of Scotland, 1880–1980* (Cambridge: White Horse Press).

Lasdun, Susan (1991), *The English Park: Royal, Private and Public* (London: André Deutsch).

Lawrence, David (2000), *Kakadu: The Making of a National Park* (Melbourne: The Miegunyah Press).

Leach, Melissa and Fairhead, James (1996), *Misreading the African Landscape: Society and Ecology in a Forest–Savanna Mosaic* (Cambridge: Cambridge University Press).

Lehrman, Jonas (1980), *Earthly Paradise: Garden and Courtyard in Islam* (London: Thames and Hudson).

Lewinsohn, Richard (Morus) (1954), *Animals, Men and Myths: A History of the Influence of Animals on Civilization and Culture* (London: Victor Gollancz).

Little, Bryan (1975), *Prior Park: Its History* (Bath: Prior Park College).

Lothian, William (1976–81), *A Brief History of Canada's National Parks*, 4 vols. (Ottawa: Parks Canada).

Loudon, J. C. (1840), 'A Catalogue of Trees and Shrubs', Derby Local Studies Library.

Louis XIV (1982), *The Way to Present the Gardens of Versailles* (Paris: Réunion des Musées).

Lovett, Anthony and Maranian, Matt (1997), *LA Bizzaro!: The Insider's Guide to the Obscure, the Absurd, and the Perverse in Los Angeles* (New York: St Martin's Press).

Lowry, Philip (1986), *Green Cathedrals* (Manhattan, KS: AG Press).

Lowry, W. (1994), *Capacity for Wonder: Preserving National Parks* (Washington, DC: Brookings Institution).

MacEwen, Ann and MacEwen, Malcolm (1982), *National Parks: Conservation or Cosmetics?* (London: George Allen and Unwin).

MacEwen, Ann and MacEwen, Malcolm (1987), *Greenprints for the Countryside? The Story of Britain's National Parks* (London: George Allen and Unwin).

Mackay, Donald (1995), *Scotland's Rural Land Use Agencies* (Aberdeen: Scottish Cultural Press).

MacKenzie, John (1988), *The Empire of Nature: Hunting, Conservation and British Imperialism* (Manchester: Manchester University Press).

Magoc, Chris (1999), *Yellowstone: The Creation and Selling of an American Landscape, 1870–1903* (Albuquerque: University of New Mexico Press).

Maguire, Henry (2000), 'Gardens and Parks in Constantinople', *Dumbarton Oaks Papers* 54, 251–64.

Malone, Patrick M. and Parrott, Charles A. (1998), 'Greenways in the Industrial City: Parks and Promenades along the Lowell Canals', *Industrial Archaeology*, 24/1, 19–40.

Mandler, Peter (1997), *The Fall and Rise of the Stately Home* (London: Yale University Press).

Manning, A. and Serpell, J. (1994), *Animals and Human Society* (London: Routledge).

Manuel, Frank and Manuel, Fritzie (1979), *Utopian Thought in the Western World* (Cambridge, MA: Belknap Press).

Marling, Karal Ann, ed. (1997), *Designing Disney's Theme Parks: The Architecture of Reassurance* (Paris: Flammarion).

Marsh, John S. and Hodgins, Bruce W., eds (1998), *Changing Parks: The History, Future and Cultural Context of Parks and Heritage Landscapes* (Toronto: Natural Heritage/Natural History).

Marx, Leo (1964), *The Machine in the Garden: Technology and the Pastoral Ideal in America* (New York: Oxford University Press).

McCullough, Edo (2000 [1957]), *Good Old Coney Island: A Sentimental Journey into the Past* (New York: Fordham University Press).

McKibben, Bill (1990), *The End of Nature* (London: Viking).

Midgeley, Mary (1984), *Animals and Why They Matter* (Athens, GA: University of Georgia Press).

Mighetto, Lisa (1991), *Wild Animals and American Environmental Ethics* (Tucson: University of Arizona Press).

Milstein, Michael (1996), *Yellowstone: 125 Years of America's Best Idea* (Billings, MT: Billings Gazette).

Milton, John (1674), *Paradise Lost* (London: S. Simmons).

Ministry of Housing and Local Government (1962), *Caravan Parks: Location, Layout, Landscape* (London: HMSO).

Misrach, Richard (1990), *Bravo 20: The Bombing of the American West* (Baltimore: Johns Hopkins University Press).

Mitchell, Anthony (1996), *Prior Park Landscape Garden* (London: National Trust).

Mitchell, W. J. Thomas, ed. (2002), *Landscape and Power* (Chicago: University of Chicago Press).

Mitman, Gregg (1999), *Reel Nature: America's Romance with Wildlife on Film* (Cambridge, MA: Harvard University Press).

More, Thomas (1965 [1516]), *Utopia* (London: Penguin).

Muir, John (1981 [1901]), *Our National Parks* (Madison: University of Wisconsin Press).

Muir, John (1962 [1912]), *The Yosemite* (New York: Doubleday).

Muir, Richard (2004), *Landscape Encyclopaedia: A Reference Guide to the Historic Landscape* (Macclesfield: Windgather Press).

Nash, Roderick (1970), 'The American Invention of National Parks', *American Quarterly*, 22/3, 726–35.

Nash, Roderick (1977), 'The Confusing Birth of National Parks', *Michigan Quarterly Review*, 216–26.

Nash, Roderick (1982), *Wilderness and the American Mind* (New Haven: Yale University Press).

Newby, Howard, ed. (1995), *The National Trust: The Next Hundred Years* (London: National Trust).

Norwich, John Julius (1976), *The Kingdom of the Sun, 1130–1194* (London: Faber & Faber).

Nye, Russel B. (1981), 'Eight Ways of Looking at an Amusement Park', *Journal of Popular Culture*, 15/1, 63–75.

Olwig, Kenneth (2002), *Landscape, Nature and the Body Politic* (Madison: University of Wisconsin Press).

Peiss, Kathy (1986), *Cheap Amusements: Working Women and Leisure in Turn-of-the-Century New York* (Philadelphia: Temple University Press).

Petty, Mike, ed. (2001), *Eden: The Guide* (London: Eden Books).

Pregill, Philip and Volkman, Nancy (1993), *Landscapes in History: Design and Planning in the Western Tradition* (New York: Van Nostrand Reinhold).

Prest, John (1981), *The Garden of Eden: The Botanic Garden and the Re-creation of Paradise* (New Haven: Yale University Press).

Price, Jennifer (1999), *Flight Maps: Adventures with Nature in Modern America* (New York: Basic Books).

Prince, Hugh (1967), *Parks in England* (Isle of Wight: Pinhorns).

Project on Disney (1995), *Inside the Mouse: Work and Play at Disney World* (Durham, NC: Duke University Press).

Pyne, Stephen J. (1998), *How the Canyon Became Grand: A Short History* (New York: Penguin).

Rackham, Oliver (1986), *The History of the Countryside: The Full Fascinating Story of Britain's Landscape* (London: J. M. Dent).

Raitz, Karl B., ed. (1995), *The Theater of Sport* (Baltimore: Johns Hopkins University Press).

Raz, Aviad E. (1999), *Riding the Black Ship: Japan and Tokyo Disneyland* (Cambridge, MA: Harvard University Press).

Reed, Michael (1990), *The Landscape of Britain* (London: Routledge).

Register, Woody (2001), *The Kid of Coney Island: Fred Thompson and the Rise of American Amusements* (New York: Oxford University Press).

Reps, John W. (1965), *The Making of Urban America: A History of City Planning in the United States* (Princeton: Princeton University Press).

Rieu, E.V. (1946), *The Odyssey* (Harmondsworth: Penguin).

Ritter, Lawrence (1992), *Lost Ballparks: A Celebration of Baseball's Legendary Fields* (New York: Penguin).

Ritvo, Harriet (1987), *The Animal Estate: The English and Other Creatures in the Victorian Age* (Cambridge, MA: Harvard University Press).

Ritzer, George (1993), *The McDonaldization of Society* (Thousand Oaks, CA: Pine Forge).

Ritzer, George, ed. (2002), *McDonaldization: The Reader* (Thousand Oaks, CA: Pine Forge).

Roper, Laura (1983), *FLO: A Biography of Frederick Law Olmsted* (Baltimore: Johns Hopkins University Press).

Rosenberg, Nathan (1976), *Perspectives on Technology* (Cambridge: Cambridge University Press).

Rosenzweig, Roy and Blackmar, Elizabeth (1992), *The Park and the People: A History of Central Park* (Ithaca, NY: Cornell University Press).

Rothfels, Nigel (2002), *Savages and Beasts: The Birth of the Modern Zoo* (Baltimore: Johns Hopkins University Press).

Runte, Alfred (1979), *National Parks: The American Experience* (Lincoln: University of Nebraska Press).

Runte, Alfred (1984), *Trains of Discovery: Western Railroads and the National Parks* (Flagstaff, AZ: Northland Press).

Runte, Alfred (1990), *Yosemite: The Embattled Wilderness* (Lincoln: University of Nebraska Press).

Russell, Osborne (1965), *Journal of a Trapper*, ed. Aubrey Haines (Lincoln: University of Nebraska Press).

Samuel, Raphael (1996), *Theatres of Memory: Past and Present in Contemporary Culture* (London: Verso).

Sanback, F. R. (1978), 'The Early Campaign for a National Park in the Lake District', *Transactions of the Institute of British Geographers*, new series 3/4, 498–514.

Sands, Mollie (1987), *The Eighteenth-Century Pleasure Grounds of Marylebone* (London: The Society for Theatre Research).

Saxon, A. H. (1989), *P.T. Barnum: The Legend and the Man* (New York: Columbia University Press).

Schama, Simon (1995), *Landscape and Memory* (London: HarperCollins).

Schleifman, Nurit (2001), 'Moscow's Victory Park: A Monumental Change', *History and Memory*, 13/2 (Fall/Writer), 5–34.

Schuyler, David (1986), *The New Urban Landscape: The Redefinition of City Form in Nineteenth-Century America* (Baltimore: Johns Hopkins University Press).

Sellars, Richard West (1997), *Preserving Nature in the National Parks: A History* (New Haven: Yale University Press).

Shaffer, Marguerite (2001), *See America First: Tourism and National Identity, 1880–1940* (Washington, DC: Smithsonian).

Sheail, John (1975), 'The Concept of National Parks in Britain, 1900–1950', *Transactions of the Institute of British Geographers*, 66, 41–56.

Sheail, John (1984), 'Nature Reserves, National Parks and Post-war Reconstruction in Britain', *Environmental Conservation*, 11/1, 29–34.

Short, John Rennie (1991), *Imagined Country: Society, Culture and Environment* (London: Routledge).

Sievert, James (1999), 'Abruzzo National Park: Land of Dreams', *Environment and History*, 5, 293–307.

Smith, Ron (2003), *The Ballpark Book*, rev. edn (St Louis, MO: Sporting News Books).

Smollett, Tobias (1771), *The Expedition of Humphry Clinker* (London: Hutchinson & Co.).

Smout, T. C. (2000), *Nature Contested: Environmental History in Scotland and Northern England since 1600* (Edinburgh: Edinburgh University Press).

Smout, T. C., ed. (2001), *Nature, Landscape and People since the Second World War* (East Linton: Tuckwell).

Soja, Edward (1989), *Postmodern Geographies: The Reassertion of Space in Critical Social Theory* (London: Verso).

Solnit, Rebecca (1994), *Savage Dreams: A Journey into the Landscape Wars of the American West* (New York: Vintage Books).

Sorkin, Michael, ed. (1992), *Variations on a Theme Park: The New American City and the End of Public Space* (New York: Hill and Wang).

Soulé, Michael and Lease, Gary, eds (1995), *Reinventing Nature* (Washington, DC: Island Press).

Spence, Mark David (1999), *Dispossessing the Wilderness: Indian Removal and the Meaning of National Parks* (New York: Oxford University Press).

Stamper, Paul (1988), 'Woods and Parks', in *The Countryside of Medieval England*, ed. Grenville Astill and Annie Grant (Oxford: Blackwell), 128–48.

Stegner, Wallace (1998), 'The Best Idea We Ever Had', in *Marking the Sparrow's Fall: The Making of the American West*, ed. Page Stegner (New York: Henry Holt), 137.

Steiner, Michael (1998), 'Frontierland as Tomorrowland: Walt Disney and the Architectural Packaging of the Mythic West', *Montana: The Magazine of Western History*, 48/1, 2–17.

Stevenson-Hamilton, James (1952 [1937]), *South African Eden: From Sabi Game Reserve to Kruger National Park* (London: Cassell & Co.).

Stewart, Charles (1904), 'A National Park for Scotland', *Nineteenth Century and After*, 55/327, 822–6.

Stroud, Dorothy (1952), 'Our Landscapes Debt to the 18th Century', *Geographical Magazine*, 9–20.

Stroud, Dorothy (1975), *Capability Brown* (London: Faber & Faber).

Sutter, Paul (2002), *Driven Wild: How the Fight against Automobiles Launched the Modern Wilderness Movement* (Seattle: University of Washington Press).

Sutton, S. B., ed. (1971), *Civilizing American Cities: A Selection of Frederick Law Olmsted's Writings on City Landscapes* (Cambridge, MA: MIT Press).

Tabliabue, John (1995), 'A Comic-Strip Gaul Battles Disney', *New York Times*, 9 August .

Taigel, Anthea and Williamson, Tom (1993) *Parks and Gardens* (London: B. H. Batsford).

Tate, Alan (2001), *Great City Parks* (London: Spon Press).

Taylor, Dorceta E. (1999), 'Central Park as a Model for Social Control: Urban Parks, Social Class and Leisure Behavior in Nineteenth-Century America', *Journal of Leisure Research*, 31/4, 420–77.

Thomas, Keith (1984), *Man and the Natural World: Changing Attitudes in England, 1500–1800* (Harmondsworth: Penguin).

Thompson, E. P. (1991), *Customs in Common* (London: Merlin Press).

Thoreau, Henry David (1991), 'Walking', in *Ralph Waldo Emerson/Henry David Thoreau, Nature/Walking* (Boston: Beacon Press), 69–122.

Thoreau, Henry David (1993), *Three Complete Books: The Maine Woods, Walden, Cape Cod* (New York: Gramercy).

Topos: European Landscape Magazine, eds (2002), *Parks: Green Urban Spaces in European Cities* (Munich: Callwey).

Trench, Charles Chenevix (1967), *The Poacher and the Squire: A History of Poaching and Game Preservation in England* (London: Longmans, Green and Co.).

Walcott, Susan M. (2003), *Chinese Science and Technology Industrial Parks* (Aldershot: Ashgate).

Wasko, Janet (2001), *Understanding Disney: The Manufacture of Fantasy* (Cambridge: Polity).

Waycott, Angus (1983), *National Parks of Western Europe* (Southampton: Inklon).

Weideger, Paula (1994), *Gilding the Acorn: Behind the Façade of the National Trust* (London: Simon & Schuster).

Weltman-Aron, Brigitte (2001), *On Other Grounds: Landscape Gardening and Nationalism in Eighteenth-Century England and France* (Albany, NY: State University of New York Press).

White, Lynn Jr (1971), 'The Historical Roots of Our Ecologic Crisis', in *Sunshine and Smoke: American Writers and the American Environment*, ed. David Anderson (Philadelphia: J. B. Lippincott), 472–81.

White, Richard (1999), 'The Nationalization of Nature', *Journal of American History*, 86/3, 976–86.

Whyte, William (1980), *The Social Life of Small Urban Spaces* (Washington, DC: Conservation Foundation).

Williams, Raymond (1976), *Keywords: A Vocabulary of Culture and Society* (London: Fontana).

Williamson, Tom (1995), *Polite Landscapes: Gardens and Society in Eighteenth-Century England* (Baltimore: Johns Hopkins University Press).

Wills, John (2001), ' "Welcome to the Atomic Park": American Nuclear Landscapes and the "Unnaturally Natural" ', *Environment and History*, 7, 449–72.

Wills, John (2002), 'Digital Dinosaurs and Artificial Life: Exploring the Culture of Nature in Computer and Video Games', *Cultural Values*, 6/4, 395–417.

Wills, John (2003), ' "On Burro'd Time", Feral Burros, the Brighty Legend, and the Pursuit of Wilderness in the Grand Canyon', *Journal of Arizona History*, 44/1, 1–24.

Wilson, Alexander (1992), *The Culture of Nature: North American Landscape from Disney to the Exxon Valdez* (Cambridge, MA: Blackwell).

Woodbridge, Kenneth (1970), *Landscape and Antiquity: Aspects of English Culture at Stourhead* (Oxford: Oxford University Press).

Woodbridge, Kenneth (2002), *The Stourhead Landscape* (London: National Trust).

Wordsworth, William (1952 [1810]), *A Guide through the District of the Lakes* (Bloomington: Indiana University Press).

Worster, Donald (1994), *Nature's Economy: A History of Ecological Ideas* (Cambridge: Cambridge University Press).

Worster, Donald, ed. (1989), *The Ends of the Earth* (New York: Cambridge University Press).

Wright, George M., Dixon, Joseph S. and Thompson, Ben H. (1933), *Fauna of the National Parks of the United States: A Preliminary Survey of Faunal Relations in National Parks*, Contributions of Wildlife Survey Fauna Series no.1 (Washington, DC: Government Printing Office).

Yard, Robert Sterling (1917), *The National Parks Portfolio* (Washington, DC: Government Printing Office).

Zucker, Paul (1959), *Town and Square: From the Agora to the Village Green* (New York: Columbia University Press).

Index